CHARTING
the
ECON●MY

CHARTING
the
ECON●MY

Early 20th Century Malaya
and Contemporary Malaysian Contrasts

SULTAN NAZRIN SHAH

OXFORD
UNIVERSITY PRESS

OXFORD
UNIVERSITY PRESS

Oxford New York
Auckland Cape Town Dar es Salaam Hong Kong
Karachi Kuala Lumpur Madrid Melbourne Mexico City
Nairobi New Delhi Shanghai Taipei Toronto

© Sultan Nazrin Shah 2017

The moral rights of the author have been asserted.

First published 2017

ISBN 978 983 47 2014 8

Perpustakaan Negara Malaysia   Cataloguing-in-Publication Data

Sultan Nazrin Shah
     CHARTING the ECONOMY : Early 20th Century Malaya and
     Contemporary Malaysian Contrasts / SULTAN NAZRIN SHAH.
     Includes index
     Bibliography: page 210
     ISBN 978-983-47-2014-8
     1 Economics--History--Malaysia.
     2. Malaya--Economics--conditions--20th century. I. Title.
     330.9595

Impression: 10 9 8 7 6 5 4 3 2 1

Text reviewed by David Demery and Frank Harrigan
Chapter opening photographs courtesy of the National Archives Malaysia
(Chapter 1. 2001/0025947, Chapter 2. 2001/0041524, Chapter 3. 2001/0046243,
Chapter 4. 2001/0053385, Chapter 5. 2001/0053349, Chapter 6. 2003/0000303,
Apendices. 2010/0011549)

Text set in 11 point ITC Cheltenham Std by
Far East Offset & Engraving Sdn. Bhd., Selangor Darul Ehsan
Printed by Percetakan Jiwabaru Sdn. Bhd., Selangor Darul Ehsan
Published by Oxford Fajar Sdn. Bhd. (008974-T)
under licence from Oxford University Press,
4 Jalan Pemaju U1/15, Seksyen U1
40150 Shah Alam
Selangor Darul Ehsan, Malaysia

For my parents who have been the guiding star of my life

My mother Tuanku Bainun

In loving memory of my father

Sultan Azlan Shah

Foreword

The defining characteristics of the second half of the 20th century were rapid economic growth and structural transformation in many Asian and Latin American economies. During that half century these economies joined the agricultural and industrial revolutions that had been largely confined to Europe, North America and Japan. But these transformations often had origins that are little known or appreciated; many of these economies had begun a transformation process, without industrialisation, much earlier in the first half of the 20th century and in a few cases even earlier.

The structural changes in the first half of the century were less well known for two major reasons. The first is that in Asia and Africa these countries were mostly colonies of one or another European (and American and Japanese) power, and their history was seen mainly in the context of the growth of European empires and the contests between them. The second reason is that there were few studies of the economies of these colonies and most of what was known about them dealt only with the role of the businesses of the ruling colonial power.

This limited focus was combined with the fact that the concept of gross domestic product (GDP) (as used here GDP also includes the closely related concepts of gross domestic expenditure and national income) that is so essential to any analysis of economic structural transformation was not even invented (by Simon Kuznets) until 1937. It was not widely applied even to high income countries until after the Second World War. Once reporting on GDP became standard practice for the statistical offices of high income countries, economists in those offices and other scholars soon made efforts to extend the series back not only to the first half of the century but also to the 19th century.

No such effort occurred in most of the former colonies that gained independence after World War II. They did calculate GDP for the post-independence period but not for the years prior to independence. Much of the discussion of what happened to the economies of colonies in the first half of the 20th century was instead based on often misleading qualitative evidence influenced in many cases by priori assumptions and biases.

Since the 1980s, that situation has begun to change and scholars have gone back to reconstruct the GDP accounts of a number of former colonies. Where the data have been comparatively plentiful, as for the Japanese colonies of Korea 1910–1945 and Taiwan 1898–1945, that effort began early on. Today, thanks in part to the work of scholars at Hitotsubashi University, we have fairly complete GDP records for those economies. Enough had also been done to estimate GDP for developing economies as a whole that Angus Maddison could piece together a rough estimate of world GDP by region going back many centuries. The assumptions needed to construct those rough estimates, however, limited their use for analysing structural change before those countries achieved independence.

Constructing GDP accounts for these earlier years in order to make an in-depth analysis of structural change is a formidable undertaking for most developing economies. The data are scattered in disparate sources, many not easily accessible. Assumptions based on other kinds of more qualitative or microeconomic evidence are often needed to fill in critical gaps in the quantitative data. It is not surprising, therefore, that there are no estimates of GDP in the first half of the 20th century for large numbers of countries that are former colonies or that were independent prior to World War II but not part of the European and North American progress to high income status.

This study by HRH Sultan Nazrin Shah, therefore, fills an important gap for understanding what happened to the Malayan (later Malaysian) economy prior to the country's independence. The substantial structural changes in that economy were different in kind from the structural changes in the industrialised countries at that time (and earlier). The changes in Malaya, however, did have much in common with the structural changes occurring at the same time in a great many other colonies of European and American powers. Understanding what happened in Malaya is thus a guide to what probably happened in many other places at that time—and to some degree is still happening today, notably in parts of Africa.

As this study makes clear, the economy of the Malay Peninsula was anything but stagnant. Despite the impact of World War I in 1914–1918, and the Great Depression of the 1930s, Malaya's economy grew on a real per capita basis at an average of 2.9 per cent a year for nearly four decades. The growth was not steady, however. It was based almost entirely on two commodities, tin and rubber. Commodity prices fluctuate widely and that was certainly the case in Malaya from 1900–1939. The demand for rubber depended on the size and growth of the automobile industry, mainly in the US, and that industry was deeply affected by World War I and even more by the Great Depression.

Despite these fluctuations, the impact of rubber and tin on both Malayan society and the economy was enormous. The Malay labour force was small and did not grow during most of the early 20th century years; most Malays preferred to stay with their traditional farming and fishing occupations. So labour had to come from overseas: Chinese initially in the tin mines, and Indians to work in rubber planting and tapping.

Ownership of the rubber plantations was mostly British and, when large dredges were introduced, the same was true for tin mining. Chinese ownership using simpler mining technologies gave way to the British-owned dredges. When prices were high, profits from the plantations and mines were large but were mostly repatriated by the British owners to Great Britain. Incomes of the workers in these mines and plantations did rise during 1900–1939 but only very slowly at 1 per cent a year. A dynamic emerged of rapid growth in GDP while wages and incomes grew at a much smaller pace, leaving significant poverty. Although perhaps a familiar pattern now, it was quite unusual in the second half of the 20th century.

In certain ways, among countries today whose economies depend largely on commodity exports (petroleum, copper and so on), workers still get low wages while the profits are shared between the foreign investors and the governments of these countries (rather than all of the profits going to the foreign investors or colonial powers). In Malaysia, this government revenue does flow in a large part into benefits for the people of the country, so household incomes and expenditures have grown as rapidly as GDP, unlike during the colonial period. But in many other countries government revenue has been squandered on projects of little value to the people or siphoned off into the pockets of a few powerful politicians. This 'resource curse' is more true for minerals than for agricultural crops such as rice, rubber, oil palm and coffee, where small holders account today for a much larger share of production, with profits often going directly to the farmer.

The 'colonial drain' is not unique to Malaya or to British colonial policies. There are many examples from the colonial past of other countries where high GDP growth was combined with only limited growth in the incomes and expenditures of the workers in mines and plantations. A prime example is the Dutch East Indies, now Indonesia. Not only did per capita food consumption actually decline during the peak of Dutch exploitation from 1880–1905, but Dutch economic management during the Great Depression was so bad that Indonesian GDP per capita fell between 1913 and 1950, as Malaya's economy grew by 1.5 per cent a year.

A major issue for anyone interested in developing economies today is how this earlier growth and structural change affected what happened later after independence. Was the colonial legacy mostly negative or at best neutral in the sense of having only a modest if any impact on the standard of living of anyone other than the colonial rulers? Or, despite the obvious rising inequality with benefits going mainly to people who were residents of the colonial homeland, was a foundation laid that contributed to faster development after independence? This study provides insights into this question as well.

The colonial era did provide Malaysia with what for the 1950s was good infrastructure in the form of paved highways and a railroad system that linked the major centres on the west coast of the Malayan Peninsula, together with electricity and even potable water in the major cities. These were developed originally to serve mining and plantation interests but were equally suitable for many other purposes. Education of a Malaysian elite at the University of Malaya in Singapore (and later in Kuala Lumpur) during late colonial times provided the country after independence with a higher quality civil service than in many other developing countries immediately after independence. But colonial policies also helped create an economy where occupations were closely associated with race. Chinese Malaysians dominated most of commerce, construction and industry employment. The Malays were largely confined to farming and, after independence, to the civil service, security and uniformed services, especially the police and military. Living standards, particularly of Malay farmers, were still very low and much lower than those in urban occupations.

In 1969, this situation would lead to riots that traumatised the country and ushered in policies designed among other things to eliminate the connection between occupation and race. Overall the colonial era produced both positives and negatives, and there probably is little to be gained by trying to estimate which outweighed the others. Malaysia at independence was clearly in a better position to launch sustained economic development efforts than most other developing countries, including such neighbours as Indonesia.

The book ends with suggestions about where future research could build on the foundation laid by the estimates and analysis in this excellent study.

Dwight H. Perkins   **C. Peter Timmer**
Belmont, Massachusetts   Sonoma Valley, California

Preface

My fascination with Malaysia's economic history began almost a generation ago when I was studying for a doctoral degree at Harvard. I committed to undertake research that would deepen my knowledge of the country's economic transformation in the 20th century.

The study of long-run economic growth and development in Malaysia has been constrained by the absence of a statistical series on national income accounts for the period prior to 1947. This is not surprising as it was only after the Great Depression that economists and statisticians in the industrialised countries began to develop the analytical tools to compile the accounts. The regular household income and expenditure surveys that have been a feature of the statistical landscape of the post-World War II era had not yet begun.

As part of my PhD dissertation, I attempted to make some initial estimates of Malaya's gross domestic product (GDP) for the first four decades of the 20th century. To make real progress I needed to access British colonial records located at the National Archives in Kuala Lumpur and the Public Records Office in London (renamed the National Archives Office and relocated to Kew, Surrey in 2004). From the vast amount of materials gathered, I began to piece together the relevant time series required for computing GDP and its components.

Malaya did not exist as a single administrative unit with a unified statistical system at the beginning of the 20th century. This made the task particularly demanding since I had to work with up to 11 sets of statistical reports, compiled with varying levels of completeness and detail. Inevitably this necessitated using a variety of direct and indirect methods to gather the data required to construct the national income accounts.

After graduating from Harvard I started a research project to continue my investigations. Having completed an improved time series of GDP estimates, I attempted to situate the results in the context of the prevailing geopolitical, economic and social settings of that time, and to draw some conclusions about Malaya's economic performance while under British colonial rule, as compared with economic growth and development in contemporary Malaysia. This book is a narrative of the findings.

It has been a long journey, and it will continue. I am indebted to many people and institutions for their wonderful cooperation without which this research would not have been possible. It gives me great pleasure to acknowledge and thank those, too numerous to mention all here, who have willingly and generously shared ideas, information and data, and supported the project in one way or another.

I want especially to express my appreciation to my PhD advisors, Dwight H. Perkins, C. Peter Timmer and Joseph J. Stern who have stimulated and encouraged my interest in economic history. I am extremely grateful to Dwight and Peter for graciously agreeing to write the foreword to this book.

Shahril Talib helped me to establish the Malaysian economic history project at the Asia-Europe Institute of the University of Malaya. I am deeply indebted to him. The Institute continues to provide outstanding institutional support and resources, and I would like to thank its current executive director, Azirah Hashim, as well as previous executive directors. I would also like to thank the Department of Statistics-Malaysia for generously meeting my substantial data requests over many years. Gnasegarah s/o C. Kandaiya led my statistical team and was ably assisted by Harbans Singh s/o Sohan Singh, both of whom were formerly from the Department of Statistics-Malaysia.

We received valuable support from several research assistants, including Ichiro Sugimoto, Tin Htoo Naing, Dang Minh Quang, Roslaili binti Mohd Din, Zulfakar bin Harun and Tuah bin Yussoff.

The project benefited from the helpful comments of many visiting scholars, including Jan Luiten van Zanden, Thomas Lindblad, Riitta Hjerppe, Tsubouchi Yoshihiro, Yujiro Hayami, Om Prakash and Ramesh Chander.

Over the years, I have also benefited enormously from the insights and ideas of many individuals in Malaysia and across the globe. I have learned a lot through engaging with them in stimulating exchanges and through discussion of often competing ideas. I express my deep appreciation to all those who have so freely shared their insights and knowledge.

These include: Afifi al-Akiti, Annuar Zaini, Jonathan Bate, Farhan Nizami, Peter Frankopan, Jean and John Harding, Jomo Kwame Sundaram, Kalimullah Hassan, Ibrahim Ahmad Bajunid, Khoo Kay Kim, Kwok Kwan Kit, Lin See-Yan, Nabiel Makarim, Mohamed Ariff, Mohamed

Jawhar Hassan, Anthony Milner, Munir Majid, Muthiah Alagappa, Pilar Ramirez, Rajah Rasiah, Shanmughalingam Murugasu, Ranjit Ajit Singh, Visu Sinnadurai, Richard Smethurst, Sulaiman Mahbob, Tan Eu Chye, John Thomas, Steven Wong, (the late) Zainal Aznam Yusof and Zarinah Anwar. They have all influenced my thinking about issues of economic growth, development and history, whether directly or indirectly.

In January 2016, I decided that the project should enter a new phase and established a roadmap for the research outputs over the next two years. This book is the first in a series of publications that will document the outcome of our extensive research. Another important output is the project website at www.ehm.my. This is where the vast amount of historical data on Malaya's GDP and its components that has been compiled can be readily accessed. I am delighted that Richard Leete has agreed to manage the project and share his insights and extensive experience.

The wonderful support and encouragement of my wife Tuanku Zara and the forbearance of my children, Raja Azlan and Raja Nazira, during the countless hours I was preoccupied with researching and writing this book have been a continuous source of inspiration.

Sultan Nazrin Shah
Istana Iskandariah

Contents

CHAPTER 3

Estimating Historical GDP and Its Components 50

Boxes

Appendix Boxes

Figures

Box Figures

Tables

Box Tables

Appendix Tables

Maps

Abbreviations

APC	Average propensity to consume
AUV	Average unit value
CPI	Consumer Price Indices
EGS	Exports of goods and services
EUVI	Export unit value index
FELDA	Federal Land Development Authority
GDP	Gross domestic product
GFCE	Government final consumption expenditure
GFCF	Gross fixed capital formation
GNI	Gross national income
GNP	Gross national product
HICOM	Heavy Industries Corporation of Malaysia
HP	Hodrick-Prescott
IGS	Imports of goods and services
IS	Increase in stocks
IUVI	Import unit value index
MA	Moving Average
MPC	Marginal propensity to consume
M&E	Machinery and equipment
NDP	Net domestic product
NEP	New economic policy
NNI	Net national income
PFCE	Private final consumption expenditure
PWD	Public Works Department
R&D	Research and Development
ROW	Rest of world
SNA	System of National Accounts
TFP	Total factor productivity
UK	The United Kingdom of Great Britain and Northern Ireland
US	The United States of America

Overview

This book charts the course of Malaya's commodity-dependent economy during the first 40 years of the 20th century while under British colonial control, contrasting that course with economic growth and development in contemporary Malaysia. It asks: what is the economic legacy of British colonialism in the Malay Peninsula, and how differently has the economy performed under national management? By deriving estimates of Malaya's GDP and its components for the period 1900–1939, and analysing trends and their interrelationships, this book aims to deepen understanding of the dynamics of economic performance during these four decades and subsequently.

The study of long-run economic growth in Malaysia has till now been held back by the absence of comprehensive statistical data on national income before World War II. Today most countries keep detailed national accounts that are routinely compiled by government statistical agencies. Such records are fundamental for measuring and understanding the anatomy and evolution of economies, and for planning and managing them. This book for the first time provides a full historical time series for the country for the period 1900–1939.

The Malayan Economy and Its People

During the late 19th century and in the first half of the 20th century, most of the Malay Peninsula, like much of Southeast Asia, was under colonial control (Chapter 2). As the geopolitical spheres of influence of the colonial and ruling powers ebbed and flowed, territorial boundaries were frequently redrawn and renamed.

Colonialism facilitated the control of lands, institutions and peoples as well as the exploitation of natural resources. British control over the territories of the Malay Peninsula was progressively established from the last quarter of the 19th century to the second decade of the 20th century. British Malaya comprised three loosely integrated territories: the Straits Settlements, the Federated Malay States and the Unfederated Malay States. Singapore, which was a Straits Settlement, is not part of this study.

The present-day structure of the Malaysian economy is broad-based and reasonably diversified. The share of agriculture and mining in GDP has declined to less than 20 per cent combined, while that of services has grown to more than 50 per cent. By contrast, the economy of Malaya a century ago was largely agrarian, supported by two primary commodity pillars—tin and rubber—that were produced to meet the needs of the industries and people in Europe and North America following their industrial revolutions. These countries required continuous inflows of raw materials to produce manufactured goods as well as supplies of food for their populations. Colonial territories, such as India and Malaya, served as sources for such supplies.

An important feature of British-governed Malaya was its trade openness and free enterprise. Tin mining led the Peninsula's economic development, but it was later eclipsed by rubber. By 1904, Malaya was producing more than half the world's tin to meet the growing demand from Europe, especially following the surge in the use of tin cans for food preservation. It was around the early 1900s that the British began promoting the commercial production of rubber. Generous assistance to plantation companies included long-term security of land tenure and freedom to recruit low-cost foreign labour. Incentives were provided to encourage an industry that was dependent on substantial capital investment, and where the period for returns on investment was long—it took 5–7 years after land clearing and seeding before trees could be tapped. The massive trade boom in rubber during the first decade of the 20th century was due to rising world demand, fuelled in large part by the remarkable development of the US motor industry and the related demand for rubber tyres.

Malaya's early 20th century economic development was closely intertwined with population dynamics. The tin mining and rubber industries (before the introduction of new technologies) were highly labour intensive, and their development could not be sustained with local labour supply. Large inflows of foreign workers were recruited from China and India, with the result that the population shares of these two communities increased substantially. Most Chinese were drawn to the new towns developing around the tin mines and to the port cities, while the Indians lived and worked mainly on the rubber estates. Migration markedly changed the Peninsula's ethnic composition, making it delicately balanced.

Estimating Historical GDP

In constructing historical GDP estimates for Malaya for the period 1900–1939, the expenditure components—consumption, government spending, investment, exports and imports—were derived (Chapter 3). The expenditure method was employed without the benefit of controls from the production (value added) or income estimation approaches. The detailed enterprise censuses or surveys on which these need to draw did not occur until after independence, and the first set of comprehensive national accounts—featuring production, income and expenditure estimates—were collated for Malaysia only in the input-output accounts of 1978.

Each of the GDP components was assessed based on the concepts and definitions used, the availability of data, the estimation method employed and the choice of the most suitable deflators to obtain constant price series. The base year was taken as 1914, as it was a relatively stable year. Rubber prices had fallen from a peak in 1910 and had stabilised in 1914, and tin prices were also relatively stable for that year. In putting together expenditure estimates for this period, the most significant challenge was estimating consumption spending, as it accounted for a large proportion of GDP. The approach adopted used direct and indirect estimation.

Growth and Volatility of Malaya's Economy

The historical national accounts series provide the quantitative evidence for assessing important questions about the growth and cyclical trends in the Malayan economy (Chapter 4). Real per capita GDP (valued in 1914 prices), widely used as an indicator of economic welfare, was Straits$86 at the beginning of the 20th century. It had more than doubled to Straits$197 by 1919, and by 1939 it had reached Straits$269, more than three times the level in 1900. Unsurprisingly, given the critical importance of the tin and rubber industries, exports were a dominant component of GDP, accounting on average for about 60 per cent of Malaya's GDP in nominal terms over the 40 years. The gap between Malaya's gross domestic savings and its investment, the so-called investment gap, increased during World War I and remained sizeable until 1939. The counterpart to this large investment gap was an equally large trade surplus, the difference between export earnings and imports. The bulk of Malaya's commodity export earnings were repatriated to colonial plantation and mine owners, with comparatively little being reinvested in the local economy.

A striking aspect of annual GDP growth is that, while income trended upwards, growth fluctuated wildly. Aggregate GDP growth can be partitioned into the contributions of its component parts: private consumption spending, government spending, investment, and export and import demand. The most conspicuous feature is the dominance of export and import demand in influencing Malaya's aggregate growth. Changes in export and import volumes accounted for the bulk of growth, and so drove much of its volatility. Growth of the domestic expenditure components (consumption, government spending and investment) appears to have played only a subsidiary role. This analysis suggests that the Malayan economy rode 'a commodity roller-coaster' between 1900 and 1939.

Three large outside shocks were the main underlying causes of the economic downturns and booms: World War I (1914–1918), the so-called Roaring Twenties (1920–1929), and the onset of the Great Depression (1929–1932). The most prominent feature of 1914–1918 is that Malaya's GDP growth was maintained because of buoyant exports. Real GDP grew over this period at an average rate of 9.4 per cent per annum. The Roaring Twenties was a decade of high economic growth and prosperity, driven by recovery from World War I and a catching-up with postponed spending. It heralded a revival of Malaya's rubber and tin industries after European shipping restrictions were lifted. In the Great Depression, most countries, and in particular the US, experienced very sharp economic declines. Malaya, by then heavily reliant on the US market for its exports, was not spared from the economic crisis and its real GDP contracted very sharply in 1931–1932 due to an unprecedented collapse in exports.

Volatility and Sources of Growth in Historical and Contemporary GDP

Economic volatility, identified with short-term fluctuations in real GDP around its longer-term trend, and its impact on economic growth are assessed using data for Malaya in the years 1900–1939, and contrasted with post-independence Malaysia over the period 1970–2009 (Chapter 5).

Benchmarked against wider experience, volatility in pre-war Malaya was intense. Year-to-year swings in real GDP growth of 10 percentage points or more were common. The volatility in pre-war colonial Malaya, both in the frequency and the magnitude of shocks, is probably without modern precedent.

The harmful effects of volatility, operating through reduced investment in built and human capital, have been found to outweigh any benefits from resource booms. The evidence for Malaya supports this contention and shows that extreme volatility had a depressing impact on long-run growth. Real annual exponential GDP growth for the period 1900–1919 was 7 per cent when volatility was lower, compared with 4 per cent for the period 1920–1939 when volatility was significantly higher. Stronger economic growth was accompanied by greater stability in post-colonial Malaysia.

In pre-war Malaya, investment was even more volatile than GDP. Extreme volatility in exports, particularly rubber, and the consequent volatility in income was associated with even more pronounced volatility in investment. Low and highly volatile investment rates held back economic diversification which weakened the defenses against volatility and entrenched commodity dependence. While investment rates in post-independence Malaysia also fluctuated, levels of investment were much higher than those in the colonial era, averaging well above 20 per cent of GDP and peaking at over 40 per cent on the cusp of the Asian Financial Crisis in 1997.

As an indicator of well-being, real per capita consumption, though imperfect, is of interest insofar as it reflects the material standard of living of the general population. Well-being is also usually considered to be linked to the volatility of consumption, with greater volatility eroding welfare. Consumption volatility was more pronounced in the first four decades of the 20th century than in the period 1970–2009. This is probably due to the dependence of employment and income during the earlier period on exports of rubber and tin, which demonstrated extreme volatility. After independence, successful efforts to diversify the economy created more—and more varied—employment opportunities.

Growth accounting suggests that, for the four decades from 1900 to 1939, of the annual average 5.5 per cent real GDP growth rate, growth of capital stock accounted for 1.7 percentage points and growth of employment another 1.8 percentage points. Total factor productivity

(TFP) growth accounted for 2.0 percentage points. The corresponding estimates for the first half of these four decades show that growth of capital stock and TFP was markedly higher than in the second half. One caveat in interpreting these data is the likely presence of unknown and possibly large measurement errors that are conflated with the TFP estimates.

Considerable debate about the sources of growth has directed researchers to learn more about growth processes. It has also made countries more conscious of the importance of the role of productivity in economic growth. Malaysia, since the mid-1990s, has focused on enhancing innovation and productivity to transform itself from being an input-driven economy to a knowledge-based one.

From Colonial Control to National Economic Management

The colonial authorities adopted a *laissez-faire* economic system (Chapter 6). They gave the British-dominated private sector—plantation and mining companies, agency houses, banks and middlemen—*carte blanche* to maximise profits, and provided a supportive legislative and institutional environment. Agency houses were thus able to repatriate substantial profits.

Laissez-faire practices led to highly uneven development, with economic growth and prosperity concentrated in and mainly benefiting the Peninsula's west coast states. These were the centres of the tin and rubber industries with better physical and social infrastructure, which served the commercial interests of the export-oriented private sector. A *laissez-faire* approach also led to high levels of inequality in the ownership and control of the economy.

Real per capita GDP in Malaya was three times larger in 1939 than in 1900, equivalent to an exponential annual growth rate of 2.9 per cent. In post-independence Malaysia between 1970 and 2009, real per capita GDP grew at a cumulative average annual rate of 3.7 per cent.

Consumption per capita in real terms, however, was just 51 per cent higher in 1939 than in 1900. While this improvement was welcome, it raises the question as to why advances in the general standard of living, equivalent to growth of just 1 per cent per year, lagged so far behind GDP per capita growth.

Real GDP growth in the post-independence period led to rapid advances in the average standard of living and to reductions in absolute poverty. From 1970 to 2009, per capita consumption advanced at an average annual rate of 3.5 per cent, only marginally less than average GDP growth of 3.7 per cent. The consumption dividend from growth over the period 1900–1939 was modest in comparison. Differences in the structure of the economy (primary export dependence) and in the structure of ownership (colonial control) are the likely explanations.

Investment rates in real terms for the period 1900–1939, averaging less than 10 per cent per year, were also very small, as was government expenditure. This suggests that little of the production surpluses was reinvested in the domestic economy. Pre-World War II inequality in consumption was also striking, with expenditures of the top 1 per cent of the population more than 21 times higher than the average for all other population groups.

Unbalanced development, poverty and inequities in corporate ownership structures were addressed after independence. In the first 10 years following independence, much was achieved in terms of growth, the expansion of infrastructure, rural development and increases in living standards. But less was achieved in terms of poverty reduction, employment creation and addressing economic imbalances among people, states and regions.

The New Economic Policy was launched by the government in 1971 following the May 1969 racial clashes to rectify the inequalities of the colonial era. Foreign-owned natural-resource companies were restructured through equity buyouts by public-sector enterprises, and placed initially under government control and management. Resource revenues were used to redistribute income and reduce poverty through multiple pathways. National control over economic management was accompanied by a long-term vision for a more unified and socially just nation. That led to considerable achievements in employment creation, welfare gains and poverty reduction.

CHAPTER 1

Labour intensive tin mining in Malaya

Introduction

Malaysia is widely considered an example of successful development that serves as a model for lesser developed countries. The country's wise macroeconomic management has delivered growth with equity. The absolute poverty in which most of the population lived at independence in 1957 has been almost eradicated, according to the national poverty line income. Structural transformation of the economy has been accompanied by massive investment in the social sector, especially in health and education, which has led to broad-based and high levels of human development. Malaysia has become a modern urban industrialised nation, and its diverse, multi-cultural population enjoys safety, security and prosperity. A secure institutional environment has in turn encouraged high levels of national and foreign investment.

Malaysia has not succumbed to the resource curse of over-reliance on its natural resources, as have some other countries with a similar colonial heritage and rich natural resource endowments. While it has had high economic growth over the past half century to 2015, some resource-rich countries have experienced little more than short-lived resource booms, their economies expanding rapidly while resources last, but contracting once these have been exhausted. Some have also succumbed to Dutch disease, whereby local currency appreciation leads to cheaper imports and more expensive exports. This in turn can result in declining exports of manufactures, rising unemployment and slowing of growth in non-resource sectors.

Malaysia has used the rents from its natural resource endowments to invest in diversifying its productive base, in improving infrastructure and in strengthening human capital. Diversification was initially within agriculture, from rubber to oil palm, and subsequently within manufacturing, from textiles to electrical products, such that Malaysia has become a leading exporter of electrical and electronic products. Exports of manufactures have long overtaken natural resource exports in value. Commodity exports, now dominated mainly by hydrocarbons and palm oil, amounted to only around one third of total merchandise exports in 2014, and contributed around one quarter of gross domestic product (GDP). Services have become the leading sector of the economy.

As well as enlarging its mix of export products, Malaysia has broadened its range of trading partners. It has increasingly diversified its export markets, with much less reliance on the advanced economies of the US, Japan and Europe, and a greater concentration on the countries of East Asia and the rest of the world.[1]

Challenges remain, particularly in relation to raising productivity, nurturing a competitive business environment, creating internationally competitive and high-tech industries, increasing educational attainment standards and strengthening national unity.

Malaysia today is a world away from what it was at the beginning of the 20th century when the Malay Peninsula was just coming under British colonial control, and its economy was beginning to thrive. At that time, the Malay Peninsula was a territory with an abundance of land and natural resources, but with a small population of just 1.7 million. Relative to the needs of its expanding economy, it had acute shortages of people and skills which were overcome by migration from three of Asia's most populous countries—China, India and the Dutch East Indies (Indonesia). The British encouraged large inflows of low-cost migrant workers to meet the needs of the Peninsula's rapidly growing economy, markedly changing the population balance between its three main communities, the Malays, the Chinese and the Indians.

This growing population was engaged principally in the production of tin and later rubber as well as the provision of a broadening range of support services, and subsistence and small-scale agriculture. The developing economy was heavily reliant on its two commodity exports of tin and rubber which it sold primarily to the US and the UK. Commodity exports accounted for almost all of the country's merchandise exports from 1901 to 1939, and contributed about 60% of GDP. The Malay Peninsula was also a market for imported British manufactures. This dependence left the country highly vulnerable to the impacts of external events over which it had no control, which contributed to the extreme volatility of export earnings and growth identified by this study.

---

1   For key economic and financial data on the status of the Malaysian economy, readers should consult Bank Negara Malaysia (2016) and Economic Planning Unit-Malaysia (2016).

The more commodity-dependent an economy is (that is, the higher the share of primary goods in a country's exports), the more vulnerable it will be to commodity price shocks. Excessive instability in export earnings and economic growth, as experienced by primary commodity-producing countries, is closely associated with highly volatile commodity prices. The inelastic nature of both the supply of and the demand for tin and rubber contributed to their excessive price volatility, which arguably reduced growth over the study period. The 5–7 year lag between planting and production of rubber means that while oversupply can last for a long time, it is difficult to boost production quickly during shortages.

Britain, which ruled over the Malay Peninsula for most of the period until independence, provided much of the capital, technology and management skills to help realize the potential of the country's natural resource abundance. It had the capital to invest heavily in its tin mines and rubber plantations, while the Peninsula's low cost raw materials were essential inputs propelling growth in British and US industry. But ultimately this reliance on the extraction and export of the country's natural resources was unable to provide a sound basis for sustainable development. As is demonstrated by the comparison with the country's post-Independence development trajectory, a much more comprehensive national development strategy has been necessary to achieve this, including the more productive reinvestment of the wealth generated by natural resource endowments.

Purpose, Organisation and Coverage

Purpose

The primary objective of this book is to chart the course of Malaya's commodity-dependent economy during the first 40 years of the 20th century while it was under British colonial control. A detailed analysis is made of long-run trends and short-run fluctuations in economic growth, of economic volatility and its impact on growth, and of the sources of growth. Some key aspects of Malaya's economic performance during this period are contrasted with economic growth and development in contemporary Malaysia.

Among the important broader questions that this book attempts to shed light on are: what is the economic legacy of British colonialism in the Malay Peninsula? Were the immense profits generated from the Peninsula's rubber and tin industries used to finance the foundations of post-independence national development? To what extent were the profits derived from the export of these natural resources used to increase the welfare and well-being of the Malayan population?

The study of long-run economic growth in Malaya (and post-1963 Malaysia) has been impeded by the absence of a statistical series on national income accounts for the pre-World War II period. Literature on Malaya's economic development for that period has been mainly confined to studies on specific sectors of the economy and particular geographic areas. By and large, these studies have focused on the rubber-planting and tin-mining sectors, the twin pillars of the economy which provided employment for a significant share of the country's labour force.

Before begining the analysis of Malaya's economy, therefore, it is necessary to develop a new set of national income accounts from the fragmented available data. National accounts are essential for measuring and understanding the evolution of economies as well as for planning and managing them. Nowadays, Malaysia and most countries keep detailed national accounts that are routinely compiled by government statistical agencies as a priority function. These accounts are based on statistical data sources, methods, concepts and definitions that follow international standards so as to ensure consistency over time and to allow comparisons with other countries. Another key aim of this book is thus to document in some detail the reconstruction of estimates of Malaya's national income accounts for the period 1900–1939, that is, up to the time of the Japanese occupation (1941–1945), a period for which no data are readily available.

Based on the results of this exercise, a detailed analysis is undertaken of the trends in GDP and its components in order to better understand the dynamics of Malaya's economic performance during these four decades. The findings are intended to fill important gaps in knowledge about the evolution of Malaya's commodity-dependent economy during British colonial rule, and its responses to wider developments affecting the international economy, particularly World War I, the boom years of the 1920s, and the Great Depression. Through comparisons of economic performance under colonial rule with post-independence Malaysia, the analysis presented here will also lead to a better understanding of longer-term trends in economic growth and well-being.

Organisation

Following this introduction, Chapter 2 provides an overview of the geopolitical setting of Southeast Asia during the late 19th and early 20th centuries, together with a detailed account of the economic, political and social context of Malaya. It also includes an analysis of population trends and an assessment of the contribution of labour migration to these trends.

Chapter 3 describes and explains the application of the national accounts expenditure method to derive estimates of historical GDP. It outlines the statistical approach used in computing each of the components of Malaya's GDP through direct and indirect estimation procedures. Some time series data on GDP and its components are given in a limited set of tables in Appendix 2. A full set of the national income accounts produced as part of this study can be accessed online at www.ehm.my. A secondary reason for presenting this detailed methodological description is to demonstrate an approach that can estimate GDP from very limited data, and from data drawn from areas under different administrations as was the case in Malaya at this time. It is hoped that the methodology employed here may be helpful to other efforts to construct historical GDP estimates in similarly challenging cases.

Chapter 4 analyses the series of GDP estimates that have been derived using a national accounting balance framework. It focuses on the long-term trends and short-term fluctuations of the economy, and in particular on the impact of the three major external shocks— World War I, the boom years of the Roaring Twenties, and the Great Depression. The chapter assesses the variations in the growth of the components of GDP and the role of exports in the considerable volatility that was experienced. A decomposition analysis of the growth of tin, rubber and other exports is also presented. The chapter concludes by comparing Malaya's GDP trends with those of other benchmark countries, particularly its major trading partners—the US and the UK.

Chapter 5 explores and contrasts the different experiences of economic volatility and its impacts on growth during the earlier colonial period (1900–1939) as compared with post-independence Malaysia (1970–2009). The chapter also provides some estimates of the sources of economic growth for the earlier period, with the application of growth accounting allowing for the identification of the contributions of capital and labour. This in turn generates an estimate of the residual, or total factor productivity, which reflects the contribution to growth of increased efficiency, including through technological progress.

Chapter 6 provides a detailed assessment of the vulnerabilities of the natural resource-dependent Malayan economy and the role of British colonial interests in shaping an unbalanced form of economic development. It examines trends in per capita GDP growth and consumption during the period of colonial administration, with its *laissez-faire* economic policy, and compares these with those of contemporary post-independence Malaysia, when a deliberately interventionist national economic policy was put in place. The chapter analyses the impact of these different approaches, especially in relation to the distribution of rents from natural resource extraction and export. The book concludes with the identification of some areas for future research arising from this study.

Coverage

Malaya did not exist as a unified administrative entity during the first half of the 20th century, which compounds the difficulties of preparing national accounts. At that time, the Malay Peninsula was made up of 12 separate administrative units or territories (Map 1.1)[2]:

- The British Colony of the Straits Settlements, comprising the territories of Penang, Malacca and Singapore.[3]
- The Federated Malay States of Perak, Selangor, Negri Sembilan and Pahang.
- The Unfederated Malay States of Perlis, Kedah, Kelantan, Trengganu and Johore.

Malaya, which corresponds geographically to present-day Peninsular Malaysia, should be distinguished from British Malaya or Pan-Malaya, both terms commonly used to refer to Malaya and Singapore combined (Chapter 2).

---

2 Spellings used here for the various states of Malaya are based on those used in Mills (1958).

3 The Straits Settlements also included the Christmas Island (from 1900), the Cocos Keeling Islands (from 1903), and the Dindings territory (from 1826 until its retrocession to the state of Perak in 1935). The Dindings, presently the Manjung District in Perak, comprising Pangkor Island, Lumut and Sitiawan, was initially ceded to the British by Perak as part of the 1826 Burney Treaty, albeit not taken-up by them until 1874, when confirmed in the Pangkor Treaty (Chapter 2).

Map 1.1 **The Malay Peninsula c. 1925**

In 1957, the Straits Settlements (excluding Singapore), the Federated Malay States and the Unfederated Malay States were combined to form the Federation of Malaya. In 1963, the Federation joined with Sabah and Sarawak (on the island of Borneo), and with Singapore, to form Malaysia. Singapore separated from Malaysia in 1965.

There are no consolidated statistical reports for Malaya for the period 1900–1939. Each of the 11 administrative units published its own independent set of annual reports, the coverage and quality of which varied considerably between administrative units and also over time. Generally, there is more statistical information relating to the more urbanised Straits Settlements, less for the Federated Malay States, and even less for the overwhelmingly rural Unfederated Malay States.

This study makes use of primary source materials wherever possible. Fortunately, there is a large amount of archival material from the British colonial period that can be drawn upon to piece together a reasonable time series on each of the aggregate demand components. This consists mainly of official documents in the form of annual reports of the various state governments, government financial statements, annual returns on exports and imports, official correspondences, departmental statistics on government revenues and expenditures, and population censuses conducted by the colonial administrators.

The first step was to locate as many of the relevant historical source materials as possible. Many can be found in the National Archives in Kuala Lumpur and the Public Records Office in London. The next step was to transform all the quantitative information into a format appropriate for the computation of national income statistics. Since different historical source materials were used, the data contained in them were in many instances not comparable, and it was necessary to make various adjustments in order to make the data internally consistent.

There were also many gaps in the data which had to be bridged by making estimates based on various assumptions, some of which were formulated of necessity on limited evidence. The data deficiencies, gaps and limitations as well as the assumptions made in estimating the individual components of GDP are described in Chapter 3 and Appendix 1. A concise historical perspective on national income accounting now follows.

National Income Accounting in Historical Perspective

The keeping of national accounts has a relatively recent history. It came about as a response to the economic information gap experienced during the Great Depression of the 1930s. National accounts provide planners with tools to better understand economies and guide them towards meeting policy objectives. National accounts data are also used for indicator analysis of past and present macroeconomic growth and development. GDP per capita, tracked over time, is the most widely used measure of aggregate economic performance. National accounts data are also used in econometric modelling to make projections. With time series data, studies of the growth and the changing structure of the economy can be undertaken.

Although the concept of national income accounting goes back as far as the 17th century (Maddison, 2003; Bolt and Van Zanden, 2014), it was not until the 1930s that the first comprehensive set of national accounts was created, based on the pioneering work of Nobel laureate Simon Kuznets in the US (Fogel, 2001).[4] In the UK, another Nobel laureate, Richard Stone, also made an important contribution towards the development of modern concepts of national accounting (Pesaran and Harcourt, 2000). In the US, the first set of accounts was presented in a report to Congress in 1937 and in a research report entitled *National Income, 1929–1935* (Abraham, 1969). The first formal national accounts were published in 1947 in the US, and many European countries followed soon after. From then on, the compilation of national accounts became an annual exercise both in the US and Europe.

The preparation of national accounts in most developing countries took somewhat longer to materialise, however, hampered by the lack of relevant data, weak statistical systems, the substantial costs involved, and limited capacities and expertise to handle the complexity of the task.

In the immediate post-World War II years, a committee of experts chaired by Richard Stone and convened by the United Nations Statistical Office and the Organisation for European Economic Cooperation (now the Organisation for Economic Co-operation and Development) made a concerted effort to improve and standardise national income accounting. Their work eventually led to the publication in 1953 of a United Nations Report entitled *A System of National Accounts and Supporting Tables (SNA)*. In the years subsequent to its publication, the construction of national income accounts started to spread with the encouragement and support of the United Nations, the World Bank and various other international organisations.

Following several regional consultations, the first of what has become a series of major periodic revisions to the SNA was published in 1968. This *System*, which has evolved over time to try to keep pace with the growing complexity of national economies, is intended to serve as a guide on standards for all countries. Reflecting in part the fact that a growing share of services and the production of increasingly complex products make the measurement of output much more complicated than in the past, the SNA has grown from around 50 pages in 1953 to more than 700 pages in its latest 2008 version (Coyle, 2014).

---

4   For a detailed reader-friendly account of the origins and evolution of GDP, see Coyle (2014), who contends that while the changing and increasingly complex nature of the modern economy in the 21st century constrains the use of GDP, there is no alternative for measuring economic growth. Expressing similar concerns with GDP and other leading indicators, Karabell (2014) suggests adopting a new paradigm through the use by individuals of Big Data to construct and measure bespoke indicators of the economy.

Income Accounting in Malaya and Malaysia

The first attempt at compiling national income statistics in the Malay Peninsula was undertaken in 1932 by the Retrenchment Commission, and covered the Federated Malay States. This Commission had been appointed by the Federated Malay States' government to look into the territory's sources of taxation. As a rough measure of what the tax base was likely to be in the 1930s, the Commission made a calculation of national income for the Federated Malay States in 1931, and provided estimates for the years 1932–1937.

The Commission noted that it 'is impracticable…in the conditions of the Federated Malay States to obtain any approach to accurate information of individual incomes'. Lacking such information, the Commission accepted 'as a sufficiently close approximation' to national income, the 'sum of two quantities more readily capable of measurement, viz., the figures of primary production and the gross profits of foreign trade', with the caveat that the 'figures are intended to represent tendencies rather than precise numerical forecasts' (Federated Malay States, 1932, pp. 2, 5).

The Commission's figures as reproduced in Table 1.1—showing that more than half of the Federated Malay States' income during this period was derived from rubber and tin exports—do not amount to 'national income' in the modern sense. Neither the theoretical insight nor the methodology was sufficiently developed to meet modern requirements for the measurement of GDP. Nor was the primary objective of the exercise to estimate national accounts as understood today. Rather the purpose was to estimate government revenue in response to the serious economic crisis of the early 1930s.

Benham's *The National Income of Malaya 1947–1949*, published in 1951, contains the earliest estimates of national income accounts derived using modern concepts.[5] That study used the output method to construct GDP at market prices and also made estimates for the components of gross national product (GNP) and national income. Although Benham was not able to prepare national income estimates based on the income and expenditure methods, he nevertheless provided estimates for some of the components. A World Bank

---

5   Dr F. C. Benham served as an economic adviser to the Commissioner-General for the UK in Southeast Asia during the early post-World War II era (Benham, 1951).

Table 1.1 National income, Federated Malay States, 1931–1937

Year	Rubber	Tin	Other produce	Profits of trade	National income
Straits\$[6] million					
1931	54	51	49	26	**180**
1932	38	32	52	18	**140**
1933	37	35	55	18	**145**
1934	45	47	58	23	**173**
1935	53	56	61	27	**197**
1936	60	60	64	30	**214**
1937	63	69	67	33	**232**
Share (%)					
1931	30.0	28.3	27.2	14.4	**100**
1932	27.1	22.9	37.1	12.9	**100**
1933	25.5	24.1	37.9	12.4	**100**
1934	26.0	27.2	33.5	13.3	**100**
1935	26.9	28.4	31.0	13.7	**100**
1936	28.0	28.0	29.9	14.0	**100**
1937	27.2	29.7	28.9	14.2	**100**

Source:
Federated Malay States (1932a, pp. 5).

report of 1955, *The Economic Development of Malaya*, provided a detailed statistical appendix containing GDP estimates for the years 1949–1953 (International Bank of Reconstruction and Development, 1955). Subsequently, Wilson estimated GDP at market prices for 1954 (Rao, 1976).

The estimates by Benham for 1947–1949, the World Bank for 1949–1953, and Wilson for 1954 were on a Pan-Malayan basis, comprising present-day Peninsular Malaysia and Singapore. The data were not separated into Malayan and Singaporean components.

Subsequent attempts to compute Peninsular Malaysia's GDP shares from the Pan-Malayan estimates of Benham, the World Bank and Wilson were made by Lim (1967) and Lee (1968). Walters prepared

---

6   The Straits dollar was introduced in Malaya in 1903 following the establishment of a Currency Board in 1897. It was initially exchangeable at par with sterling, but in 1906, the rate was fixed at 2 shillings and 4 pence. This stable rate was maintained until 1939, when the Straits dollar was replaced at par by the Malayan dollar. The Currency Board system endured until 1967, when the currency was split, with Malaysia, Singapore and Brunei all issuing their own currencies. This also marked the end of the sterling exchange standard for Malaysia and Singapore (Lee, 1990).

the first set of national accounts for Peninsular Malaysia for the years 1955–1960 based on the 1953 SNA guidelines (Harvie, 1960). Significant contributions were also made by Abraham and Gill (1969a, 1969b), who estimated the sectoral GDP series for the period 1956–1966, and the GDP expenditure components for the years 1960–1966. Since then, the Department of Statistics-Malaysia has updated the national accounts on a continuing basis, incorporating the periodic revisions made to the SNA guidelines.[7] As part of his historical study of the world's economy, Maddison (2003) has also made some basic estimates of GDP for Malaysia stretching back to 1914.[8]

Drawing on the earlier estimates, Rao (1976) assembled the national accounts of Peninsular Malaysia for the 25-year period from 1947–1971 at current and constant 1959 prices. Noteworthy was his attempt to revise the national accounts data of the late 1940s and 1950s to achieve consistency with the 1960–1971 official estimates (Department of Statistics-Malaysia, 1975).

Malaya's immediate postwar national accounts were derived using imprecise estimation techniques due to the severe data limitations. The authors were acutely aware of the imperfect nature of their estimates and emphasised the need for caution in their use. Benham pointed out that his estimates 'involve a considerable amount of guesswork', and that 'a large number of gaps have had to be filled in by estimates, in some cases, so rough that they are only informed guesses' (Benham, 1951, pp. 1). Lim (1967, pp. vii) noted that 'statistics in underdeveloped Malaya are also underdeveloped and this underdevelopment of statistical data, much to our regret, has imposed its limitations in various ways and in varying degrees on a study of this nature depending as it does so much on historical statistical facts'. Similarly, Rao (1976) had reservations about the reliability of the data for the earlier years where guesses had to be made in the absence of accurate data.

Malaysia's first comprehensive national accounts using all three methods—production, income and expenditure—were computed in

7   In the 1960s, a branch of economic history called Cliometrics, or new economic history, was established. The new economic history was able to develop quickly because its foundations had been laid by the earlier development of historical national accounting. This produced a stock of quantitative knowledge, and provided a clearer picture of the timing and sources of economic growth.

8   The critical importance of historical national accounts for charting the economic development of a country is underlined by Horlings (1995) in his account of the economic development of the Dutch service sector in the first half of the 19th century. For an account of Finland's economic development, see Hjerppe (1989).

the input-output accounts of 1978. Similar sets of accounts have since been compiled on an annual basis.

The GDP estimates made in this study were derived using the expenditure method, which looks at the final uses of output. Box 1.1 illustrates this approach and situates it within a model of the circular flow of income in a national economy.

Box 1.1   Circular flow model of income

Income is a flow that circulates within an economy over an interval of time. In the simplest economy, firms pay households for the services that they provide and households spend their income in exchange for the output produced by firms. In practice, the flows of income are more complicated (Box Figure 1.1). There are other economic actors in addition to firms and households, and there are both withdrawals and injections into the circular flow of income.

A more complete model recognises the presence of government, financial institutions, and an *overseas* or *rest of the world sector*. Income leaks from the circular flow in the form of taxes (net of subsidies), but government spending injects income. The savings that are deposited with financial institutions (or even hoarded) also constitute a leakage from the system. But the investment that these savings finance is an injection. When firms, households, or other domestic entities buy imports, this too is a leakage. Conversely, output sold to the rest of the world, exports, is an injection.

These withdrawals and injections into the circular flow of income correspond to financial surpluses and deficits of the private sector (savings less investment), government (taxes less government spending), and overseas sector (imports less exports). As the claims that arise from institutional financial surpluses and deficits must net out (each asset has a counterparty liability), it follows that in an accounting sense, aggregate injections must be equal to aggregate leakages.

Box Figure 1.1 **Flows of income**

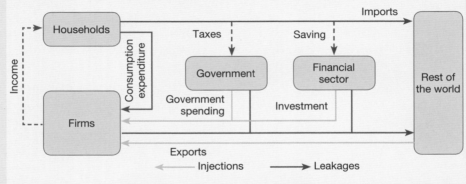

Beyond GDP

GDP is essentially a measure of the output of market-based economic activity rather than of social well-being, although the two are generally closely correlated. National economic performance has traditionally been tracked using GDP and other macroeconomic indicators. Since the 1990s, composite indices such as the United Nations Development Programme's Human Development Index, which measures a range of social welfare indicators including health and education, have become increasingly popular. But there has also been growing recognition that success in relation to national development goals cannot effectively be captured through the use of such indicators alone. One reason is that rising economic prosperity has, in many cases, been accompanied by other serious challenges such as environmental degradation.

Continuing efforts to address the shortcomings of existing measures include the establishment by then French President Nicolas Sarkozy of a Commission on the Measurement of Economic Performance and Social Progress (Stiglitz *et al.*, 2009). The Commission concluded that a range of separate indicators is required to capture the different elements of well-being, with GDP still used to measure economic or market activity, supplemented by social well-being and environmental indicators. Traditional objective measures of well-being can themselves be further strengthened through the use of subjective or self-reported indicators (Deaton, 2013). So while much of this book focuses on measures of GDP and material well-being, it is recognized that a broader range of indicators is necessary to monitor more fully trends in development and prosperity.

*   *   *

The next chapter situates the subsequent estimation and analysis of Malaya's economic performance within the prevailing geopolitical setting of Southeast Asia. It also gives an overview of the nature of Malaya's economy and its people—who they were, where they came from, what they were doing and where they lived.

CHAPTER 2

Extracting latex by tapping a rubber tree

The Malayan Economy and Its People

During the late 19th century and in the first half of the 20th century, most of the Malay Peninsula, like much of Southeast Asia, was under colonial rule. Territorial boundaries were frequently redrawn and renamed as the geopolitical spheres of influence of the colonial and ruling powers ebbed and flowed. By the late 19th century, colonial domination in Southeast Asia was primarily concentrated among three European powers (the UK, the Netherlands and France) and the US, which had gained control of the Philippines from Spain in 1898 (Map 2.1). All were engaged in developing and exploiting the region's vast natural resources to meet the growing needs of a rapidly industrialising Europe and North America.

Map 2.1 Southeast Asia during the high colonial age, 1870–1914

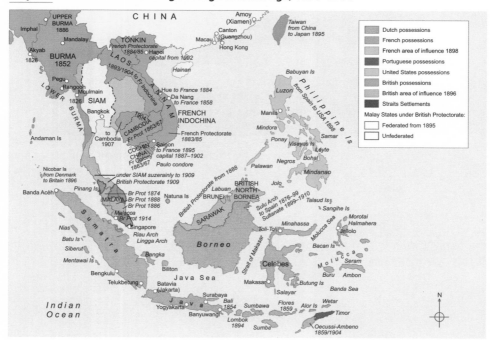

Source:
Adapted from O'Brien and University of London (1999).
Note:
Country boundaries are approximate and are intended for illustration purposes only.

Colonialism facilitated the control of lands, institutions and peoples as well as the exploitation and depletion of natural resources. It changed the mode of production from peasant farming and fishing in subsistence economies to wage employment in order to promote and further the economic interests of the colonial powers. It created unbalanced development, with resource revenues rarely used to promote human well-being or for capital formation to diversify and develop economies for the benefit of indigenous communities.[9]

To further its economic interests, British control over most of the territories of the Malay Peninsula was progressively established from the last quarter of the 19th century to the second decade of the 20th century. The Pangkor Treaty of 1874 was a critical milestone in the formal relationship between the UK and the Malay states, and in the subsequent extension of British rule across the Peninsula. British authority was gradually formalised and consolidated throughout British Malaya, which comprised three loosely integrated geographical entities: the Straits Settlements, the Federated Malay States and the Unfederated Malay States (Smith, 1963). In the early 20th century, there was little sense, if any, of a national identity among the people living in British Malaya, with their allegiance being either to their state of residence or, for foreign migrants, to their country of origin. British Malaya was essentially an assembly of political entities without a common vision for national development.

British Malaya
The Straits Settlements

From April 1867, the three strategically-located port cities of Penang, Malacca and Singapore came to be ruled directly as the British Crown Colony of the Straits Settlements, having been earlier controlled as one administrative unit by the British East India Company.[10] These ports were initially used to bolster and protect the East India Company's

---

9   British colonialism did nevertheless establish institutions and systems that were built upon after decolonisation, including a well-functioning Malayan civil service (Heussler, 1981) and institutions that supported British business interests (Barlow, 1978).

10 Following treaties with the Dutch and the Siamese, the East India Company, with the support of its own army, gradually extended its influence over the independent Malay states through trade and treaties. While the rulers of these states looked to the Company as the arbiter of local politics, and appealed for its help in settling internal and external disputes, the Company itself sought deeper British commercial penetration (Thio, 1969).

lucrative trading routes to China and other locations in Asia. The bulk of the world's trade to eastern Asia passed through the Strait of Malacca. Penang island in the north of the Peninsula was the first settlement to be secured through a treaty with Kedah in the late 18th century. Singapore, with its even more favourable trading location in the south, followed through a treaty with the Johore Sultanate in 1819. Malacca had already been surrendered by the Dutch, and this arrangement was formalised through the Anglo-Dutch Treaty of 1824, which divided the Malay Archipelago into a British zone in the north and a Dutch zone in the south.

Each of the three Straits Settlements had free port status, meaning that shipping and cargo could enter and leave without taxation. The Settlements, and in particular Singapore, which was a flourishing centre for the ever-growing trade in commodity exports and Western and Asian imports, served as a springboard for British expansion of control over the Peninsula's Malay states. They also benefited from the Malay states coming under British protection.

Through a series of treaties, the UK progressively gained suzerainty over the nine Malay sultanates on the Peninsula (Penang and Malacca were not sultanates). Four of these were eventually grouped together as the Federated Malay States, and five as the Unfederated Malay States.

Federated Malay States: The Pangkor Treaty

Formulated by the British government and the local hereditary Malay leaders of Perak, the Pangkor Treaty of January 1874 resolved a Perak royal succession dispute in favour of Raja Abdullah, and muted disputes between Chinese groups over control of the Larut tin mines (Swettenham, 1975; Barlow, 1995; Cheah, 2001). The rapid growth of the tin trade from around the mid-19th century had brought with it an influx of Chinese labour to the tin-producing west coast states of Perak, Selangor and Negri Sembilan. Fierce competition emerged between Chinese secret societies and rival business and social groups, which were formed around dialect and clan membership. This coincided with disputes over the control of imposts on tin (Khoo, 2003). The British, responding to sections of the Straits Settlements trading community who were financing the mines, intervened to safeguard and strengthen their commercial interests in lands that they perceived to be rich in natural resources.

The Pangkor Treaty provided for the appointment of a British Resident to advise the Sultan of Perak in all matters affecting general administration including maintaining peace and security, overseeing the collection of revenue from taxation and encouraging economic development. The Residential system thus involved British control over all aspects of the administration other than those touching on Islam and Malay custom. The treaty signalled a formal departure from the hitherto official policy of non-intervention by the British in the affairs of the Malay states. Similar treaty arrangements were reached around the same period with the rulers of Selangor, Negri Sembilan and Pahang, with each accepting a British-appointed Resident.[11]

In 1896, the Federated Malay States—combining the three neighbouring states of Negri Sembilan,[12] Selangor and Perak on the western side of the Peninsula, and Pahang on the eastern side—formally came into existence through the Treaty of Federation, with Kuala Lumpur designated as the administrative capital of the four British-protected states. The Federated Malay States were administered by a Federal Council, headed by a British High Commissioner and assisted by a Resident-General, with the UK being responsible for defence and foreign affairs (Ho, 2009). For administrative purposes, each state was subdivided into districts managed by British District Officers.

Unfederated Malay States

In 1826, the UK, through the East India Company, signed a secret treaty known as the Burney Treaty with the Kingdom of Siam (Marks, 1997; Cheah, 2001). The rulers of the four northern and eastern Malay states of Kedah, Perlis, Trengganu and Kelantan were not present during the signing of the agreement. The British acknowledged Siamese sovereignty over those states, and Siam accepted British ownership of Penang and Province Wellesley (now Seberang Perai), a narrow

---

11 These states were not annexed due to the Victorian preference for informal rather than formal rule. They remained sovereign entities, with the Malay rulers as the sovereign heads of state, although in practice the substance of power gradually passed into British hands (Thio, 1969).

12 In view of the complicated political and clan organisations in the districts of Negri Sembilan and ongoing disputes, the exercise of British influence and control over the state was a gradual process, beginning initially with the district of Sungai Ujong and then extending to all other districts some years later (Gullick, 2003).

hinterland opposite the island of Penang, and allowed the East India Company to trade freely in Trengganu and Kelantan. In 1909, the Anglo-Siamese Treaty was signed by the same parties, and through it, Siam agreed to give up its claim over Kedah, Perlis, Trengganu and Kelantan which formally came under British protection. Pattani meanwhile remained a Siamese territory.

Johore, in the south of the Peninsula, accepted a treaty of protection with the UK in 1885, and in 1914 yielded to British pressure to accept a resident British Advisor (Nadarajah, 2000). Despite accepting protectorate status, Johore remained outside of the Federated Malay States. Johore, which was multi-ethnic and had benefited economically from its proximity to Singapore, was comparable to the Federated Malay States in its level of development.

In contrast to the Federated Malay States, the Unfederated Malay States were more autonomous, with their rulers enjoying some political discretion, and they were not administered collectively (Heussler, 1981). Each had a British Advisor in its administration. Apart from Johore, which was more developed, these states were largely rural and predominantly Malay, with employment being overwhelmingly concentrated in traditional agriculture and fishing.

Sabah and Sarawak

Sabah and Sarawak, which acquired colonial status in 1946, were administered separately from the Malay states on the Peninsula as well as from each other. Separated from the Malay Peninsula by some 500 kilometres of the South China Sea, these two vast, under-populated and resource-rich states were a world away from the political and economic life of Malaya.

In 1881, the British North Borneo Chartered Company was estab-lished, and began administering a territory on Borneo island that had been ceded by the Sultan of Brunei and the Sultan of Sulu (Purcell, 1967). This territory of North Borneo, which was later to be known as Sabah, was made a British Protectorate in 1888, still administered by the Company.[13]

---

13 The Company also administered the island of Labuan until 1906, when it was joined to the Straits Settlements.

Sarawak also became a British protectorate in 1888, and continued to be governed by the Brooke family (Jackson, 1968). The Sultan of Brunei had elevated James Brooke, a British adventurer, to the position of Rajah of Sarawak in 1841 as a reward for his help in calming a rebellion in Brunei. Sarawak was gradually enlarged with additional grants of land from the Sultan, along with the River Lawas area bought from the North Borneo Chartered Company in 1905.

Following the end of Japanese occupation in 1945, Sabah and Sarawak came under 17 years of direct British colonial rule. In September 1963, they became the largest member states of the Federation of Malaysia, although they lagged behind the states in the Peninsula economically. Under the Federal Constitution, Sabah and Sarawak have retained greater control over immigration, education and the civil service as compared to states on the Peninsula.

Towards Malaysia

While there was no blueprint for self-determination, British colonial dominance of the Malay Peninsula had been irreversibly weakened by World War II in general, and by the Japanese occupation in particular (Harper, 1999). After the Japanese surrender, a short period of British Military Administration ensued until March 1946, when an attempt was made by the British to impose a centralised Malayan Union (Lau, 1991; Rais Yatim, 2007). The Straits Settlements were dissolved. Penang and Malacca were then grouped with the Federated Malay States and the Unfederated Malay States to form the Malayan Union on 1 April 1946 (Figure 2.1).

The Union was to have a single sovereignty and a common citizen-ship by transferring jurisdiction over the states from the sultans to the British Crown, and by offering citizenship to Malays and non-Malays on equal terms. There was, however, widespread and fierce opposition to this British-imposed politically unified system of administration. This was particularly marked among the Malays in the Unfederated Malay States who feared the encroachment of the other ethnic groups. The Union was untenable.

In February 1948, the British colonial government proposed a new agreement to replace the Malayan Union in the form of the Federation of Malaya. This comprised the 11 states on the Peninsula, with the Malay rulers playing an important role in its administration through a federal legislative council and an executive council presided over

Figure 2.1 **Evolution of Malaysia**

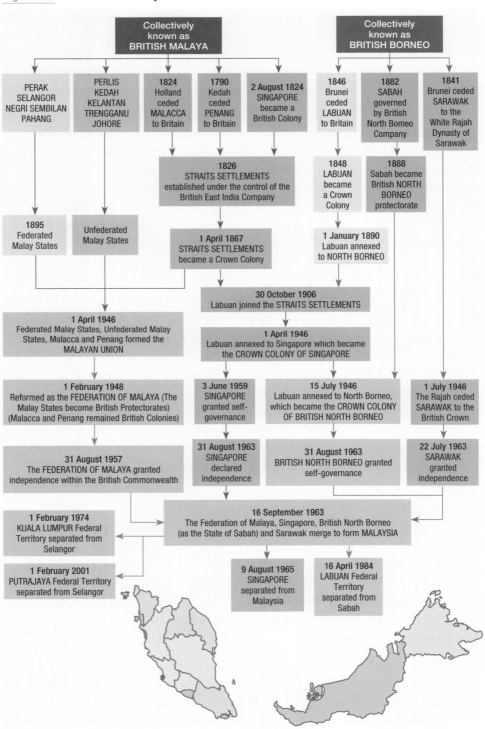

Source:
Adapted from Wdcf (2010).

by the British High Commissioner. The federation, which survived despite various secession attempts by Penang, Kelantan and Johore, provided the foundation for subsequent British decolonisation and the achievement of full independence in August 1957.

The evolution of the various territories that eventually came together to form Malaysia in 1963, and which all shared a common background of British colonial administration, is summarised in Figure 2.1.[14]

Malaya's Economy

The present-day structure of the Malaysian economy has become broad-based and reasonably diversified. The shares of agriculture and mining in GDP have declined markedly to less than 20 per cent combined, while that of manufacturing is around one quarter and modern services around half. This structural change is consistent with a transformation towards a fully developed economy. By contrast, the economy of Malaya a century ago was largely agrarian. It was supported by two primary commodity pillars, tin and rubber, produced to meet the needs of the industries and people in the western hemisphere which had been experiencing an industrial revolution since the first half of the 19th century (Mokyr, 1985).

Industrialising countries required continuous inflows of raw materials to produce manufactured goods as well as supplies of food for their population. Colonial territories, such as India and Malaya, served as important sources for such supplies. While India was the jewel in the crown of the British Empire, among other British-governed territories, Malaya was its natural resource cash cow.

The Straits Settlements' port-cities of Penang, Malacca and Singapore hosted *entrepôt* trading, with business enterprises that were small-scale, mainly localised and family-based (Zainal Aznam Yusof and Bhattasali, 2008). Malaya's economy was dependent on the primary sectors of agriculture and mining with relatively little manufacturing, and only an infant services sector to support the expanding plantation and mining economy (Box 2.1).

---

14 Following the end of World War II and the defeat of the Japanese, within a period of two decades, most Southeast Asian countries attained independence, starting with Vietnam and Cambodia which gained independence from France in 1945; Indonesia which gained independence from the Netherlands in 1945; the Philippines which gained independence from the US in 1946; Burma which gained independence from the UK in 1948; and Laos which gained independence from France in 1949.

Malaya's employment structure by industry

Time trends of Malaya's employment structure of economically-active persons by industry during the first four decades of the 20th century are not available on a comparable classification basis. However, analysis of data from the 1921 census (Nathan, 1922) provides a snapshot of the distribution of workers according to a limited number of broad industrial sectors (Box Figure 2.1). The employment structure of 1921 is likely to be reasonably representative of the pattern of employment by industry prevailing in the two decades immediately before and after 1921.

Overall, about two thirds of workers in Malaya in 1921 were employed in the agriculture and fishing industry. But this proportion is shown to vary markedly by location, reflecting the striking differences in levels of economic activity and development in different parts of Malaya. In the more urbanised and commercial states of Penang and Malacca, this share was just 52 per cent compared to 60 per cent in the Federated Malay States and 79 per cent in the Unfederated Malay States.

Outside of the agricultural sector, employment in manufacturing and mining was next most important and, as expected, the share of employment in this sector was highest at 14 per cent in the Federated Malay States where tin mining was concentrated.

Box Figure 2.1 Workers by industry, Malaya and component territories, 1921

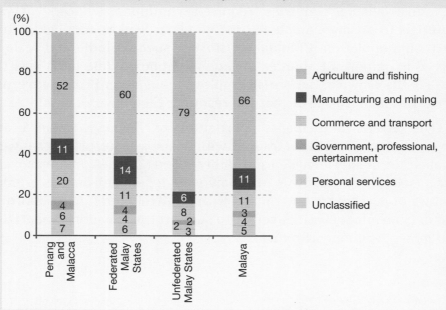

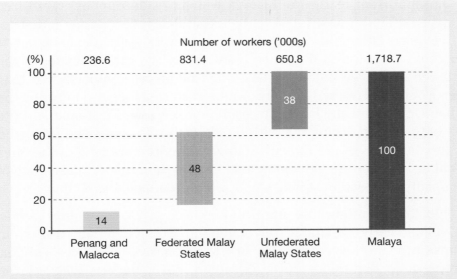

Source of data:
Nathan (1922).

Variations in the employment structure of the Straits Settlements, the Federated Malay States and the Unfederated Malay States mirrored the prevailing differences in the ethnic composition of these three territories. The Chinese were heavily concentrated in the Settlements, whereas the Malays dominated the Unfederated Malay States. In the Federated Malay States, the rapid growth of tin mining and, subsequently, the rubber industry had created a more evenly balanced labour force, although Chinese and Indian workers together outnumbered Malay workers.

The notion that the Chinese came to Malaya primarily to work in the tin mines is not borne out by the evidence, even in those states where mining was concentrated. According to the 1921 census, of the 154,000 Chinese workers recorded for the state of Perak, just 27 per cent were employed in tin mining, with 32 per cent working in agriculture, generally as unskilled labourers. In the Straits Settlement of Penang, the Chinese were the largest community among the working population and were employed in all sectors of the economy, particularly the modern sectors of commerce and transport.

With the continued growth of the Malayan economy and its subsequent diversification in the decades that followed, it was to be expected that the share of employment in the agricultural and fishing sectors would gradually decline as compared with 1921, while the share in the non-agricultural and more modern sectors would rise.

An important feature of Malaya was its trade openness and free enterprise. Trade constituted a substantial share of economic activities, with exports and imports accounting on average for 60 per cent and 41 per cent of nominal GDP respectively during the early decades of the 20th century. Even before British rule, the Malay Peninsula had long been a centre of trade due to its unique seafaring location between the Indian Ocean and the Far East. Trade between the Peninsula and the rest of the world during the period of British rule was greatly boosted by the demands of the Industrial Revolution, the opening of the Suez Canal in 1869 and the Panama Canal in 1914, and the increased use of steamships instead of sailing ships, which reduced travel time.

Tin, a non-renewable natural resource, was the initial driver propelling early economic development. But its impact was soon eclipsed by another commodity of transformative influence—rubber, a renewable natural resource (Drabble, 1973; Barber, 2008). From 1915 onwards, rubber increasingly became Malaya's main export earner (Figure 2.2). Other key exports were copra, pineapples, arecanuts, gambier, tapioca and later palm oil. Plantation agriculture was encouraged by the colonial administration through a liberal land policy that incentivized companies to invest in large areas of land at low cost, with a conducive regulatory environment and a permissive labour policy. Sugar and coffee plantations proved to be uneconomic, however, and several such estates had already been abandoned by the early 20th century.

Figure 2.2 **Share of exports at current prices, Malaya, 1900–1939**

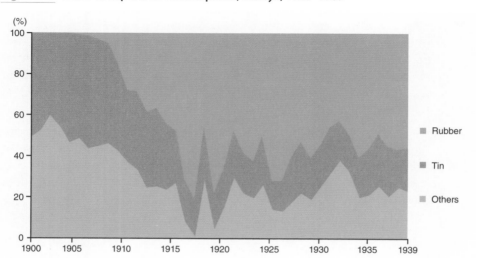

Copra, the dried meat of coconuts, was another important commodity export. It was used mainly to generate coconut oil for the soap and margarine industries, with the resulting residue made into coconut oil cake for livestock feed. Copra was produced primarily in the Federated Malay States, predominantly in Perak, both on plantations and by smallholders. It provided an important source of income to the latter, especially when the price of rubber was low. Copra was shipped mainly to the UK, other European countries, and the US.

Tin

Malays had been mining tin on a very limited scale for centuries (Lim, 1967; Yip, 1969; Thoburn, 1977). However, the discovery of large tin deposits in Perak and Selangor in the first half of the 19th century led to significant investments of capital by wealthy Chinese merchants living in the Straits Settlements, and to the influx of migrant workers from mainland China to develop the industry (Mills, 1958; Wong, 1965; Burns, 1982). By 1904, Malaya was producing 50,000 tons of tin annually, more than half of world output, to meet the growing demand from Europe, especially following the surge in the use of tin cans for food preservation.

Tin mining was initially a predominantly Chinese enterprise, and functioned in a largely unregulated environment with considerable rivalry between different clans. This situation changed markedly when, with the support of the colonial administration, European, and predominantly British, companies injected large amounts of capital, managerial expertise and new technology into the industry. They introduced hydraulic sluicing and other scientific methods to mine the alluvial tin deposits. They extended the use of machinery and were the first to attempt underground mining. The introduction of the gravel pump, and of the dredging machine in 1912, transformed the industry, while at the same time establishing British control over it. Simultaneously, the colonial government of the Federated Malay States invested heavily in rail and road infrastructure which helped to lower production costs. The government also provided land concessions to new companies. The net result was that, whereas in 1912 some 80 per cent of Malaya's tin production was under Chinese management, by 1931 British firms accounted for more than 65 per cent of total production (Kennedy, 2007).

Rubber

The first attempt in the Malay Peninsula to plant rubber on a commercial scale was in 1896 (Drabble, 1973; Barlow, 1978). By 1900, the British had begun to promote the potential commercial production of rubber and sought to attract experienced European planters to the Peninsula.[15] As the planting of rubber is very capital intensive, with a long lag before returns on the investment are realised, the government provided generous assistance to planters including long-term security of land tenure and the freedom to recruit low-cost labour from overseas. The high capital requirement of estate rubber reflected the cost of buying the land, clearing the jungle, planting, cultivating and tending the growing trees for up to seven years before they became productive. Most rubber planting took place in Perak, Selangor, Negri Sembilan and Johore—states where transport and communication links were already in existence and growing.

Rubber was mainly used in the UK and elsewhere at the turn of the century for bicycles and footwear. The massive boom in the rubber trade came in the first decade of the 20th century as prices rose due to the remarkable development of the automobile industry in the US and the consequent demand for rubber tyres. As global demand for natural rubber increased, rubber production became highly profitable and plantations spread all over the Malay Peninsula. The area under estate cultivation rose from just 2,400 hectares in 1900 to 18,600 in 1905, a phenomenal achievement especially in the absence of mechanical aids for land clearance (Lim, 1967).

All communities benefited from the rubber industry's growth, with the Europeans, the Chinese, the Malays and the Indians all having a stake in ownership (Lim, 1967). But European plantation companies were the dominant players and beneficiaries as a result of their ability to mobilise large amounts of capital through joint-stock companies, especially in London. Other communities had fewer opportunities for mobilising capital. The Europeans employed about 258,000 plantation workers in 1929, of whom 80 per cent were from South India (Hagan and Wells, 2005). Rubber plantations were also subsuming land meant for other cash crops, such as sugar and tapioca.

---

15 Expansion of production of both the rubber and tin industries depended on an efficient system of land administration that was managed and overseen by the District Officers in an ever growing civil service, dominated at the higher levels by Colonial Office–appointed British staff (Heussler, 1981).

High rubber prices and the expectation of a regular flow of cash income encouraged large numbers of smallholders to plant rubber. They tended to use family labour to clear a few hectares which were planted with free or cheap seed from neighbouring estates (Barlow *et al.*, 1994). By 1921, smallholders accounted for 48 per cent of the total rubber cultivated area in Perak (Azrai Abdullah *et al.*, 2012). New planting had already reached 186,000 acres by 1913 as private investment grew strongly. By the 1930s, Malaya had become the world's largest natural rubber producer. The use of an improved method of tapping to extract the maximum flow of latex with the minimum damage to the trees also helped increase supply.[16]

While the colonial government endeavoured to create the enabling conditions for the exploitation of the Peninsula's bountiful natural resources, for example, by granting land concessions to open up rubber plantations, there was growing concern about the sale of traditional or hereditary Malay land to non-Malays and its potentially disruptive effects on Malay settlements. With the surge in the rubber trade, many companies had bought large areas of land, predominantly in the west coast states, which intruded into traditional areas of Malay subsistence cultivation.

While not wanting to curb what it saw as legitimate land transactions, often with significant windfall profits, the government of the Federated Malay States in 1913 passed the Malay Reservation Enactment which imposed restrictions on the disposal of Malay land (Lim, 1977). The legislation, supported by the Malay rulers, stated that no Malays could dispose of *kampung* land, usually land on which there was a house and mixed cultivations, to any non-Malay within an area designated and gazetted as Malay reservation land by the state Resident through his District Officers. This legislation, which was revised in the early 1930s and provided the basis for each of the Unfederated Malay States to enact similar legislation, remains in force and is safeguarded in the Federal Constitution.

The upturn of tin and rubber prices in the early 1900s saw a dramatic rise in foreign investment, particularly British, supported by the tools of imperialism (Box 2.2). A total of 129 European companies were operating in the Federated Malay States by 1939, most of which were joint stock companies registered in London. The mainly European

---

16 The Rubber Research Institute contributed to these and other productivity advances. This Institute was established by the colonial administration in 1925 to conduct research and development, with a sizeable cadre of European managerial and technical staff.

capital investment in the rubber industry came in primarily through merchant houses that were actively promoting investment in the London capital market. High prices for rubber and tin contributed to substantial profits and incomes for plantation houses and smallholders during this period, as well as for those joint stock companies that had invested in these industries. The profits were huge, with dividends from some of the bigger and stronger-performing plantation companies ranging from 20 to 80 per cent (Barber, 2008).

Box 2.2 **Joint stock companies, agency houses, British banks and the Colonial Office**

Malaya's tin and rubber industries required substantial capital investments for the purchase and clearing of large land holdings, for the introduction of new technology, and for the payment of large numbers of workers. The preferred vehicle for raising capital was the British public joint stock company through the London capital market. Investments in Malaya, where there were no restrictions on foreign capital inflows, were initially seen as riskier than those in colonies such as Ceylon, a maturing economy run more professionally.

In the first decade of the 20th century, especially as rubber prices spiked, these companies paid huge profits to their shareholders. Unsurprisingly, these large dividends increased interest in investing in primary commodity production, and encouraged demand from other investors when new mining and plantation offerings came to the market.

British agency houses—prominent among which were Guthrie and Company, Edward Boustead and Company, Harrisons and Crosfield, Sime Darby, and Barlow and Company—helped to promote investment in Malayan commodities, and to raise money on the London stock market. They were already promoting trade in Malaya and elsewhere in the region, and had considerable experience in providing a wide range of ancillary services such as in sales, supplies, shipping and insurance.

With offices in London and Malaya, agency houses had wide international networks which included commercial representatives and government officials, and were a classic expression of British advantage in trade (Darwin, 2013). They understood the volatility in commodity trading, and bridged the gap between the planters in Malaya and the shareholders in Britain. Without their involvement, overseas investment would have been lower and the participation of local interests, mainly Chinese, would have been larger (Barlow, 1978).

The agency houses supported plantation owners by underwriting new crops, providing fertilizers and harvesting equipment, acting as sales agents and purchasing output, thereby helping to ensure the success of the plantation and its investment. They took responsibility for book-keeping and for raising finance, and sent visiting agents to inspect the plantations. In this way, the fledgling plantations benefited from high-quality advice on both the financial and agricultural aspects of the business. The agency houses charged agency fees and commissions for their services.

However, there was sometimes a blurring of interests, with the agency houses acquiring estates, floating them as public companies, appointing estate managers, taking profits and retaining substantial share interests (Puthucheary, 1960; Drabble, 1973).

In support of the advancement of British trading activities and encouraged by the British Colonial Office, several major British banks established branches, initially in the Straits Settlements and later in Malaya's tin and rubber commercial centres. These included Chartered Bank, Hong Kong Bank and Mercantile Bank (Cheah, 2001; Wong, 2004). The banks and agency houses, headquartered overseas, had close business relations. The banks provided the agency houses with crucial financing. While their role was initially limited, they increasingly provided investment advice, short-term credit lines and foreign exchange.

The British Colonial Office, through its control of government and its use of other networks in Malaya, including exclusive social recreational clubs, provided a supportive legislative, institutional and policy environment. This served to nurture the commodity-trading companies and to further their economic interests as well as to protect them in various ways during periods of low prices and recessions.

New rubber planting also added to gross fixed capital formation. The nominal value of external capital in Malayan rubber companies in 1918 was 54.6 million pounds, while local companies (mostly Chinese) were capitalised at 1.67 million pounds (Barber, 2008). Rising exports added to wage income and also boosted government revenues. With a significant revenue base, Malaya's colonial rulers were able to invest in strengthening the transport and communications infrastructure as well as in social services such as basic education and sanitation in the towns, all of which contributed to the growth of GDP.

The early 20th century thus constituted a major phase in the opening of Malaya. The commercial production of rubber on estate plantations as well as small-holdings to meet the growing demand from industrial countries led to Malaya becoming the global leader in rubber supply. As the century progressed, trade expanded significantly, with rubber overtaking tin as the main export earner. But there was considerable year-to-year trade volatility, with Malayan rubber and tin exports being markedly affected during and as a result of World War I and the Great Depression (Box 2.3).

Box 2.3   World War I and the Great Depression

As an open trading economy, Malaya was profoundly influenced by factors affecting the global economy. Two major external events—World War I and the Great Depression—had vastly different effects. During World War I, there was robust growth of Malayan GDP. By contrast, the Great Depression resulted in a severe downturn of the economy (Chapter 4).

World War I

World War I began on 28 July 1914 and lasted until 11 November 1918. More than 70 million military personnel, including 60 million Europeans, were mobilised. About 9 million combatants and 7 million civilians died as a result of the war. The war involved all the world's leading economic powers grouped into opposing alliances: the Allies comprising the British Empire, France and the Russian Empire, and the Central Powers of Germany and Austria-Hungary. These alliances expanded as more nations entered the war: Italy, Japan and the US joined the Allies, while the Ottoman Empire and Bulgaria joined the Central Powers.

International trade was affected as shipping was disrupted, especially on routes to and from Europe. The war years of 1914–1918 had a major impact on Malaya's exports and real GDP growth. Malaya's rubber exports by that time accounted for the largest share of the country's total merchandise exports.

The fortuitously-timed introduction of the assembly-line technique in automobile production in 1913 in the US reduced the construction time per car from 14 hours to 1½ hours. This led to a period of extraordinary growth in the industry. The resulting increase in the demand for rubber tyres generated double-digit growth in Malaya's rubber exports, especially between 1914–1917, notwithstanding a fall in prices.

Although cargo space for rubber on routes to the UK decreased due to the war, more vessels, especially from Japan, were available in the Pacific for direct shipments to the US. This was aided greatly by the opening of the Panama Canal in 1914, which substantially reduced the distance from Malaya to American east-coast ports (Drabble, 1973).

Tin prices rose between 1914–1918, due mainly to the difficulty of transportation to Europe as a result of a shortage of shipping facilities (Box Figure 2.2) (Yip, 1969). The quantity of tin exported declined each year throughout this period, but this was more than compensated by the consistent yearly increase of the average unit value of tin exported. Consequently, Malaya's export revenue from tin increased each year from 1914–1918, and by 1918 had reached a record Straits$95 million, a figure that was only exceeded seven years later in 1925.

Box Figure 2.2 **Rubber and tin prices, GDP at constant 1914 prices, Malaya, 1900–1939**

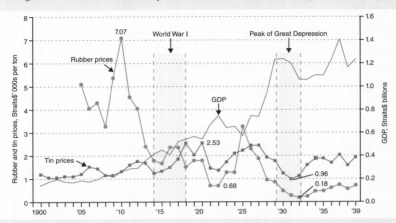

Sources of data: Drabble (1973); Heath (1951); McFadyean (1944); British Malaya (1921–1925, 1928, 1934, 1937 and 1939); Federation of Malaya (1951).

The Great Depression

The Great Depression of the 1930s saw a severe worldwide economic decline. The Depression began in the US, after a dramatic fall in stock prices that started in September 1929, and spread globally. Between 1929 and 1932, worldwide GDP fell by an estimated 15 per cent. Unemployment was high and poverty increased as international trade plummeted. It was a period of economic gloom.

Urban economies were devastated, especially those dependent on heavy industry. Construction virtually ceased in many countries. Rural areas suffered as crop prices fell. Facing plummeting demand, and with few alternative sources of jobs, areas and territories dependent on natural resource industries also suffered. Some economies started to recover by the mid-1930s, but for others the negative effects of the Great Depression lasted until the beginning of World War II. International trade remained low as countries imposed import tariffs and quotas. Currency exchange rates were extremely volatile, and banks and companies were reluctant to grant credit as insolvencies grew.

Malaya was not spared, and its real GDP registered large negative growth rates in 1931–1932, due mainly to an unprecedented collapse of its external trade. In 1931, Malaya's total exports registered a negative growth rate of 4.3 per cent (Box Figure 2.2). The year 1932 represented the worst of the depression years as Malaya's total exports contracted by 17.2 per cent. The scale of human suffering was far-reaching, especially in the west coast states, with massive lay-offs, huge reductions in wages leading to lower living standards, high unemployment and destitution, and many tin mining and plantation workers being repatriated, especially the Indians (Ramasamy, 1994).

The economic effects of World War I and the Great Depression are discussed in more detail in Chapter 4.

Transport, Communications and Electrification

Malaya's transport and communications began to develop in the late 19th century to support its increasing international trade. Up to that point, the primary means of communication within and between the states of the Peninsula was along river networks, with the rivers and seas forming natural highways. Coastal ports served as links for trade with the rest of the world.

British control of state revenues facilitated spending on economic and social infrastructure in support of colonial interests. As Frank Swettenham, the first Resident-General of the Federated Malay States, rationalised:

> 'The lesson is that, in the administration of a Malay State, revenue and prosperity follow the liberal but prudently-directed expenditure of public funds, especially when they are invested in high-class roads, in railways, telegraphs, waterworks, and everything likely to encourage trade and private enterprise' (Swettenham, 1975, pp. 294).

The establishment of a modern railway system began in 1885 with the opening of the first line between Taiping and Port Weld in the state of Perak (Cheah, 2001). This was highly significant because the inland town of Taiping, which was the distribution point for the Larut tin mines, was thereby linked to the nearest port. Around the same time, a railway line was also built linking the main mining areas in Selangor with its local port. A few years later in 1893, Ipoh and Telok Anson (now Teluk Intan) were connected, providing links to the Kinta Valley which had the world's largest tin mine (Yip, 1969).

As the cost benefits of transporting tin and rubber in this way became apparent, the construction of the Peninsula's rail network was progressively extended to support its export industries and to advance the economic interests of European investors (Kaur, 1985). By 1910, Johore Bahru in the southern tip of the Peninsula was connected by rail to Province Wellesley in the north. Over the next 20 years, the rail network connected almost all of the main towns and ports, running through the major tin-mining and rubber-growing hubs on the west and east coasts as well as to Siam (Thailand). With an expanded railway network, new centres of population and commercial activity emerged, and with them, the demand for goods and services grew further.

Before the railways were built, tin was transported by river. This practice was time-consuming and inefficient. In the early 1900s, the Federated Malay States Railways was established. It gradually acquired all the dispersed railway systems in order to expand and integrate them into a unified transport system. Investments and budgets for building and maintaining the railways were by then being met by both federal and state governments. The new centres of economic activity became magnets for migrants.

The first trunk road in Malaya also linked the main tin-mining towns of Seremban (in Negri Sembilan), Kuala Lumpur (in Selangor), Ipoh and Taiping (both in Perak), with the main purpose of transporting resources from the states to the ports. Malaya's subsequent road network development similarly had its origins in efforts to promote its commodity exports. Each state established a Public Works Department to support road construction and maintenance.

As well as facilitating the bidirectional movement of goods and people, the expansion of Malaya's rail and road systems, and port development, also contributed to government fixed capital formation, or government investment. Substantial sums were spent from government revenues on the construction of buildings, bridges and roads amounting to a total of Straits\$12.8 million in 1927, compared with a mere Straits\$0.2 million a year earlier (Federated Malay States, 1927, 1928). Expenditure on special services of the Federated Malay States amounted to Straits\$21.7 million and Straits\$15.1 million in 1928 and 1929 respectively (Federated Malay States, 1928, 1929). Up until those years, the Malayan railways had been highly profitable, with substantial annual budget surpluses, but with the Great Depression and the increasing competition of road transport, this comfortable economic situation changed (Lim, 1967).

Investments in electricity began in the late 19th century, predominantly in the Federated Malay States and the Straits Settlements. Private supplies of electricity had preceded public provision. From the early 1890s, the landed elite began purchasing small electric generators for home use. In 1894, the first application of electricity to power mining pumps was made in Selangor's tin-mining town of Rawang. Private supply for street lighting was extended to the town, and subsequently to the new railway station in neighbouring Kuala Lumpur. In 1900, the first power station, the Sempam Hydroelectric Power Station in Raub, Pahang, was built to support the local gold mining industry, after which public electricity supply was progressively expanded.

With improvements in living standards, demand for electricity rose markedly over time. To meet this demand, large amounts of capital were provided from government revenues, supplemented much later by private domestic and foreign investments.

Health and Education

Advances in the social sectors during this period were influenced more by the need to ensure the success of colonial economic activities than by any vision of social development for the people of Malaya. They did nevertheless have positive impacts on the well-being of the general population. Investments in healthcare and education mainly benefited the colonial administrators and elite families living in the towns, with only very limited medical services and schooling reaching rural areas. Where they did exist, out-of-town clinics served primarily to protect the health of Europeans, and only secondarily, to maintain the health of the labour force working to support colonial economic interests (Manderson, 1996).

Hygiene and sanitation in the towns were poor, and working and living conditions in and around the tin mines and rubber plantations were harsh. Annual death rates from malaria and other infectious diseases were high and exceeded birth rates. Population and labour force growth resulted instead from the net inflows of foreign workers. This migrant population introduced infections into the local population and, at the same time, migrants were exposed to local endemic diseases. Health and sanitation programmes began in the Straits Settlements and in the towns of the Federated Malay States, and were gradually extended after 1911 with the establishment of a federal health department in Kuala Lumpur. Government hospitals were supplemented by private medical providers in the bigger tin mines and rubber estates.

An increasing number of European medical practitioners came to Malaya to work in government hospitals and outpatient clinics where they began applying the findings of medical research carried out at the London School of Hygiene and Tropical Medicine, and the Liverpool School of Tropical Medicine, both of which had been founded around the turn of the century. The application of their new knowledge, which included an awareness of the need for improved hygiene and safe sanitation, contributed to the control of diseases and improvements in health (Kennedy, 2007). Town Sanitary Boards were established to supervise street cleaning and lighting, road upkeep, the building of drains and management of markets.

These various measures progressively contributed to a gradual reduction in mortality rates, although the lack of complete and reliable mortality data for the Peninsula as a whole makes it difficult to quantify the magnitude of improvement. Evidence from the Straits Settlements on infant mortality trends, which provides a gauge for overall mortality in this territory, suggests that, while in 1900 about one in four babies would die during the first year of life, this had fallen to one in five in 1920, and one in six by the late 1930s (Manderson, 1996). Levels of infant mortality would almost certainly have been higher elsewhere in the Peninsula, however.

Colonial rule, with its concomitant economic expansion and demand for Chinese and Indian labour, gradually transformed the formerly Malay-speaking states into a multilingual society, particularly on the more developed west coast. With the expansion of the British bureaucracy in Malaya, English became increasingly used in the civil service despite the misgivings of some of the Malay rulers, and the fact that Malay was recognised by the British as the language of governance. English was also the foremost means of communication in the local and federal legislative councils, as well as among the professional classes (Lee, 2007).

Malaya's education system evolved following this pattern of cultural pluralism rather than through an education policy designed to create a unified and common national identity. The children of rural Malay families attended government-funded schools, which provided only four years of basic elementary education in the Malay language. Children of the Malay ruling elite generally attended the expensive English-medium schools together with children of the Europeans. Foremost among these was the Malay College in Kuala Kangsar, founded in 1905, which was administered along the lines of an English public school, and aimed to prepare the sons of privileged families for future government service. Chinese and Tamil vernacular schools also began to grow in number in line with the increase in Chinese and Indian school-aged children.

The provision of education in government schools began before World War I, and by 1938 there were some 800 Malay schools, 700 Chinese schools, 600 Tamil schools and 200 English schools (United Nations Country Team, Malaysia; Economic Planning Unit-Malaysia,

2005). Education in the Straits Settlements and the Federated Malay States had begun much earlier, however, in the early 19th century, largely through the efforts of Christian missionary organisations, Chinese associations and other vernacular groups (Kennedy, 2007). These mission or trustee schools were funded by voluntary donations which were often uncertain in times of recession, together with some grant support from the governments of the Straits Settlements and the Federated Malay States.

While the vernacular school system served to reinforce the group identity of the different ethnic communities, attendance at English schools tended to weaken traditional cultural loyalties. One outcome was the social and cultural isolation from each other of the Malays, Chinese and Indians educated in their own languages. Another was the emergence of a cosmopolitan Westernized elite, drawn in varying proportions from all three of the main communities, whose common bond was English (Chai, 1977).

People

Due to the overwhelming dependence of its growth on foreign workers, Malaya's early 20th century economic development cannot be separated from its demographic patterns. High labour force growth, predominantly of young male migrant workers, drove volatile GDP growth. Ultimately, it is the population who produce and consume, invest, and export and import goods and services. By doing so, they generate economic growth.

Patterns of settlement in Malaya have been strongly influenced, *inter alia*, by the physical relief of the country and the distribution of its natural resources. Early settlement by the Peninsular Malays took place along the coast and inland along the rivers. The Malays were traditionally engaged in maritime trade, fishing and agriculture. Those living on the more rural east coast, in particular, tended to maintain a traditional way of life and did not acquire skills that would support their social mobility. This suited the prevailing order, serving to limit the accumulation of wealth and maintain traditional deference to rank (Kinney, 1975; Milner, 1994).

With the growing colonial influence, tin mining and commercial agriculture began to flourish, which led to substantial inflows of foreign workers, mainly from China and India, to overcome local labour shortages. The Chinese were mainly drawn to the newly prospering towns around the tin mines, to the port cities and to the plantations, while the Indians, whose numbers were always much lower, mainly lived and worked on the rubber estates.

Population census-taking in the Malay Peninsula began during the British administration, with censuses being conducted in the same years as in the UK and according to similar methods. The geographical coverage of the censuses was associated with the historical backgrounds of the Peninsula's different territories. The first sequence of censuses in the Straits Settlements began in the mid-19th century, and continued in 1901 and 1911. The first census for the Federated Malay States was conducted in 1891, and repeated in 1901 and 1911. The first census covering the Unfederated Malay States was conducted in 1911. In 1921, the first unified census on a Pan-Malayan basis was conducted, involving the Straits Settlements, the Federated Malay States and the Unfederated Malay States. Thereafter, censuses were held decennially, except for the planned 1941 census, which was postponed until after the end of the Japanese occupation.

According to these censuses, the population living on the Malay Peninsula rose dramatically between 1901 and 1947, increasing from 1.7 million to 4.9 million. This growth was due mainly to net inflows of migrants from China and India, with natural increase—the difference between birth and death rates—close to zero throughout much of this period. Net migration flows, approximated by the annual average growth rates shown in Table 2.1, were subject to considerable variation, both across the different periods and according to ethnic community.

International migration had a significant impact on the ethnic composition of the Peninsula during this period. In 1901, Malays comprised some 63 per cent of the Peninsula's population. By 1931, their share had fallen to 49 per cent despite substantial immigration of Malays from the Dutch East Indies (Gullick, 1998). Migration from elsewhere in the Malay Archipelago was encouraged as part of colonial policy in order to increase local food production, especially of rice, to feed the growing population not engaged in agriculture.[17]

---

17 While there were substantial inflows of Malays from Sumatra to the Peninsula throughout the early decades of the 20th century, this did not lead to a significant growth in padi production, due mainly to the ready availability of low-cost rice imports from neigbouring countries (Lim, 1977). Only a small proportion of these Malays worked in estate rubber plantations, although many became rubber smallholders (Barlow, 1978).

The substantial rise in the number and proportion of Chinese occurred in the period 1921–1947, when their population share rose from 29 per cent to 38 per cent (Table 2.1). The proportion of Indians more than doubled in the years between 1901 and 1921, from just 6 per cent to 15 per cent. It then fell back to only 11 per cent by 1947, as many Indian plantation workers had been repatriated during the Great Depression. There were also very high death rates among all communities during this period. By 1931, the ethnic composition of the Peninsula was delicately balanced, with the Malays comprising slightly less than half of the total. It remained so for the next two decades and beyond (Fell, 1957; Leete, 1996).

Table 2.1 Population size, distribution and growth by ethnic group, Malaya, 1901–1947

Year	Malays	Chinese	Indians	Others	Total
Numbers ('000)					
1901	1,088.9	508.5	107.7	28.6	1,733.7
1911	1,369.8	693.2	239.2	36.8	2,339.1
1921	1,568.6	855.9	439.2	43.1	2,906.7
1931	1,863.9	1,284.9	571.0	68.0	3,787.8
1947	2,427.8	1,884.5	530.6	65.1	4,908.1
Distribution (%)					
1901	62.8	29.3	6.2	1.7	100
1911	58.6	29.6	10.2	1.6	100
1921	54.0	29.4	15.1	1.5	100
1931	49.2	33.9	15.1	1.8	100
1947	49.5	38.4	10.8	1.3	100
Average annual growth (%)					
1901–1911	2.3	3.1	8.0	2.5	3.0
1911–1921	1.3	2.1	6.0	1.3	2.1
1921–1931	1.7	4.1	2.7	4.4	2.7
1931–1947	1.6	2.3	–0.5	–0.1	1.6

Sources of data:
For 1901: Hare (1902); Innes (1901). Estimates were made for the Unfederated Malay States. For 1911: Cavendish (1911); Marriott (1911a and 1911b); Pountney (1911). For 1921: Nathan (1922). For 1931: Vlieland (1932). For 1947: Del Tufo (1949).

Apart from the small elite group of Europeans, most of whom were British citizens and who enjoyed a markedly higher standard of living than other groups, and a small number of Japanese and Arabs, the plural society that evolved within the British colonial economy consisted mainly of Malays, Chinese and Indians. The latter three groups were themselves far from homogeneous, with numerous subcultural, religious and linguistic differences within each as well as between them (Sidhu and Jones, 1981).

While their different occupational activities created an economic divide between the Peninsula's ethnic groups, their different religious and cultural customs generated further social barriers. The physical, social, religious and cultural distance which separated the communities precluded the development of a sense of common identity. The maintenance of a class structure in which the elite of all ethnic groups cooperated with the British in order to ensure their own access to privilege, rank and wealth was a central element of the colonial enterprise (Andaya and Andaya, 2001).

Migrants from China and India helped to facilitate the Peninsula's transition from a trading outpost to a leading global commodity producer. The European planters were responsible for recruiting a large proportion of the Indian migrant workers on whom they and the government depended for low-cost labour. Access to cheap labour, which was initially indentured but later hired through a contract system, helped to ensure the success and profitability of the rubber industry. Since there was work available for wives and older children on the rubber estates, Indian migration sometimes included whole families, who were then housed on the plantations in labour lines. But their low wages, indebtedness, poor social status and physical isolation kept estate Indians apart, and they tended to exercise little influence on Malayan society.

Indians had been migrating to the Malay Peninsula in relatively small numbers for generations, but their numbers increased markedly under the British. They were recruited for public works as police and guards, and were also well-represented in the lower ranks of the colonial bureaucracy. Indian migration to the Straits Settlements was legalised in 1872, and to the protected Malay States in 1884. Most came from Tamil areas in south India. Tamils were considered to be more accustomed to British rule and more amenable to discipline than the Chinese, and to be willing to work for lower wages than the Malays.

The Chinese worked in the tin mines and on the plantations, and operated the revenue farms which collected various taxes for the government including those from the lucrative opium trade (Lee and Tan, 2000). They were also engaged in numerous other economic activities, working as market-gardeners, artisans, shopkeepers, contractors and financiers. The Chinese made a valuable contribution to Malaya's economic development, especially but not exclusively in the west coast states, through their industrious work ethic as well as through their contribution to opium revenues (Chapter 3).

The Malays were mainly fishermen and rubber smallholders. Immigration increased the size of the Malay population. The first generation of these migrants, mainly from Sumatra and Java, clustered together and for a time preserved their own identity. But the distinctions disappeared for the migrants' descendants, and most local-born migrant offspring referred to themselves as Malay. This shifting self-identity was made possible because of a basic similarity of appearance, their perception of the Peninsula as their native land, the use of Malay as a common language and, above all, their shared religion of Islam.

The sex-selective nature of the inflows of foreign workers contributed to an imbalanced sex ratio in the overall population. In 1921, the sex ratio was 154 males for every 100 females, but it had been even higher earlier in the century. This was due to the extremely high proportion of young males among the Chinese and Indian migrants, who were either single or, if married, had generally left their wives behind before entering Malaya. The sex ratios of these communities became much more evenly balanced in the 1930s and 1940s as the government introduced special schemes to encourage existing migrants to bring their wives and settle more permanently in the Peninsula. The result was that during these decades, the net inflows of Chinese female migrants rose faster than those of males (Caldwell, 1963). Malay migrant inflows were always much less sex-selective.

Another demographic impact stemming from the migrant inflows was on the age structure, with a much smaller share of children than would be expected in a settled population. As a result, the population was heavily concentrated in the young working ages.

Yet another impact was the high proportion of the foreign-born as a share of the total population. This share was especially high in the

Federated Malay States, where in 1911, 63 per cent of the population was foreign-born, according to the census of that year. Disaggregated by community groups, 17 per cent of Malays and 92 per cent of Chinese and Indians were born outside Malaya at this time (Pountney, 1911). The proportion of each community born outside of Malaya fell sharply subsequently due to stricter controls on inflows of migrants as well as rising natural increase rates.

Population Distribution and Urbanisation

Malaya's population distribution has long been highly uneven, with settlements being concentrated in coastal areas and inland along river banks. At the beginning of the 20th century, Perak (19 per cent), Penang (14 per cent), Kelantan (13 per cent) and Kedah (11 per cent) together accounted for 58 per cent of the total population (Map 2.2). The concentrations of population changed markedly over the course of the next half century, reflecting flows of predominantly international labour migrants.

By 1947, Selangor, the site of Malaya's administrative capital of Kuala Lumpur, had grown the most. Its population share had risen to 15 per cent from 10 per cent in 1901. However, this was still smaller than the share of Perak, which accounted for about one fifth in both years (Map 2.3). Another major growth area was the southern state of Johore, the population share of which rose from 8 per cent in 1901 to 15 per cent in 1947. The growth in Johore, as in Selangor and Perak, was linked to its high rates of economic growth, driven by its diversified agricultural exports. By the early 1930s, Johore was beginning to benefit from the cultivation of oil palm, in addition to rubber, coconuts, tapioca, gambier and other crops (Winstedt, 1992).

The population of Pahang, the Peninsula's largest state in terms of land area, was one of the smallest, with its share being around 5 per cent throughout this period. Interestingly, and reflecting the uneven pattern of economic development in the Peninsula, the population shares of the east coast states of Kelantan and Trengganu fell sharply during the first half of the century. In these states, commercial agriculture was limited, consisting primarily of coconut estates, and while tin and gold mining contributed significantly to state revenues, their importance faded as the century progressed (Shahril Talib, 1984 and 1995).

Map 2.2 Share of population by state, Malaya, 1901

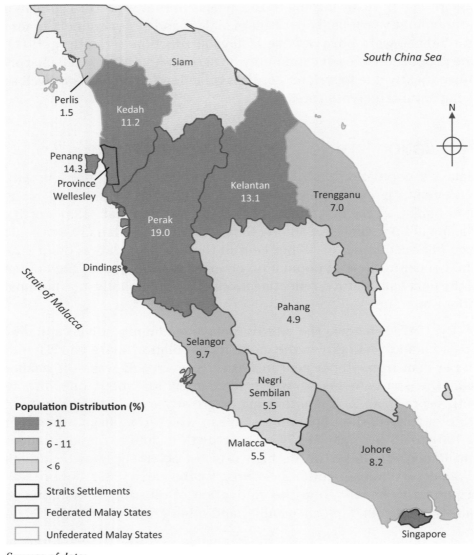

Sources of data:
Hare (1902); Innes (1901). Estimates were made for the Unfederated Malay States.

The share of Malaya's urban population grew from 11 per cent in 1911 to 19 per cent in 1947. The annual urbanisation rate during this period of 3.6 per cent exceeded the growth of the total population, which was 2.1 per cent.[18] This growth was due mainly to the concentration

---

18 Urban areas are defined as gazetted areas with a population of 10,000 or more.

Map 2.3 **Share of population by state, Malaya, 1947**

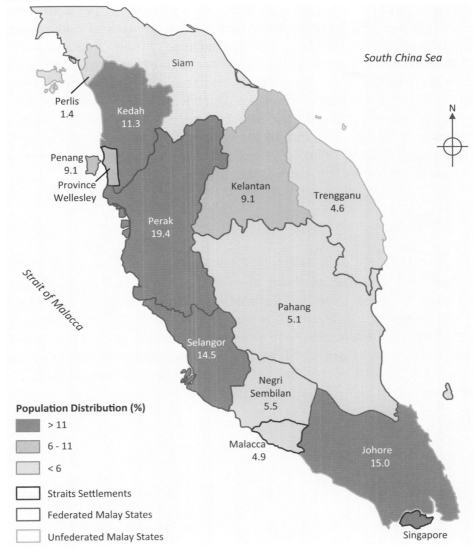

Population Distribution (%)

- > 11
- 6 - 11
- < 6

- Straits Settlements
- Federated Malay States
- Unfederated Malay States

Source of data:
Del Tufo (1949).

of international migrant settlement in towns such as Kuala Lumpur, Ipoh, Klang, Georgetown and Johore Bahru, the formation and growth of which could be traced to the development of tin, rubber, commerce and related infrastructure (Saw, 1988).

By 1947, the most urbanised states were Penang (53 per cent), Selangor (33 per cent), Malacca (23 per cent), Perak (17 per cent) and Johore (15 per cent) due to their being major centres of commerce, transport and administration, and also because of their close links with the tin and rubber industries. These west coast urban centres and port towns were much more ethnically diverse than the rural areas of these states, as well as the east coast states which were predominantly Malay. British colonial policy had the effect of perpetuating the traditional economic structure and way of life of the Malay population living in these areas (Kinney, 1975). Levels of urbanisation were much lower in the east coast states throughout this period.

*   *   *

The next chapter sets out the methods, concepts, definitions and data sources used for estimating a time series of GDP and its components for Malaya for the period 1900–1939. No similar comprehensive estimates have previously been constructed. Unless other data sources are cited, statistics from this new GDP database have been used to derive the various tables and figures throughout this book.

CHAPTER 3

Kuala Lumpur railway station hub: transportation
system in early 20th century Malaya

Estimating Historical GDP and Its Components

This chapter starts by summarizing the approaches that can be used to measure GDP and its components. It describes how the expenditure method is employed here to derive a new series of historical GDP estimates for Malaya for the period 1900–1939 from the limited available data.[19] Two series of GDP estimates are then constructed—a current and constant price series, with 1914 the base year for the latter. For each of the GDP components, details are given of the concepts and definitions employed, sources of data, estimation techniques and underlying assumptions. The definitions and methods are taken from the System of National Accounts, or SNA, of 1968 (United Nations Department of Economic and Social Affairs [UNDESA], 1968).[20] This was used rather than that of 1953 as it is more comprehensive, but still appropriate for the level of development of Malaya at that time.

The information base used to derive the series draws on numerous disparate data sources of varying quality and completeness, and for several elements in the estimation process, judgements had to be made. The resulting estimates of GDP and its components are, therefore, necessarily imperfect and some caution is required in their interpretation. They form the basis of the statistical and econometric analyses in Chapters 4, 5 and 6.

Deriving GDP Estimates

Estimates of GDP for a country or area can be derived in one of three

---

19 The series of GDP estimates in this book supersedes the earlier estimates that were contained in my PhD (Raja Nazrin, 2000). This new series is based on a much more comprehensive database and improved estimation methods. A fuller account of the methodology summarised here will be given in a forthcoming publication. Singapore was excluded from this study so that the estimates made here could be linked with a post-independence series for Malaysia.

20 The SNA of 1968 (UNDESA, 1968) was used in conjunction with the explanatory Handbook of National Accounting (UNDESA, 1986).

ways (Box 3.1).[21] As the three approaches (production, income and expenditure) are conceptually equivalent, they should yield identical estimates. In practice, reliable and complete data are rarely available to make independent estimates of GDP using all three approaches, particularly in developing countries. While the use of more than one approach is desirable, especially for validation purposes, in practice data limitations frequently necessitate the use of only one. For this reason, the GDP estimates derived in this study were computed using the expenditure method only.[22] The conceptual framework of this approach is set out as follows:

GDP at purchasers' values = Private final consumption expenditure of households (PFCE)

plus   Private final consumption expenditure of non-profit institutions serving households (PFCE/NPI)

plus   Government final consumption expenditure (GFCE)

plus   Increase in stocks (IS)

plus   Gross fixed capital formation (GFCF)

plus   Exports of goods and services (EGS)

less   Imports of goods and services (IGS).

Two of these components were excluded:

- *PFCE of non-profit institutions*, such as fraternal societies, trade unions, religious institutions and foundations for which data were not available.[23]

- *Increase in stocks*, which were relatively insignificant and for which data were also not available. When official statistics first became available in 1955, this item accounted for only 0.3 per

---

21 The Department of Statistics-Malaysia currently adopts a combination of three estimation approaches, and its reports generally contain the following core tables: (i) expenditure on gross national product; (ii) industrial origin of gross domestic product at factor cost; (iii) national income by type of organisation; (iv) distribution of national income; (v) the finance of gross domestic capital formation; (vi) composition of gross domestic capital formation; (vii) receipts and expenditure of private enterprises and households; (viii) composition of private consumption expenditure; (ix) general government revenue and expenditure; (x) composition of general government consumption expenditure; and (xi) international transactions.

22 The expenditure methodology used in estimating Malaya's GDP for the period 1900–1939 has also been employed in estimating Singapore's historical GDP over the same time span (Sugimoto, 2009, 2011 and 2015). The application of this approach for estimating GDP in the Netherlands in the 19th century can be found in Smits *et al.* (2000).

23 Private non-profit institutions serving households include societies, trade unions, religious institutions, schools, hospitals, foundations, clubs, and political parties, which have been established by associations of individuals without the aim of making a profit (UNDESA, 1986).

cent of Malaya's GDP, and it averaged only 0.2 per cent from 1955–1964 (Department of Statistics-Malaysia, 1965 and 1975).

Box 3.1 Three methods for estimating national income

The data required for the construction of a complete set of national income accounts are extensive, and only in highly developed statistical systems are such data systematically collected, processed and published.

The *production method*, or value added method, of estimating national income requires a production census or a survey of establishments/enterprises with adequate coverage. For each establishment/enterprise, value added at market prices is calculated as the market value of its output, less the value of intermediate goods and services it consumes in the production of its output. From value added *at market prices,* indirect production taxes are deducted, and production subsidies added, to obtain value added at factor cost. Subtraction of depreciation allowances yields *net* value added (UNDESA, 1986).

Gross domestic product (GDP) at market prices (factor cost) is obtained as the sum of value-added at market prices (factor cost) over all establishments/enterprises, and should also include an imputed value for the rent of owner-occupied dwellings. Gross national income (GNI) adds net overseas primary income (net property income and compensation received, less net indirect taxes, less subsidies paid) to GDP (Box Table 3.1).

The production method of estimating national income has the benefit not only of providing an aggregate measure of economic activity, but also of mapping the structure of output in the economy. As measures of national income are generally produced annually, the use of the production method can make large demands on resources. Reductions in the cost of computing power and improvements in data processing technology have reduced costs, but production censuses or extensive establishment/enterprise surveys still make heavy demands on statistical agencies.

The *income method* looks at national income through the lens of the distribution of profits, compensation of employees, rents and interest on capital. In many countries, there will also be a category of *mixed income* for small businesses and households that engage in production. Income estimates are typically embedded in broader efforts to measure production and value added. For any enterprise, value added at factor cost (the market value of gross output, less intermediate consumption, less indirect taxes, plus subsidies) should, in principle, be equal to the sum of employee compensation, profits, royalties, interest on capital and rent (which are all payments for factor services), plus depreciation.

Where production censuses or establishment/enterprise surveys do not exist, income can be measured using other sources. These could include household income surveys, labour force surveys and business surveys. In economies with developed taxation systems and where the bulk of economic activity falls within the formal economy, tax data may usefully supplement these other sources.

The *expenditure method* looks at what is spent on *final* goods and services (that is goods and services not consumed in production). This requires separate estimates of household consumption spending, government spending on final goods and services (those that are not used in the production of public services), business investment spending including inventory changes, the value of all domestic output exported, and goods and services consumed by non-profit entities (other than in the delivery of services). So as to obtain an estimate of GDP at market prices, the total value of imports should be subtracted (Box Table 3.1).

Box Table 3.1 **Differences between product- and income-based measures of national income**

	Domestic product (within the country boundaries)	National income (received on an ownership basis, and irrespective of location)	National product
	1	2	3
Gross (no allowance for the depreciation of capital)	Gross domestic product at market prices (GDP) = Value added = Value of gross output – Value of intermediate goods	Gross national income (GNI) = GDP – (Indirect taxes + Subsidies on production and imports) – Primary income paid abroad + Primary income received from abroad	Gross national product (GNP) = GDP – Income received by non-residents from domestic production + Property income received by residents abroad
Net (capital depreciation subtracted)	Net domestic product (NDP) = GDP – Depreciation	Net national income (NNI) = GNI – Depreciation	Net national product = GNP – Depreciation
Factor cost	= GDP – Indirect taxes + Subsidies		

Estimating income in this way requires the combination of data from a variety of sources, including household expenditure surveys, business surveys, government accounts and balance of payments estimates. These data are typically collected by different agencies and so may need to be reconciled with one another. In countries where estimates of income have been made independently of the production accounts, one component of final expenditure can be treated residually to ensure consistency between expenditure and production estimates of GDP. Consumption expenditure, which is often the largest component of final spending, usually plays this balancing role.

In estimating the historical GDP series for Malaya, the expenditure method has been employed without the benefit of *controls* derived from the production (value added) or income approaches. The detailed establishment/enterprise surveys on which these are based did not occur until after independence, and the first set of comprehensive national accounts (featuring production, income and expenditure estimates) were only computed in the input-output accounts of 1978. In putting together these expenditure estimates, the most important challenge was in estimating consumption spending, as this accounted for a large proportion of GDP.

Box Table 3.1 summarises the differences between product- and income-based measures of national income, between national and domestic measures, and between gross and net measures. Historically, GDP (column 1) and gross national product (GNP) (column 3) have been the main metrics used in national income accounting, but the latter has now been replaced by Gross National Income in the official 2008 SNA.

The computation of Malaya's GDP thus consisted of five components, namely: PFCE, GFCE, GFCF, EGS and IGS. The definition of each component, and the categories of which it is comprised, were, as mentioned, taken from the 1968 SNA. Each component of GDP was then considered according to the availability of data, method of estimation used, and choice of the most suitable price deflator to obtain a constant price series. The base year was taken as 1914 as it was a relatively stable year—rubber prices had fallen from a peak in 1909 and had stabilised by 1914, and tin prices were relatively stable for that year.

Private Final Consumption Expenditure

Concepts and Definitions

In the 1968 SNA, PFCE is defined as all expenditure, including imputed expenditure, incurred by resident households on individual consumption of goods and services.

PFCE of resident households is usually derived by adding to PFCE of residents and non-residents in the domestic market, the direct purchases that resident households make abroad, and deducting the purchases non-resident households make in the domestic market. For the purposes of this study, however, it has been assumed that expenditures made abroad by residents were equal to expenditures by non-residents in the domestic market.[24]

For this study, PFCE has been estimated on a per capita rather than on a per household basis because of the limited data on consumption at household level. Malaya's large migrant community consisting of predominantly single males was another factor justifying this approach.

Data Sources

The computation of PFCE according to the 1968 SNA required data on consumption expenditure for:

- Food, beverages and tobacco.
- Clothing and footwear.
- Gross rent, fuel and power.
- Furniture, furnishings, and household equipment and operation.
- Medical care and health expenses.
- Transport and communication.
- Recreation, entertainment, education and cultural services.
- Miscellaneous goods and services (for example, personal care and effects; expenditure in restaurants, cafes and hotels; holiday travel; and financial and other services not classified elsewhere).

Details on data availability together with their limitations are described in Appendix 1.

---

24 Official time series data for the period 1960–1965 show that the average expenditure incurred abroad by residents less expenditure in the domestic market of non-residents as a share of nominal PFCE was less than 0.4% (Department of Statistics-Malaysia, 1966).

Computing PFCE at Current Prices

There are several methods for estimating PFCE: through the use of household expenditure surveys, commodity flows, retail valuation and retail sales. A lack of relevant data precluded the use of these methods, however. Instead, a combination of direct and indirect approaches was employed to construct the PFCE series at constant and current prices.[25] The direct approach was used where data were available from official records, and where data were lacking, an indirect approach was employed. Miscellaneous items were then calculated as a proportion of expenditures estimated through the indirect approach. Combining the expenditures from the two approaches with those on miscellaneous items then provided the total PFCE series (Figure 3.1).

Direct Approach

The direct approach was used to estimate expenditure on medical services and education, utilities, passenger transport by rail and ferry, and opium/*chandu*. Consumer expenditure on medical services and education was obtained from information on the total medical fees collected by government hospitals and outdoor dispensaries, and on the school fees collected by government and government-aided schools. Final private consumption expenditure on utilities was obtained from revenue collected by the electricity and water boards. Expenditure on passenger transport (rail and ferry) was estimated based on the revenue collected by the Railway Department.

Consumption of opium, or *chandu* in its cooked form, was obtained from the government's gross revenue receipts for the sale of opium/chandu by the Government Monopolies Department, or estimated based on the quantity sold to consumers at retail prices (Box 3.2).

Expenditures estimated using the direct approach may not have been all-encompassing, or fully representative of actual total consumption expenditure. For example, expenditure on private health care and education were excluded. Evidence suggests that these expenditures were minimal in pre-World War II Malaya. Such expenditures, although small, have been implicitly incorporated under the *miscellaneous items of expenditure* component that will be described later.

---

25 The methodology for estimating the PFCE of Malaya for the period 1900–1939 was initially presented in Tokyo in 2001 and in Helsinki in 2006 (Raja Nazrin, 2001 and 2006). It was subsequently employed by Ichiro Sugimoto in deriving the PFCE of Singapore for the years 1900–1939 and 1947–1960 (Sugimoto, 2011).

Box 3.2 Opium trade as a major source of government revenue

Opium smoking was widespread among the urban and mining Chinese community living in Malaya up to around the middle of the 20th century, and many workers spent a significant proportion of their wages on it (Box Figure 3.1) (Wu, 2003). Some even borrowed money to purchase opium, becoming indebted to their employers or money-lenders. Per capita expenditure tended to be highest in states where the Chinese proportion of the population was largest. Chinese manual labourers enjoyed smoking after a strenuous day's work, supposedly because it produced pleasant dreams and feelings of contentment. Raw opium, imported from India, had to be boiled and otherwise treated to convert it into a thick dark brown treacle called *chandu*, ready for smoking in an opium pipe.

Box Figure 3.1 Expenditure shares on opium/*chandu* at current prices, Malaya, 1900–1939

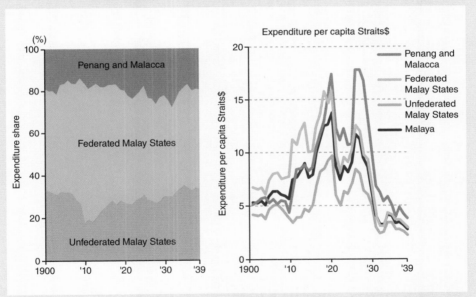

Opium was a very important source of government revenue for administrative and infrastructure spending. Other revenue sources included export duties on tin and rubber (Li, 1982). The government made money from duties on opium when it entered the country, and also benefited through licenses issued to those who sold it. Opium comprised around a third of government revenue of the Straits Settlements in 1928, and was also a substantial source of revenue in the Federated Malay States (Baker, 2008).

The right to import opium, prepare it for smoking and sell it to customers was farmed out to the highest bidder in the coastal districts—a practice followed in the Straits Settlements since the first half of the 19th century. In inland tin mining areas, mine owners were licensed at a fee to supply the substance to their opium-smoking employees. The farming system gave the farmer the sole right to prepare and sell *chandu*. The farmer issued licences to others to retail the preparation. The government regulated the price and ensured that the *chandu* met certain standards. The revenue farms contributed to the spread of opium smoking since those running them, as well as some of the mine owners, had a share in the profits generated.

The 1909 *Chandu* Revenue Ordinance gave the government exclusive control over the import and export of opium, as well as the preparation and selling of *chandu*. In 1910, the British government created the Monopolies Department to oversee all opium farms and built a factory in Singapore to convert the raw opium into *chandu*, and to pack it for distribution. *Chandu* shops were opened in every town in the Federation, with the product brought over from Singapore and sold to anyone who wanted to buy it (National Library Board, 2014).

During the early 1930s, the government decided to discourage opium smoking and every opium smoker had to register before being able to purchase opium from a government shop. Only registered smokers could now buy opium legally and no one, apart from the government, was allowed to sell it. Since it had full control over the industry, the government was able to reduce opium consumption by gradually raising the retail price. International pressure on the British Colonial Office, particularly from the US, eventually led to a diminution in opium use (Manderson, 1996).

Indirect Approach

The indirect approach was employed to estimate expenditure on food, beverages, tobacco, clothing, rent, domestic servants, passenger transport (other than rail and ferry), clubs and other miscellaneous expenditures. This involved estimating PFCE on the major consumption categories for each 'consumption standard', as defined below. It required as inputs, information on the population of each consumption standard, per capita consumption of each major consumption category for each consumption standard, consumer price indices, a real wage index and income elasticities of demand. This approach utilised an 11-step procedure as outlined in Figure 3.1.

Figure 3.1 Estimation of private final consumption expenditure, Malaya, 1900–1939

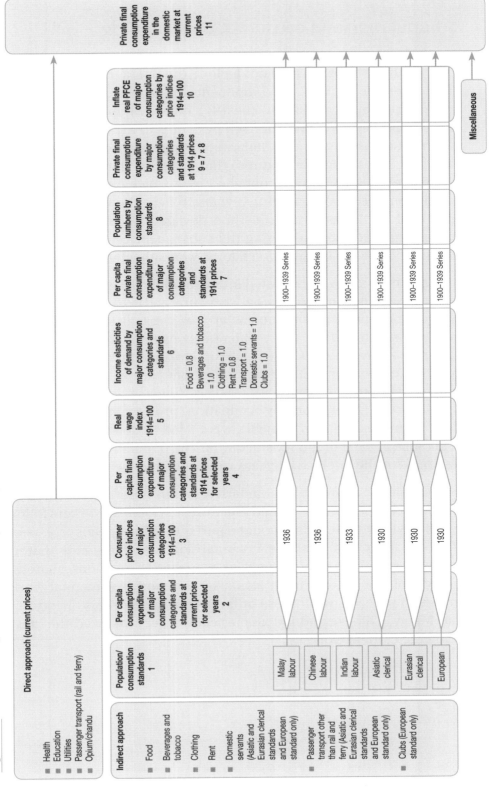

1 Population and consumption standards

Population censuses were conducted in the years 1901, 1911, 1921 and 1931. As the 1901 census did not include the Unfederated Malay States, the figures for each of its component states were calculated based on their percentage share in the 1911 census. Population figures for intercensal years were then derived by adding to the census population, natural increase and net immigration (immigration less emigration based on arrivals and departures) that occurred during the year. Data for mid-year (June 30) were obtained by averaging the beginning-year population over two consecutive years. Where the intercensal figures generated by the estimation method deviated from the actual census figures, they were revised using the subsequent census figures as the anchor and the net immigration figures were adjusted accordingly.[26]

Significant differences existed in consumption levels and expenditure patterns among ethnic groups, between rural and urban areas, and among different occupational and income groups. Six consumption standards were utilised to reflect these different consumption and expenditure patterns: Malay labour, Chinese labour, Indian labour, Asiatic clerical,[27] Eurasian clerical and European. Data from the population census of employed persons by ethnicity (Malays, Chinese, Indians, Europeans, Eurasians and Others), and by occupation (professional and managerial, clerical and related, and manual), were used to determine the number of persons in each of the six standards. The population figures for each standard for the intercensal years were obtained by interpolation.

Inclusion in a particular standard was thus determined by ethnicity and occupation. It was assumed that Eurasian manual workers followed the lifestyle of their Indian counterparts, that Europeans irrespective of occupation had a single consumption standard, and that non-Europeans holding professional or managerial positions shared the lifestyle of the Europeans. It was also assumed that manual workers adhered to the Malay, Chinese or Indian manual workers' lifestyle, and that Malay, Chinese and Indian clerical workers followed the lifestyle of Asiatic clerical workers.

---

26 The arrival and departure figures were mere departmental records and not genuine migration statistics, as was alluded to in the 1947 Population Census Report, pp. 28 (Del Tufo, 1949).

27 Asiatic clerical standard encompasses Malay, Chinese and Indian clerical standards.

2 Estimating per capita consumption expenditure of major consumption categories and standards

The method of estimating annual consumption expenditure of a *representative* individual differed for each of the six standards as determined by the available data.

European standard: The expenditure pattern of a European household in Malaya was assumed to be similar to that of a European household in Singapore. A study undertaken in Singapore in 1930 estimated the monthly living expenses of a typical three-person household at Straits$649 (Miller, 1931). This amount excluded expenditure on education and utilities, which were estimated through the direct method. It was assumed that a European household in Malaya would incur only 90 per cent of the expenditure incurred by its counterpart in Singapore.

Eurasian/Asiatic clerical standards: The procedure for deriving consumption expenditure for the Eurasian and Asiatic clerical standards was similar to that adopted for the European standard. The data were obtained from the same 1930 Singapore study, taking into account variations in household size. For these two standards, each comprising a household of five persons, the monthly household expenses were Straits$134 and Straits$130 respectively.

Indian labour standard: The consumption figure for this standard was based on the amount of Straits$4.53 per month for an Indian adult derived from the *Johore Annual Report, Labourer's Specimen Monthly Budget 1933*. The assumptions were that an adult female would consume the same amount of food and clothing as an adult male, and that a child's consumption of these items would be two-thirds that of an adult. These assumptions provided the basis for the derivation of the weighted per capita consumption. Food expenditure was revised upwards to include consumption of food produced on their own account. Per capita consumption of tobacco was based solely on the consumption of an adult male. Rental expenditure was assumed to be 5 per cent of all goods and services consumed.

Malay and Chinese labour standards: The 1936 full-meat diet scale of government hospitals was utilised to derive the food consumption pattern for a Malay and a Chinese adult. The hospital food consumption data were revised upwards as it was assumed that the normal food intake of an adult would exceed the amount of food provided in hospital. The weighted per capita consumption for the Malay and Chinese standards was estimated using a method similar to that described above for the Indian labour standard.

No data were available on the per capita consumption of tobacco, clothing and rent for 1936, the relevant year for the Malay and Chinese labour standards, but some data were available for 1949, except on rent. It was assumed that the proportion of expenditure on tobacco and clothing in relation to food observed in 1949 would have been the same in 1939, the closest year in the study period and one for which data on food expenditures were available. Using these data, it was thus possible to derive the per capita consumption values for tobacco and clothing for 1939, based on their consumption in relation to food in 1949. Data for 1936 were then obtained by applying the price deflators to the 1939 values.

Rent constituted 9.6 per cent of the per capita expenditure of the European standard in 1936. It was assumed that the share of expenditure on rent for the Malay and Chinese labour standards would be less than that for the European standard. This was taken as 5 per cent for the Malay labour standard and 6 per cent for the Chinese labour standard.

The annual expenditure of a *representative* individual in each of the six consumption standards was then calculated for each major consumption category at current prices for the selected years. Table 3.1 shows the per cent distribution of expenditure by standard for the consumption categories as well as their mean per capita monthly expenditures on the items covered by the indirect approach.

Food expenditure was by far the largest category for each of the standards, except the European standard. Food accounted for just 24% of total expenditure in the European standard on items covered by the indirect approach. This standard had the highest per capita monthly expenditure on these items of Straits$195 (Table 3.1). The Eurasian and Asiatic clerical standards, with per capita monthly expenditure of Straits$23–24, again on items covered by the indirect approach, spent about half on food. The majority of the population categorised in the Indian, Malay and Chinese labour standards had the highest expenditure share on food of between 78 and 86 per cent. Their per capita monthly expenditure on items covered by the indirect approach was just Straits$5–6.

Table 3.1 Distribution of mean monthly per capita expenditure at current prices in Straits$ for major consumption categories, Malaya, 1930, 1933 and 1936

Major categories of consumption	European 1930	Eurasian clerical 1930	Asiatic clerical 1930	Indian labour 1933	Malay labour 1936	Chinese labour 1936
			Consumption standards			
		Per cent distribution by expenditure categories				
Food	24.2	49.6	47.8	85.5	77.9	77.7
Beverages and tobacco	7.3	2.7	2.8	4.5	4.5	4.2
Clothing	12.3	9.7	10.0	4.6	12.8	12.2
Rent	12.3	22.4	23.2	5.4	4.7	6.0
Domestic servants	26.2	7.5	7.7	na	na	na
Passenger transport (other than rail and ferry)	8.2	8.2	8.5	na	na	na
Clubs	9.4	na	na	na	na	na
Total	100	100	100	100	100	100
Mean Straits$	*194.73*	*24.14*	*23.32*	*4.95*	*5.54*	*5.63*

na = Not applicable

3 Consumer price indices of major consumption categories, 1900–1939

Price indices for each of the major categories of consumption and for overall consumption were required in order to value spending by the six standards in the same base year (1914) prices. These price indices were also used to express constant price consumption in current price terms and to express nominal wage rates in real terms.

The construction of consumer price indices for the period 1900–1939 can be divided into two sub-periods of 1900–1914 and 1914–1939. Except for the years 1915–1917 and 1939, for which estimates were made, the price indices for Malaya over the period 1914–1939 were based on Singapore's annual cost-of-living indices which were available for each major consumption category of the European standard, and the Eurasian and Asiatic clerical standards. It was assumed that the price movements of Malaya's European standard, and Eurasian and Asiatic clerical standards followed those of their counterparts in Singapore. It was also assumed that the remaining three, Malay, Chinese and Indian labour standards followed the price movements of Singapore's Asiatic clerical standard.

Since no price indices were available for the period 1900–1914, even for Singapore, a set for each major category of consumption and each standard was estimated for Malaya based on a weighted average of the prices of various consumption items.

Having determined the price indices for all major consumption categories by standard for the period 1900–1914 and 1914–1939, the next step involved the computation of a weighted overall consumer price index for the entire 1900–1939 period. The consumer price indices of major consumption categories are shown in Figure 3.2.

4 Estimating per capita PFCE of major consumption categories and standards at 1914 prices

Per capita consumer spending for the six standards was estimated for different years according to the available data (1930, 1933, 1936). Per capita consumption at current prices for each major consumption category in 1930 (European standard, Eurasian and Asiatic clerical standards), 1933 (Indian labour standard), and 1936 (Malay and Chinese labour standards) was then deflated by the respective price indices using the base year of 1914. This implies, however, that the quantity consumed per capita for each major consumption category remained unchanged between 1914 and 1930, 1914 and 1933, and 1914 and 1936, depending on the consumption standard. Any changes in consumption patterns resulting from changes in income over time were thus not reflected.

5 Real wage index, 1900–1939

The construction of a real wage index was, therefore, required in order to take account of the impact of changes in real income on consumption. No continuous wage series was available for the period 1900–1939. It was possible, however, to construct a continuous surrogate series of wage data for the sub-periods of 1900–1914 and 1914–1939. In turn, the overlapping year of 1914 made it possible to link the two sub-period series. In the absence of official data, these

Figure 3.2 **Consumer 1914 price indices by major categories of consumption, Malaya, 1900–1939**

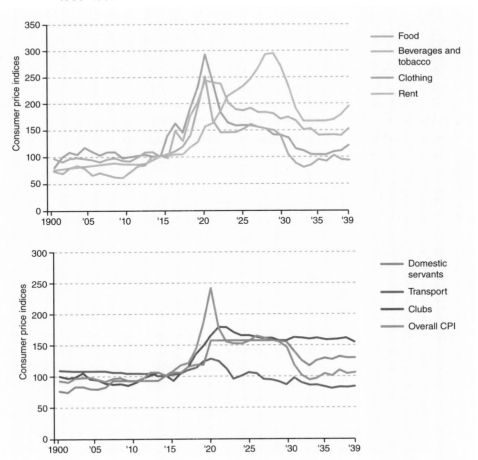

two sub-period series reflected changes in income over time in the form of wages and salaries received by employees in both cash and kind, entrepreneurial income derived from self-employment, income receipts of unpaid family workers and other income.

The wage rate series for the period 1900–1914 took into account the agricultural and non-agricultural sectors of the Malayan economy. The wage index for the agricultural sector was based on a simple arithmetic average of two elements: the wage index of Chinese estate coolies and predial (field workers and gardeners), and the wage index of the 'trades' (carpenters, joiners, blacksmiths and bricklayers). For the non-agricultural sector, the wage movements of the 'trades' were used. The wage rate series for the years 1914–1939 was similarly obtained, although the wage index of Chinese estate coolies and predial was replaced by the wage index of Indian adult male rubber tappers.

As suitable employment data for the base year 1914 were not available, the 1921 census data on employment by sector were used to weight the nominal wage indices for the agricultural and non-agricultural sectors for the period 1900–1914 and 1914–1939. The 1921 census indicated that 66.1 per cent of workers were engaged in the agricultural sector compared to 33.9 per cent in non-agriculture. The 1931 census showed that these shares had not changed significantly (67.2 per cent in agriculture and 32.8 per cent in non-agriculture). It was assumed that the sector weights in 1914 would have been similar to those in 1921, and these were, therefore, used to compute the overall nominal wage index for the period 1900–1939. The nominal wage index was then deflated by the overall consumer price index to arrive at the real wage index for the entire period 1900–1939 (Figure 3.3).

Figure 3.3 Real wage index, Malaya, 1900–1939

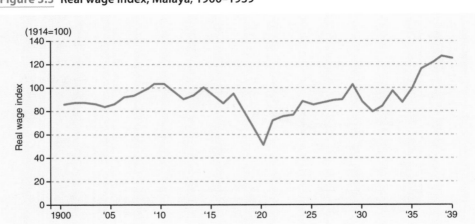

6–11 Deriving total PFCE at constant and current prices, 1900–1939 (excluding miscellaneous expenditure)

Consumer spending on each category and for each standard would have been influenced by changes in real income over time. To capture the effects of real income changes on real expenditure, income elasticities were applied to the real wage index plotted in Figure 3.3. The following income elasticities of demand were used in order to adjust the expenditure series to capture the effect of real income changes: 0.8 for food, 0.8 for rent, and 1.0 for beverages and tobacco, clothing, passenger transport other than rail and ferry, domestic servants and clubs (Box 3.3).

Box 3.3   Income and consumption patterns

A person, or household, spends on many different goods and services—the so-called *consumption basket*. Some of this spending is essential to life such as food, clothing and shelter, but other spending may be more discretionary and be influenced by habits, tastes, or other influences.

Observed consumption patterns vary greatly among households, and across time and place. The consumption patterns observed among the poor are not the same as those among the rich. The needs and preferences of the elderly are different from those who are young. The wants of large families are not the same as those of married couples with no children. Geography, climate and culture also exert an important influence on patterns of household spending. In seeking to understand these varied patterns, economists try to take all of these factors into account.

One important way to characterise patterns of consumption is to look at how spending within the household consumption basket changes as total household income changes, with all the prices of goods and services within the consumption basket unchanged. The study of how income influences consumption spending was pioneered in the 19th century by Engel (1857), who studied how food consumption among poor families in Belgium was affected by income.

Increases in income enable higher spending on all goods and services. If spending on an item rises (falls) as income rises (falls), such a good is labeled *normal*. This is what Engel observed in relation to expenditure on food among poor households in 19th century Belgium. A special type of normal good is a *superior* good. A good is superior when its share in total spending rises (falls) as income rises (falls). If income rises by 10 per cent, spending on a superior good will rise by more than 10 per cent. Engel observed that the share of food in total spending fell as the incomes of households increased, so while food was a normal good, it was not a superior good. At the other end of the spectrum are inferior goods. A good or service is considered *inferior* if spending falls (rises) as income rises (falls). A particularly important example is rice consumption in Asia (Timmer, Block and Dawe, 2010).

The characterisation of goods as normal, superior or inferior is based on observed spending behaviour—it is not intrinsic to the goods or services themselves. However, inferior goods are typically low cost, low quality goods that are widely available. Conversely, superior goods are typically high cost and scarce. For example, if low-cost cars are substituted for public transportation as income rises from low levels, public transportation is observed to be inferior, and transportation in private cars is observed to be normal, possibly superior. Then, at higher levels of income, if luxury cars are substituted for low-cost cars, low-cost cars are now inferior and luxury cars are superior.

Another way of looking at the characteristics of goods is to ask what happens to their share in spending as total income changes. If the share rises (falls) as income rises (falls), it is necessarily the case that the growth in spending on that good is larger than the growth in income. The ratio of these growth rates is what is referred to as an income elasticity. So when shares in spending rise (fall), the income elasticity is greater (less) than one. A superior good is, therefore, one whose income elasticity is greater than one. A normal good has a positive income elasticity, but it is one or less than one. In the case of an inferior good, when the share not only falls but less is consumed in absolute terms, the income elasticity is negative.

In every consumption basket, there is necessarily a mix of normal and superior goods, and possibly some inferior goods. If when income rises, all shares remain the same, all goods are normal and all would have an income elasticity of one. But this would be an extremely unusual case. In general, as income rises, some shares will rise and such goods, with *income elasticities* greater than one, would be superior. But if some shares rise, others must fall (since the shares must always add up to one), and so other goods must either be normal or inferior, and have income elasticities of less than one.

Given the high proportion of income spent on food, the income elasticity of demand for food of 0.8 represented the most important component. This figure was based on an estimate made for the income elasticity of demand for food in the Netherlands in 1938 of 0.7 (Derksen and Tinbergen, 1945), but was set slightly higher to reflect the fact that the level of development in pre-war Malaya would have been lower than that of the Netherlands. Similar levels of income elasticity of demand for food have also been calculated for the UK during the 19th century (Crafts, 1985).

By applying these elasticities, it was possible to compute the constant-price per capita PFCE for the period 1900–1939, taking as the starting point the real annual per capita expenditure on the major consumption categories for the different standards in the selected years. This computation, therefore, took into account changes in real wages and income elasticities of demand.

In basing the income effects on real wage rates, the method took no account of variations in employment over time due to either spells of unemployment or variations in labour force participation. The real wage series was calculated based on the wages of those in employment, but incomes would also have varied according to rates of labour-force participation and unemployment. Many Malay, Chinese and Indian workers were laid off in the Great Depression of 1929–1932 and in 1938, which naturally amplified the income effects already allowed for through the use of wage data. Unfortunately, unemployment data were not available for this period, and for this reason, income effects on consumption were estimated through the use of the real wage index alone.

The per capita consumption of each major consumption category was then multiplied by the total population of each standard. This provided the total PFCE for each major consumption category for each standard at constant prices for each year. The expenditure was then inflated by the price indices of the major consumption categories to obtain the total PFCE at current prices. A summation of the major categories of consumption across the standards at constant and current prices then gave the total PFCE for those items covered by the indirect approach at constant and current prices respectively.

Estimating Miscellaneous Items of Expenditure

The expenditure on miscellaneous items was computed for each year based on total PFCE at current prices as derived through the indirect approach. This expenditure was taken as 7 per cent of total PFCE. The miscellaneous expenditure in constant prices for each year was then derived by deflating the miscellaneous expenditure values in nominal terms by the overall consumer price index.

The overall PFCE for each year in real and nominal terms was obtained by summing the consumption expenditure estimates based on the direct and indirect approaches, including miscellaneous expenditure. The totals are shown in Figure 3.4.

Figure 3.4 **Trends in private final consumption expenditure, Malaya, 1900–1939**

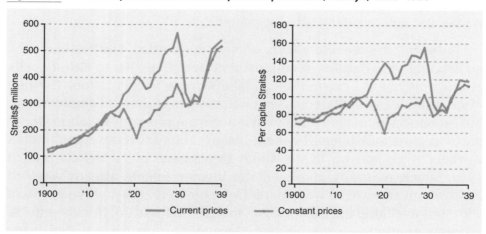

Government Final Consumption Expenditure

Concepts and Definitions

GFCE represents the expenditure of government on goods and services. It is defined as the value of gross output of producers of government services, less the value of government sales and the value of any own-account capital formation that is included in gross output. In other words, it is equal to the value of goods and services produced by the government for its own current use (UNDESA, 1986).

GFCE is not, however, equivalent to total government expenditure as the latter also includes expenditure on gross fixed capital formation and 'transfer payments and others' such as contributions to charitable foundations, grants and pensions which are not included in the calculation of GFCE.

The producers of government services include all bodies, departments and establishments of government, both central and local, that engage in a wide range of activities including administration, defence and the regulation of public order, health, educational, cultural, recreational and other social services (UNDESA, 1968). These producers of government services are considered to be the final consumers of most of the goods and services they produce, and their cost structures do not contain any element of operating surplus.

Government output, which is mainly not sold, is usually computed based on the cost of producing it, namely the sum of compensation of employees, intermediate consumption, consumption of fixed capital or depreciation, indirect taxes and own-account capital formation, if any (UNDESA, 1986). In the Malayan context, final government output has been calculated based on the first three components, as the government did not pay tax in any form nor did it engage in own-account capital formation (Box 3.4).

Box 3.4 Deriving government final consumption expenditure

The three components used to derive Malaya's GFCE are defined in accordance with the 1968 SNA, as follows:

Compensation of employees mainly consists of two general items: (i) personal emoluments, which refer to salaries and wages in cash and in kind, and (ii) employers' contributions to social security, life insurance, private pension schemes and other similar schemes.

Intermediate consumption consists of non-durable goods and services that are purchased by producers and used up in the process of production—postage and telephone charges, water, lighting, electricity, purchases of supplies such as stationery, traveling costs (reimbursement), maintenance cost of furniture and equipment, and purchases of printing and legal services.

Consumption of fixed capital, or depreciation, is a cost of production and may be defined as the decline in the current value of the stock of fixed assets owned and used by a producer as a result of physical deterioration and normal obsolescence.

Government sales, which are deducted from government output, usually include receipts from post-cards, publications sold by statistical offices, fees for medical and hospital treatment, school fees, and sales of maps. Detailed information on government sales in pre-World War II Malaya was available only for school and hospital fees. Sales of other goods and services were anyway negligible.

Data Sources

The computation of GFCE required detailed information on total government expenditure which was organized according to class of account and heads of departments. Class of account refers to the distinct categories of total government expenditure. These included compensation of employees, intermediate consumption and consumption of fixed capital or depreciation (although there was no data on this aspect), as well as fixed capital formation and transfer payments and others. Categorising information according to heads of departments allowed a distinction to be made between expenditures incurred by producers of government services (general departments) and those by industries (trading departments). Trading departments do not form part of GFCE.[28] Details on data sources and their limitations are described in Appendix 1.

Computing GFCE at Current Prices

Malaya's GFCE was computed by taking the output of producers of government services and other outlays, less the value of government sales, namely hospital and school fees. The expenditure information published in the colonial documents could not readily be used in its original form since the accounts were compiled mainly for administrative purposes. Some data processing was, therefore, required before the raw data contained in the government financial accounts could be utilised to estimate GFCE. A coding system was established to classify expenditure items into the major categories of government expenditure described above.

---

28 In the Malayan context, trading departments included (i) Post and Telegraph; (ii) Electricity Supply Department (Central Electricity Board); (iii) Public Works Department; (iv) Printing Department; (v) Drainage and Irrigation Department; and (vi) Federated Malay States Railways.

Using this coding scheme, two of the three components of the output of producers of government services were obtained—compensation of employees and intermediate consumption. Data were not, however, available for the third component, consumption of fixed capital or depreciation. Information for the 1960s for Peninsular Malaysia was used instead as an indicative guide. Based on this evidence, it was assumed that the percentage of consumption of fixed capital to total government output would have been in the region of 4 per cent. Having obtained the output of producers of government services in this way, and subtracting government sales, GFCE was then derived.

In completing the GFCE accounts, several estimates had to be made to overcome various data challenges including:

- Expenditure patterns for the years where departmental level data were not available were estimated using data for years where detailed expenditure by class of account were available.
- Where detailed data by class of account were not available for a given administrative unit, the data of another administrative unit deemed to have had a similar expenditure structure were utilised.
- For years in which separate figures were not available for general and trading departments, shares were estimated using data from years when they were available for the same administrative unit.
- The difficulties involved in the estimation of government expenditure were compounded by the changing number and names of heads of departments. This problem was overcome by using the average expenditure structure for a similar head of department.
- Gaps in data on government expenditure in intervening years were filled by interpolation, while those for single year(s) in the series were estimated by using the simple arithmetic average of adjacent years.
- Gaps in data for early and end years were filled by backward and forward interpolation respectively.

Having taken these challenges into account, the final estimates are brought together in Figure 3.5.

Figure 3.5 Trends in government final consumption expenditure, Malaya, 1900–1939

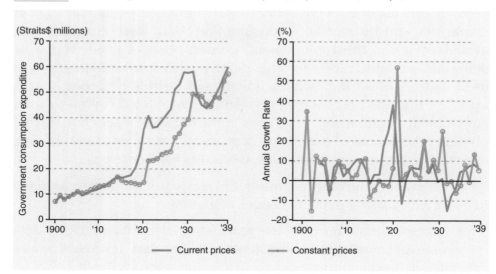

Computing GFCE at Constant Prices

The calculation of GFCE at constant prices required a judgement on which deflator would be appropriate. Since the compensation of employees and intermediate consumption comprised the bulk of GFCE (two-thirds and 30 per cent respectively), deflators were required that reflected both components. In theory, the wage rate index of government employees by department should be used for the former. For the latter, weighted producer price indices should be used to reflect government consumption of specific goods and services of intermediate consumption.

The data needed to calculate the two required indices for local and imported goods were, however, insufficiently detailed. Rather than listing items individually, expenditure statements in the colonial records generally grouped them together. It was also not generally noted whether purchases were of locally produced or imported items. These inadequacies made it difficult to construct the indices.

Rao (1976), in estimating GFCE for Peninsular Malaysia for the period 1960–1968, used a weighted average of the retail price index and an import price index (weights being 0.7 and 0.3 respectively), with 1959 as the base year. The use of the import price index is not without shortcomings since imports can consist of both intermediate goods as well as capital goods. Furthermore, this index only covers merchandise imports and, therefore, does not take into account imports of services.

Two approaches were tried—one used only the consumer price index for GFCE as a whole, while the other used a weighted consumer price index and an import unit value index (weights being 0.69 and 0.31 respectively), an approach not too dissimilar to that employed by Rao. Both approaches used 1914 as the base year. The results from these two approaches were similar, with the exception of a few years in which the differences were minor. The former approach was adopted for this study to obtain GFCE at constant prices.

Gross Fixed Capital Formation

Concepts and Definitions

According to the 1968 SNA, GFCF consists of the outlays of industries and the producers of government services and of private non-profit services to households, on additions of commodities to their fixed assets, reduced by their net sales (sales less purchases) of similar used (second-hand) and scrapped goods (UNDESA, 1968). Excluded are outlays on construction works and other durable goods that are to be used primarily for military purposes.

The 1968 SNA provides a system of classification according to the type of fixed assets, which can be grouped into four main categories:

- Construction (residential buildings, non-residential buildings and other construction except land improvement);
- Land improvement, and plantation and orchard development;
- Machinery and equipment (transport equipment, agricultural machinery and equipment, and others); and
- Breeding stock, draught animals, dairy cattle and other similar animals.

All categories were taken into account, except for the sub-element of land improvement in the second category, and the whole of the fourth category. Land improvement, which involves outlays on all land reclamation and land clearance, irrigation and flood control projects and dams, was assumed to be minimal during pre-war Malaya. The first estimate on investment in land improvement in Malaya was for the year 1955. This amounted to $2 million, which accounted for only 0.4 per cent of total GFCF and 0.04 per cent of GDP (Department of Statistics-Malaysia, 1965).

Data on breeding stock, draught animals, dairy cattle and other similar animals were available only for producers of government services. The earliest total figure was for the year 1969 when this category was estimated at $2 million, accounting for just 0.15 per cent and 0.02 per cent of Malaya's total GFCF and GDP respectively (Department of Statistics-Malaysia, 1975).

Construction refers to the value of work done on buildings that may consist entirely or primarily of dwellings, or for industrial or commercial use, or for roads, bridges, airports and harbours that are non-military in nature.

Plantation and orchard development refers to expenditure on new holdings of fruit-bearing and sap-bearing plants that take more than a year to become productive. Eight perennial crops were included: rubber, coconut, oil palm, pineapple, arecanut, coffee, tea and gambier.

Machinery and equipment (M&E) refers to purchasers' value of new and imported transport equipment (motor vehicles, vans, trucks, tractors, ships, aircraft and railway rolling stock) acquired for civilian use. It also refers to agricultural machinery and equipment including harvesters, threshers, ploughs, and other machinery and equipment such as power-generating machinery, cranes and forklifts, office equipment and furnishings.

Data Sources

As construction activity in pre-war Malaya relied heavily on imported cement, and because machinery and equipment were also predominantly imported, import statistics figured prominently amongst the data sources used for estimating GFCF. Estimating these components of GFCF required additional data, for example, to link cement imports to construction activity through the use of input-output coefficients.

Estimating GFCF for the planting of perennial crops (cultivated assets) required three types of data:

- Statistics on newly planted acreage for each year.
- Number of years for the crop to reach maturity or bearing age.
- Cost per acre of bringing the crop into bearing.

With these three data sets, GFCF for any one crop could then be calculated to obtain estimates of annual expenditure on newly planted acreages as well as the costs incurred subsequently in bringing the crop to maturity. Details on data availability together with their limitations are described in Appendix 1.

Computing GFCF at Current Prices

Planting of perennial crops

The following steps were required to calculate this component of GFCF:

- Newly planted acreage was determined as the annual difference in total planted acreage.
- For rubber and coconuts, disaggregated data were required for newly planted acreage by estate and smallholding cultivation since the cost per acre of bringing these crops to maturity differed between the two methods of cultivation. Generally smallholding acreage was obtained as a residual by taking the difference between total acreage and estate acreage.
- Cost per acre estimates were determined by data availability. For example, the cost per acre for rubber cultivation was based on five estimates: estate ordinary rubber (1913, 1924, and 1935), smallholding ordinary rubber (1924), and bud-grafted rubber (1935).
- GFCF for each of the eight perennial crops was obtained by applying the appropriate cost-per-acre estimates to the newly planted acreage. These figures were converted to current prices for each year by the use of wage indices.

Construction

The calculation of the construction component of GFCF involved the following:

- Malaya's net cement imports for the period 1921–1939 were obtained by subtracting Singapore's net cement imports from the overall net cement imports of British Malaya. The net imports of cement for Malaya for the period 1900–1920 were then estimated based on the assumption that the average ratio of Malaya's cement imports to the Federated Malay States cement imports for the period 1921–1927 of 2.0 would hold for the years 1900–1920.
- The data for Peninsular Malaysia for the period 1967–1973 consistently showed an input-output coefficient of cement to total construction output of 7 per cent. Using this figure as a basis for estimating the earlier period, it was assumed that the ratio of cement inputs to total construction was 5 per cent for the years 1900–1918, and 6 per cent for the post-World War I period 1919–1939. The rationale for using lower input ratios for the earlier years is based on the assumption that the building structures would have used less cement and more of other materials such as timber.
- From the *Survey of Construction Industries for Peninsular Malaysia* undertaken for the period 1966–1970, it was observed that around 7 per cent of total construction activity was in repairs and maintenance. This figure was used to deduct the estimated repairs and maintenance activity from the construction total over the period 1900–1939.
- Adjustments had to be made for some years as a result of the extraordinarily high construction expenditures incurred by the Federated Malay States Railways.

Machinery and equipment

Domestic manufacturing was negligible in pre-war Malaya. Machinery and equipment were largely imported. So the calculation of this component of GFCF involved the following:

- Using the relatively stable relationship between the net imports of M&E for Malaya and net imports of M&E for the Federated Malay States, which had almost complete data for the period 1900–1939.

- Imports of M&E for the period 1921–1939 were derived by subtracting the estimated retained net imports of M&E of Singapore[29] from the net import figures of M&E of British Malaya, calculated from officially published data.
- For the period 1900–1920, for which British Malayan data were not available, the 1921–1927 average ratio of Malaya's net imports of M&E to those of the Federated Malay States' was applied to the Federated Malay States' data.
- To obtain values at market prices, trade and transport margins had to be added. Based on relevant evidence, the margins for imports of M&E into Malaya during the period 1900–1939 were assumed to be in the region of 25 per cent. No commodity taxes applied at that time.
- Some items with dual or multiple uses were excluded from the M&E net import figures. It was assumed that these items constituted about 20 per cent of the total net imports of M&E in purchasers' values.

Computing GFCF at Constant Prices

To compute GFCF at constant 1914 prices, deflators were required for its three main components. These deflators were derived as follows:

- Planting of perennial crops: labour costs accounted for the bulk of expenditure required to bring crops to maturity. For the period 1900–1914, the wage deflator used was the average of the minimum annual wage rates of estate coolies in Singapore, predial workers (labourers and gardeners) in Penang and workers involved in the 'trades' (carpenters, joiners, blacksmiths and bricklayers). For the period 1914–1939, the simple arithmetic average of the minimum wage rate of rubber tappers and the wage index for the trades were utilised. These wage deflators were used to convert the GFCF in cultivated assets from current to constant prices.
- Construction: the deflator was based on the import unit value of cement, with 1914 as the base year. Data on imports of cement (quantity and value) for the Federated Malay States were used to calculate the import unit values for each year.

---

29 Retained net imports of M&E for Singapore were in part based on the average proportion of M&E net imports of Singapore to those of the Straits Settlements (1908–1912) and British Malaya (1924–1927).

■ Machinery and equipment: the price deflator was based on the price index of capital goods (plant and machinery) of the UK (given in 1913 prices), which was normalised to the base year 1914. The use of this index was justified based on the fact that a large proportion of Malaya's M&E imports originated from the UK. The index was then used to obtain constant-price GFCF in M&E (Feinstein, 1972).

The results of applying these deflators to the nominal expenditures are set out in Figure 3.6.

Figure 3.6 Trends in gross fixed capital formation at constant 1914 prices, Malaya, 1900–1939

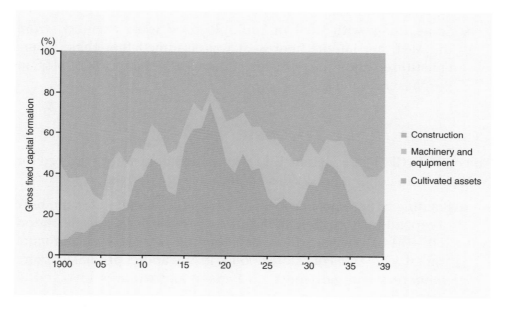

Exports and Imports of Goods and Services

Concepts and Definitions

According to the 1968 SNA, exports and imports of goods and services consist of the transactions in these items by the residents of a given country with the rest of the world (UNDESA, 1968). Estimates are generally based on international trade statistics, but these include items that are not relevant for the national accounts—for example, cross-border movements of coins and bullion—which have to be omitted. Imported goods processed by Malayan resident enterprises and re-exported were recorded as gross imports and gross exports respectively. An example is the import of rubber and tin into Malaya (particularly from the neighbouring Dutch East Indies) for the purpose of further processing before being exported. Under the 1968 SNA, these items should not be treated as imports/exports of such goods, but classified as part of services provided. Similarly, no adjustments have been made for bunker fuel and stores, which should be treated as part of transport services provided rather than classified as merchandise trade.

Data Sources

Trade data were generally more readily available than data for the other GDP components. There were no trade statistics available for Malaya as a whole, however, and these had to be compiled from the separate administrative units. Details on data availability together with their limitations are described in Appendix 1.

Computing Exports and Imports at Current Prices

The construction of a consistent historical series on exports and imports for Malaya required the separation of Singapore's trade figures from those of Malaya. Trade statistics in the official source documents, however, did not distinguish trade between these two territories. The early trade statistics for the Straits Settlements treated it as a single statistical entity. When consolidated trade data began to be published in 1921, the area covered again included Singapore.

The method used here disaggregated the data so that the trade statistics for Penang, Malacca, the Federated Malay States and the Unfederated Malay States could all be calculated separately. As there were sufficient data on Singapore's external trade, it was also possible to calculate separately for each of these administrative units, their trade with Singapore and with the rest of the world (ROW).[30] Adding together the individual figures of the various administrative units then gave an estimate of Malaya's merchandise exports and imports (Figure 3.7).

---

30 The trade flows for the Dindings with Singapore and with the ROW have not been taken into account as its share of Malaya's total trade was negligible.

Figure 3.7 Estimating exports and imports of goods by administrative unit, Malaya, 1900–1939

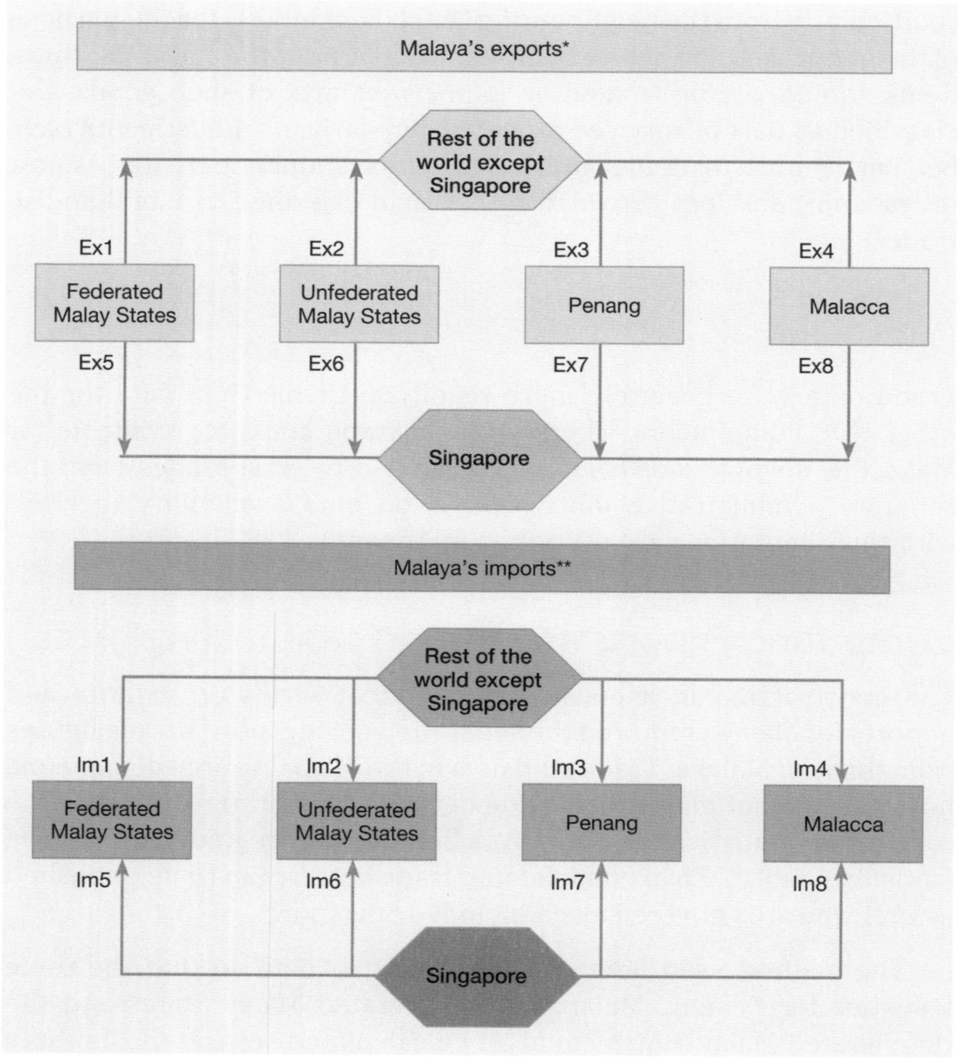

*Total exports = $\Sigma_{i=1}^{8} Ex_i$
**Total imports = $\Sigma_{i=1}^{8} Im_i$

In making these estimates, care was taken to ensure that inter-Settlement trade as well as trade between Penang, Malacca, the Federated Malay States, and the Unfederated Malay States was excluded to avoid double counting.

Some of the ways in which data limitations were overcome included the following:

- Trade between Singapore and individual Malay states was based on Malayan data sources and, when not available, on Singaporean sources. For example, no data from Malayan sources were available on the Unfederated Malay States' imports from and exports to Singapore for the years 1900–1927. However, data were available on Singapore's imports from and exports to these states, which were used to obtain each state's trade with Singapore.

- The stable relationships observed between two different trade data sets for a series of years were presumed to hold for the years for which data were not available. For example, no data were available on Penang's trade with Singapore for the period 1928–1939. Penang's imports from Singapore for this period were estimated on the assumption that the average ratio of Penang's imports from Singapore to Penang's imports from ROW for the years 1924–1927 (12.6 per cent) would also hold good for the years 1928–1939. Penang's exports to Singapore were similarly estimated.

- When data for an entity were available only for total exports/imports and for either trade with ROW or Singapore, the missing figures were obtained as a residual. For example, Malacca's trade with ROW for the period 1900–1927 was obtained by subtracting from Malacca's total exports/imports (which included interstate trade) the corresponding exports/imports to/from Singapore, Penang, the Federated Malay States, and the Unfederated Malay States.

- For exports and imports of services, no data were available for Malaya throughout the 1900–1939 period. Using later evidence, it was assumed that the share of exports and imports of services to the total trade of Malaya was 3 per cent and 6 per cent respectively.

Computing Exports and Imports at Constant Prices

Appropriate deflators were again required to calculate exports and imports of goods and services at constant 1914 prices. The following describes the construction of these deflators, separately for merchandise trade and for trade in services.

Merchandise trade

A different set of deflators was used for exports and imports of goods. The export unit value index (EUVI) was employed for the former and the import unit value index (IUVI) for the latter. These unit values were derived by dividing *values* of exports and imports by the *volumes* traded. A brief summary of the method used in the construction of these indices is given below:

- Export unit value index: Deriving a continuous unit value index series proved to be impractical due to the changing composition of exports. The sample period was divided into several overlapping sub-periods with different base years. The sub-periods were selected on the basis of the relative stability of the export shares of commodities.[31] The resulting sub-period indices were spliced to provide a single index with 1914 as the base year.
- Import unit value index: This was based on the import data of the Federated Malay States which accounted for a significant proportion of Malaya's imports. As with exports, the index was formed from a series of overlapping sub-period indices, with the sub-periods selected on the basis of a reasonably stable commodity composition. Nine sub-periods were identified for the computation of the IUVI.[32]

Services

The deflator for services was approximated using the UK's data on price indices for consumer goods and services, which used 1913 as the base year. Malaya's services trade deflator was obtained by taking the arithmetic average of the price indices of the UK's 'transport and communication' and 'other services' categories, and normalising this average to the 1914 reference year. This was applied to both the export and import figures for services at current prices that had been estimated earlier (Feinstein, 1972).

---

31 Seven intervals were identified, namely: 1900–1904, 1904–1908, 1908–1914, 1914–1920, 1920–1924, 1924–1927 and 1927–1939, with 1903, 1905, 1911, 1919, 1924, 1926, and 1936 as their respective base years.

32 These intervals were 1899–1902, 1902–1906, 1906–1912, 1912–1915, 1915–1920, 1920–1926, 1926–1933, 1933–1937, and 1937–1939, with 1900, 1906, 1908, 1913, 1918, 1925, 1930, 1935, and 1937 as their respective base years.

Malaya's exports and imports of goods and services at constant 1914 prices are shown in Figure 3.8.

*   *   *

This chapter has described the way in which a large number of disparate data sources were used to estimate GDP accounts for Malaya for the period 1900–1939. The sources varied in quality and coverage, from relatively little detailed information on consumer spending to far more accurate and complete information on exports and imports. Some further summary GDP tables are presented in Appendix 2, while the full database is available online at www.ehm.my.

The chapters that follow use these GDP estimates as the basis for assessing the cyclical fluctuations and long-term trends of Malaya's economy, and the ways in which it was buffeted by events in Europe and North America.

Figure 3.8 Trends in exports and imports of goods and services, Malaya, 1900–1939

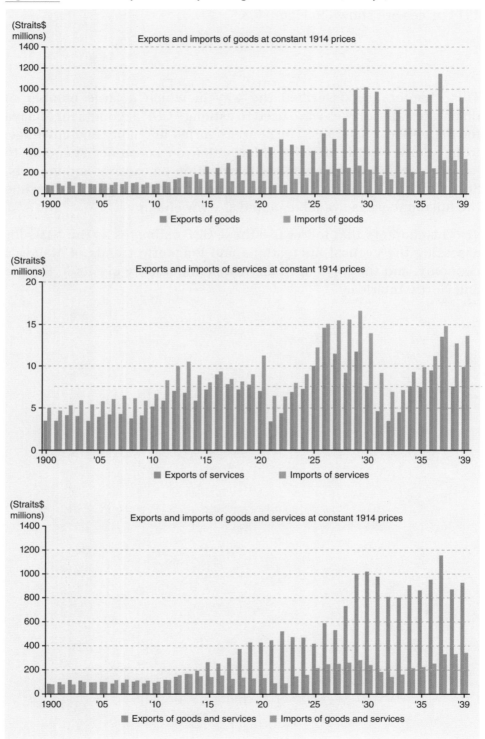

CHAPTER 4

Open cast mining in Kinta Valley employing the *lampan* or sluicing method

Growth and Volatility of Malaya's Economy 1900–1939

Malaya's historical national accounts provide the quantitative data necessary for measuring economic growth and for assessing the cyclical behaviour of the economy. They offer new insights into the economic dynamics of early 20th century Malaya.[33] Analysis of these data can help to answer important questions such as: what were the main characteristics of GDP growth from 1900 to 1939? What was the magnitude of change that occurred during that period? How was this change affected by other events, and what were the underlying causes? By comparing the study data with comparable data for other countries, it is also possible to assess similarities and contrasts, and better understand the drivers of Malaya's economic trends. This chapter helps to answer these questions through:

- An analysis of long-run trends and relationships among the components of GDP.[34]
- A short-run analysis of GDP through a decomposition analysis of its components.
- A focus on how Malaya's small open economy responded to three major external shocks—World War I, the economic boom of the Roaring Twenties, and the Great Depression.
- A comparison of trends in Malaya's GDP and its consumption and export components with selected countries for which comparable data are available.

One of the main aims of analysing economic data is to determine the underlying causes of observed changes and trends, which themselves result from a combination of factors. It would greatly

---

33 The new series also makes possible comparisons of economic performance before and after 1947, the earliest year for which relatively comprehensive data were previously available (Rao, 1976). This is discussed in Chapter 5.

34 No attempt is made in this chapter to provide extensive econometric estimation of the parameters of these relations, although some econometric analysis is reported in the next chapter.

improve understanding if the contribution of each of these factors could be viewed in isolation, as in a scientific experiment. But in economics, this is not possible. A careful analysis of external shocks to an economy can, however, help promote a deeper understanding of the dynamics at play. An analytical framework based on the national accounting balance identity is also useful for exploring the underlying causes of observed changes (Box 4.1). Both approaches are employed in this chapter.

Box 4.1 **National accounting balance**

The national accounting balance shows that for an open economy, GDP (Y) is made up of the following components:

- Private Final Consumption Expenditure, or simply Consumption (C).

- Gross Fixed Capital Formation, or simply Investment (I).

- Government Final Consumption Expenditure, or simply Government Expenditure (G).

- The difference between Exports and Imports, or simply Net Exports (NX).

This can be expressed as:

$$Y = C + I + G + NX$$

Since GDP (Y) measures the final value of all goods and services that are produced within a country in a given time period, it is the sum of expenditures of residents on domestically produced goods and services ($C^d + I^d + G^d$), and what has been exported (X).

$$\text{So} \quad Y = C^d + I^d + G^d + X$$

But expenditures of residents consist of two components, one being goods and services produced domestically (denoted by superscript ^{d}), and the other being goods and services produced in foreign countries (denoted by superscript ^{f}).

$$\text{Thus} \quad C = C^d + C^f$$
$$I = I^d + I^f$$
$$G = G^d + G^f$$

And $C^f + G^f + I^f$ are imports (M) and have to be deducted from $C + I + G$ so that they add up to Y, that is GDP.

$$\text{So} \quad Y = C + I + G + X - M \quad \text{or} \quad Y = C + I + G + NX$$

Long-run Trends and Relationship Between Components of GDP

The national accounting balance framework is employed below to analyse trends in the inter-relationships between the various components of the economy. These are GDP, private consumption, national savings and investment, and exports and imports, which may be expressed in constant and current prices (Box 4.2).

Box 4.2 Current and constant prices

National accounts are usually presented in both *current prices or nominal terms* and *constant prices or real terms*. Current prices express income and expenditure in observed monetary values. These monetary values can be conceptualised in terms of the product of a quantity and a price.

In current prices, for example, the consumption of a given food item such as fish can be expressed as the quantity of fish consumed, measured in kilos, and multiplied by the average price per kilo in dollars (over a given interval of time). If the current price (or nominal) value of the consumption of fish increases, it may be because either the quantity and/or the price of fish has risen.

Constant price measures differ from current price measures in that they utilise prices which are set at some base value. So in constant prices, the consumption of fish is the quantity consumed, measured in kilos, multiplied by the price, measured in dollars, in some reference year. Changes in constant price measures are, therefore, associated with changes in the underlying quantity (in this example, consumption of fish measured in kilos).

The main difference between *current price* or *nominal GDP* and *constant price* or *real GDP* is that real values are adjusted to take inflation into account, while nominal values are not. As a result, nominal GDP will often appear higher than real GDP during inflationary times.

The nominal values of GDP for different time periods can differ due both to changes in quantities of goods and services, and/or to changes in general price levels. As a result, it is necessary to take price levels (or inflation) into account when determining the extent of economic gains or losses across different time periods.

In this study, real GDP figures were estimated by converting each expenditure component into constant prices, using 1914 as the base year. A summary of the deflators used for each component of GDP is shown in Box Table 4.1.

Box Table 4.1 Summary of deflators used for each component of GDP

Expenditure category	Deflator 1914=100
Private final consumption expenditure	■ Consumer price index by major categories of consumption ■ Consumer price index (overall)
Government final consumption expenditure	Consumer price index

Gross fixed capital formation
  Cultivated assets
  Construction
 	
  Machinery and equipment
	
	Wage rate indices
	Cement import unit value index (Federated Malay States)
	Price index of capital goods (*plant and machinery* of the UK)

Exports of goods and services
  Goods
  Services
	
	Export unit value index
	Price indices of *transport and other services* of the UK

Imports of goods and services
  Goods
 	
  Services
	
	Import unit value index (Federated Malay States)
	Price indices of *transport and communication* and *other services* of the UK

Trends in GDP

At the beginning of the 20th century, Malaya's real GDP (1914 prices) was estimated at Straits$143 million. While real GDP increased year on year, there were marked fluctuations in years in which there were external shocks. GDP registered an average annual growth rate of 6.4 per cent and by 1919, midway through the study period, it had already nearly quadrupled to Straits$564 million.

The Roaring Twenties saw GDP increase further by leaps and bounds. Growth was temporarily arrested, however, by the worldwide Great Depression of the early 1930s, but regained momentum subsequently from 1934 onwards. Malaya's real GDP reached Straits$1.4 billion in 1937, close to 10 times the figure recorded at the beginning of the century.

Real per capita GDP is widely used as an indicator of economic welfare. It was Straits$86 at the beginning of the 20th century and increased throughout the study period, though not without interruptions, in a similar trend to that of real aggregate GDP. Real per capita GDP had more than doubled to Straits$197 by 1919, and by the end of the 40 years, it had reached Straits$269, more than three times the level recorded in 1900 (Figure 4.1).

Figure 4.1 Trends in GDP per capita, Malaya, 1900–1939

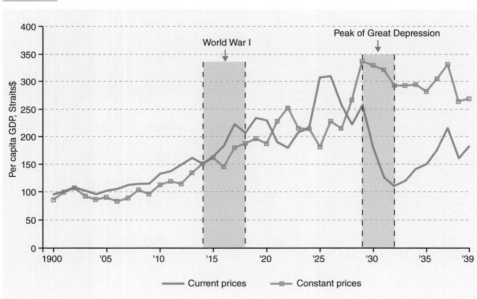

To gauge the impact of the components on GDP, it is useful to express them as ratios. Figure 4.2 shows the trends in the two largest ratios—consumption as a ratio to GDP, and net exports as a ratio to GDP. These two components accounted on average for more than 80 per cent of GDP over this period.

Figure 4.2 Decreasing weight of consumption and increasing weight of net exports in GDP, Malaya, 1900–1939

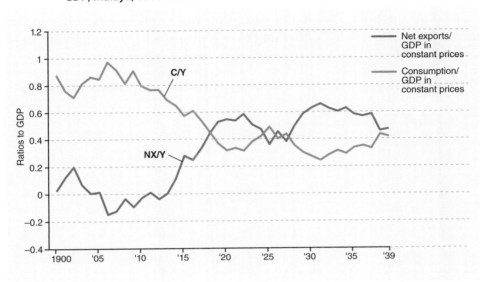

The relative importance of consumption decreased over the period, while that of net exports increased (Figure 4.2). In 1900, net exports constituted only 0.03 per cent of Malaya's GDP, but by 1939 this component formed 47 per cent of the total. Conversely, consumption had a weight of 88 per cent in 1900, but this had declined to 42 per cent by 1939. The declining trend in the proportion of consumption to GDP mainly reflected the rising proportion of corporate profits remitted overseas (Chapter 6) and, to a significantly lesser extent, increasing savings rates among those with higher incomes.

Consumption

In many countries, consumption is the largest component of GDP. The amount a household consumes out of its current income and the amount it saves for the future have significant short- and long-run consequences for any economy. In the short-run, consumption affects aggregate demand, while over the longer term it has an important impact on economic growth. Levels of consumption play a key role during booms and recessions. As it is such a major component, any changes in consumption have an immediate impact on GDP. Provided there are under-utilised resources in an economy, a stimulus to consumption should thus raise GDP quickly, other things being equal.

It may also generate additional demand for goods and services produced abroad, resulting in a rise in imports. Figure 4.3 shows the close relationship between consumption and imports in Malaya during the period 1900–1939, confirming that increases in consumption were strongly and positively correlated with increased imports.

Figure 4.3 Increases in consumption are strongly related to imports, Malaya, 1900–1939

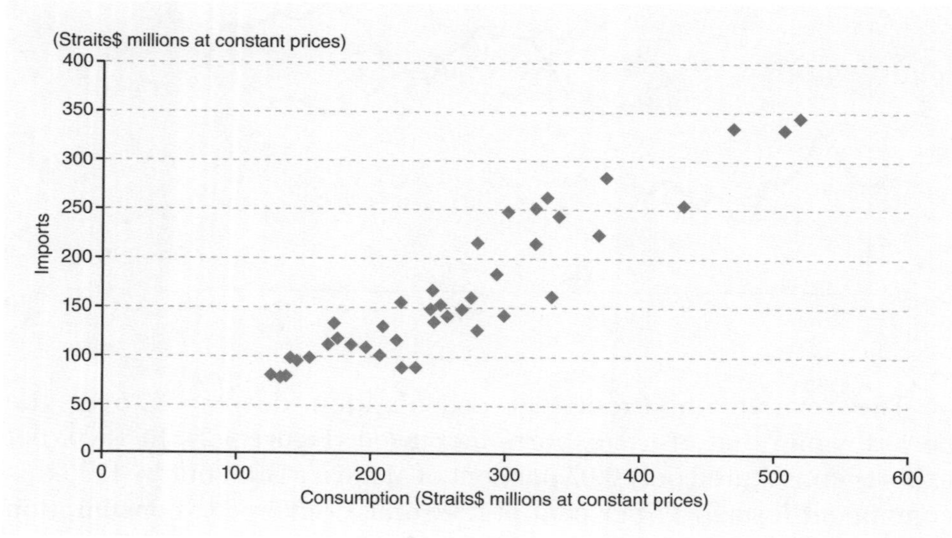

To the extent that firms make investment decisions by forecasting future demand and comparing this with present capacity, an increase in consumption may induce new investment. This expected relationship is subject to leads and lags, however, and is unstable because investment takes time to be realised and other factors also contribute to investment decisions.

Figure 4.4 compares the long-run trends of both consumption and GDP. While real GDP grew at an average annual rate of 6.4 per cent over the period 1900–1939, real consumption grew more modestly, at an average annual rate of 4.1 per cent. GDP growth was far more volatile, with the standard deviation for the growth rates of GDP 1.4 times higher than those of consumption. Variations in GDP growth were extraordinary, such as the 26.4 per cent experienced in 1917 following a decline of 8 per cent the previous year. There were further significant declines in the years 1923–1925 and 1931–1933, while spectacular growth rates of around 30 per cent were recorded in 1926, 1928 and 1929 (see Tables 4.1 and 4.2). In comparison, there were two major declines in consumption, in 1918–1920 and 1930–1931, with the substantial decline in the earlier years followed by 29 per cent growth in 1921. Malaya's economic performance during these four decades was undoubtedly highly volatile.

Figure 4.4 Long-run trends in consumption and GDP at constant 1914 prices, Malaya, 1900–1939

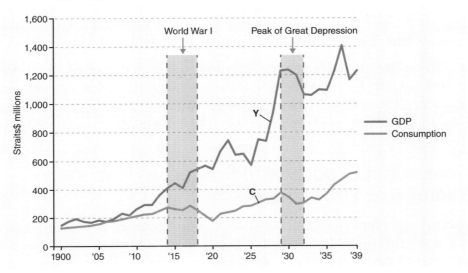

Theories of aggregate consumption predict an element of 'consumption smoothing', that is, consumption is expected to be far less volatile than income (Deaton, 1991; Carroll, 1997). Studies have shown that saving in good times, when personal income is unusually high, helps finance consumption in bad times, when income is depressed. Even so, aggregate consumption would be expected to track personal disposable income fairly closely over an extended period of four decades (Carroll and Summers, 1991). Average growth of personal income over the full period would, therefore, be expected to match that of consumption, which grew at an average of 4.1 per cent per annum.

Although it has not been possible to measure household income directly as part of this study, the index of real wages that has been constructed provides a useful proxy (Chapter 3, Figure 3.3). This real wage index has been based on reported wage rates for selected agricultural and non-agricultural occupations such as carpenters, joiners and estate workers. These occupations were dominated by the three poorest consumption standards (Malay, Chinese and Indian), which accounted for an estimated 97 per cent of the population, and for 74 per cent of total consumption on items calculated by the indirect method. Although somewhat selective in its coverage, the index provides a useful guide to overall earnings growth, suggesting that real wages grew at an average annual rate of around 1.6 per cent during the period 1900–1939, compared to the average annual population growth for the period of 2.6 per cent. If the number of working individuals grew at the same rate as the population, the real wage series would imply a 4.2 per cent average annual growth in aggregate real incomes from employment. This figure matches the growth of consumption.

The difference between the growth rates of GDP and consumption, therefore, suggests that personal income accounted for a decreasing share of GDP, with increasing income flows going to foreign companies and non-residents who repatriated much of these overseas (Chapter 6).

Role of Net Exports with Respect to National Savings and Investment

A rearrangement of the national accounting balance described in Box 4.1 is useful to highlight the link between the domestic economy and the rest of the world (ROW), as below:

$$Y - (C + I + G) = NX$$

This rearrangement shows how domestic output, domestic spending and net exports are related. If domestic output exceeds domestic spending, the difference is exported and net exports are positive. Similarly, if domestic spending is more than domestic output, the difference is imported and net exports are negative.

If we denote $Y - C - G$ as national savings S,

$$S - I = X - M$$

This shows the relationship between the international flow of funds for capital accumulation $(S - I)$, and the international flow of goods and services $(X - M \text{ or } NX)$. $S - I$ is called the net foreign investment, or the investment gap. It is the excess of domestic savings over domestic investment, and it is equal to the amount that residents are lending abroad, less the amount of foreign loans received. The second part of the identity is the net exports, or the trade balance.

For Malaya, the large positive investment gap observed during the period 1900–1939 was due to the favourable trade balance achieved from the buoyant performance of exports, principally of rubber and tin. The private European, predominantly British, companies that owned and operated the rubber plantations and tin mines made huge profits that were largely repatriated to their shareholders overseas. The colonial government offered a highly favourable tax regime, with only minimal taxation on tin and rubber exports.

Figure 4.5 shows the trends in national savings and investment. The area between national savings and investment (shaded in blue) is the investment gap, which is equal to the trade balance. This gap increased during World War I and remained sizable until 1939, indicating the huge trade surplus. If Malayan firms had invested more (I rising), or Malayan households had consumed more (S falling), the trade balance would not have been as substantial, and net exports would have been reduced (as M rose).

Figure 4.5 Long-run trends in national savings and investment at constant 1914 prices, Malaya, 1900–1939

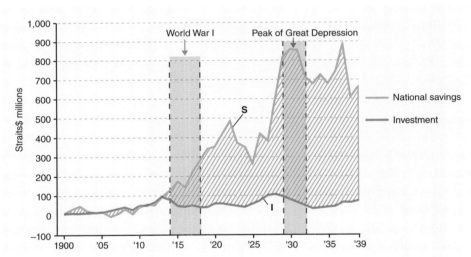

Role of Savings and Investment

Savings, or deferred consumption, affect investment directly and this in turn is the basis of future output and consumption. The ratio of national savings to GDP is thus an important indicator of the likely future performance of an economy. On the whole, an increasing savings ratio indicates scope for economic improvement. For Malaya during the period 1900–1939, this ratio increased sharply just before World War I and stabilised during the latter part of the period (Figure 4.6).

Figure 4.6 Ratio of national savings to GDP at constant 1914 prices, Malaya, 1900–1939

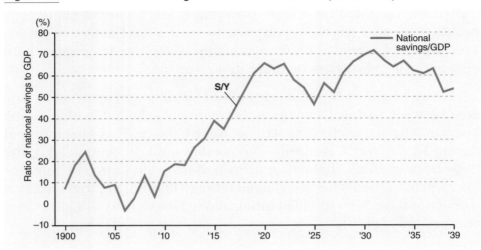

Although investment generally accounts for a relatively small proportion of GDP, it is vital for the future growth of the economy as it forms the basis of future production. For the period under review, the share of investment in GDP averaged 11 per cent. Construction was the largest component, followed by cultivated assets (planting of perennial crops), and machinery and equipment.

Major Role of Exports

As expected, given the critical importance of the tin and rubber industries, the export of goods and services was a major component of GDP during the study period. It accounted, on average, for about 60 per cent of GDP in nominal terms. Its value in real terms increased 14-fold from Straits$85 million in 1900 to reach Straits$1.16 billion in 1937, with its share of real GDP increasing accordingly from 60 per cent to 82 per cent.

The growth rates of Malaya's exports and GDP in real terms generally moved in tandem throughout the period 1900–1939. This is not unexpected given the large share of exports in GDP which significantly exceeded the share of the other components, especially from 1915 onwards. It is thus apparent that the growth rate of exports in real terms impacted heavily on the GDP growth rate, as reflected in the strong positive correlation between the two variables (Figure 4.7).

Figure 4.7 **Strong positive relationship between GDP and exports at constant 1914 prices, Malaya, 1900–1939**

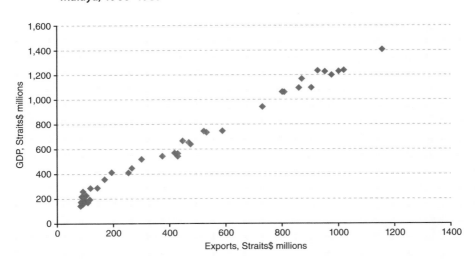

Exports were also the most volatile component, being very much influenced by the changing economic fortunes of other countries. As a small open economy that was highly dependent on only two export commodities, Malaya was particularly vulnerable to external shocks caused by sudden changes in world demand for these commodities. In addition, its exports were largely dependent on two markets, the US and the UK, so any significant downturn in these economies had a major impact on the Malayan economy.

Rubber and Tin

Malaya's rubber exports in 1905 amounted to 130 tons, or about 5 per cent of all cultivated rubber produced worldwide, and 0.2 per cent of all rubber exports for that year. Ten years later, Malaya accounted for three-fifths of the world's cultivated rubber exports, and two-fifths of total world rubber exports (Figure 4.8) (Tate, 1996).

This phenomenal expansion of rubber output was due to rising world demand, fuelled in large part by the rapid rise of automobile manufacturing in the US and the increased demand for rubber tyres that this created. Motor vehicle factory sales in the US rose from 4,100 in 1900 to 969,900 in 1915 (Carter *et al.*, 2006). This extraordinary growth

Figure 4.8 Trends in exports of rubber and tin, Malaya, 1900–1939

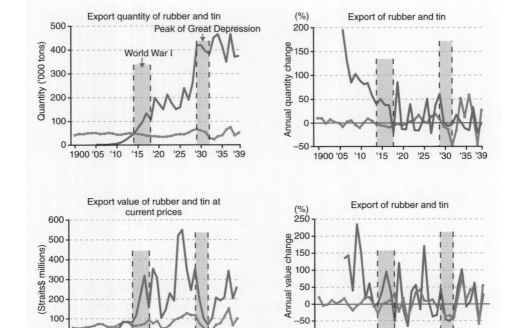

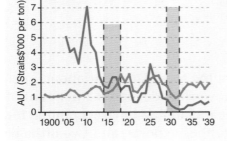

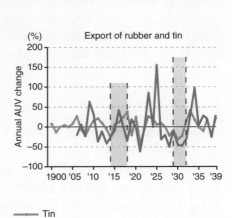

Rubber ——— Tin ———

Sources of data:
1. Drabble (1973). Rubber in Malaya 1876–1922: The Genesis of the Industry. Kuala Lumpur: Oxford University Press, Appendix VII, pp. 220 and Appendix XVI, pp. 230.
2. McFadyean (1944). The History of Rubber Regulation, 1934–1943. London: George Allen & Unwin Ltd, pp. 226–229.
3. Return of Foreign Imports and Exports, British Malaya, 1921–25, 1928, 1934 and 1937.
4. Foreign Trade of Malaya, 1939.
5. Heath (1951). Malayan Agricultural Statistics, T. 14.
6. Federation of Malaya, Mines Department, Bulletin of Statistics Relating to the Mining Industry of Malaya, 1950, T. 5, pp. 5.

continued, and sales almost doubled again over the following two years to reach 1.8 million in 1917 (Drabble, 1973). A major contributory factor was the introduction during this period of assembly line mass production, which reduced construction time per car from 14 hours to just 1.5 hours, thereby greatly reducing the cost of production.[35]

World consumption of rubber doubled between 1900 and 1910, and increased another threefold between 1910 and 1920 (Drabble, 1973). The resulting steep rise in the price of rubber provided the catalyst for the large investments into the sector during this period. In 1912, rubber replaced tin as the country's leading export for the first time, a position it retained until the end of the study period, with the exception of 1913. The share of rubber exports in total merchandise exports for the period 1912–1939 averaged about 56 per cent.

Malaya's other major export commodity during this period was tin. World output of tin in the first decade of the 19th century amounted to less than 10,000 tons (Thoburn, 1994). One hundred years later, world output exceeded 100,000 tons annually, of which close to half came from Malaya.

Two developments contributed to the remarkable transformation of the tin industry. The first was the increasing use of cans in the preservation of food. Tin's non-toxic and non-corrosive properties made it highly suitable for that purpose. The tinplate industry in Europe grew rapidly following the successful mechanisation of the hot-dipping of tinplate in 1856.

The second was the discovery of large deposits of tin in the Malay Peninsula, principally in the Larut district in 1848 and in the Kinta valley in the early 1880s (Loh, 1988; Yip, 1969). The latter was to remain the global centre of the tin-mining industry for much of the 20th century.

In the 1870s, the average annual output in the Malay Peninsula was 7,000 tons (18 per cent of world output). By the 1890s, the territory was producing an average annual output of 42,000 tons, which was more than the rest of the world combined (Lim, 1967).

Malaya's share of world tin output stood at over 50 per cent at the turn of the 20th century, but by the end of the 1920s, though still

---

35 Drabble also notes that, at this time, European rubber manufacturers, notably in the UK, were preoccupied with wartime work, leaving an opportunity for American exports of tyres to increase (Drabble, 1973).

substantial, this share had been reduced to 37 per cent. In terms of the share of Malaya's total merchandise exports, tin occupied the top position between 1900–1911 and in 1913, averaging 46 per cent for these years. From 1912 (with the exception of 1913), however, tin was overtaken by rubber, leading to the decline in its share of total merchandise exports to an average of 22 per cent over the period 1912–1939.

Imports

The share of the other components of GDP was relatively small, with the exception of imports, which averaged 41 per cent of GDP over the 40-year period. This is not unexpected since, at that time, the Malayan economy was heavily dependent on external trade, with little manufacturing activity within the territory. Malaya's imports were always lower than its exports during this 40-year period, though the two generally moved in tandem.

An indicator of the degree of import penetration of an economy is the ratio of imports to GDP. This shows the degree of dependence of the economy on imports. The higher the ratio, the more vulnerable the economy is to changes in import prices.

Import penetration, as indicated by the import-GDP ratio, shows a declining trend over the study period (Figure 4.9). In some cases, such a decline could reflect import substitution, or a set of policies aimed at

Figure 4.9 Decreasing import penetration at constant 1914 prices, Malaya, 1900–1939

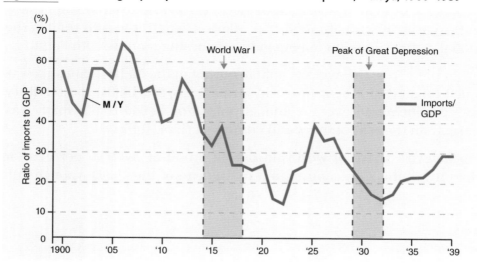

reducing reliance on imported goods by increasing local manufactures. There was little local manufacturing in Malaya at this time, however, and the declining trend of the import-GDP ratio was, in fact, the result of a faster increase in GDP than in imports. Annual GDP growth was 1.2 times larger than that of imports.

Having considered long-run trends in GDP and its components, the next two sections focus on short-run fluctuations—through an analysis of annual changes and an assessment of cyclical changes brought about by external shocks.

Short-run Fluctuations in GDP and Its Components

This section considers the main characteristics of annual GDP growth from 1900 to 1939, and explores their underlying drivers.

Perhaps the most striking aspect is that, while income rose steadily, growth oscillated wildly. In 14 out of 39 years, real GDP actually shrank. In per capita terms, there were even more reversals, with 17 in total. This extreme volatility, and the uncertainty that it inevitably created, is likely to have curtailed risk appetites and dampened investment. Planning at any level, whether in the state or private sectors, would have been very challenging in the face of such instability.

Figure 4.10 Trends in GDP, Malaya, 1900–1939

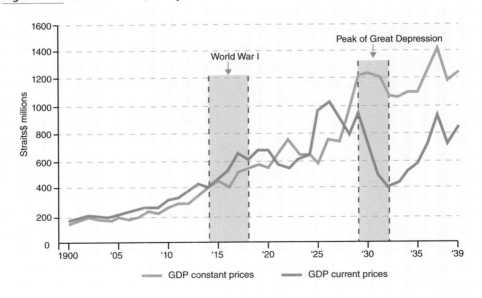

The path of GDP was even more erratic in nominal terms. By 1935, while nominal GDP had barely changed compared with the level attained in the early 1920s, it was 42 per cent below its peak in 1926, and 47 per cent higher than the deep trough of 1932. Figure 4.10 shows the trajectory of real and nominal GDP over the study period.

Aggregate GDP growth can be dissected into the contributions of its component parts: consumer spending, government spending, investment, and export and import demand. Aggregate growth in a given year is equal to the weighted average of the growth of each expenditure component in that year, with weights equal to their shares in GDP in the previous year. Such a decomposition should reveal both the underlying drivers of growth and the sources of volatility.

Figure 4.11 illustrates this decomposition analysis. Green dots locate real GDP growth for the given year (measured on the vertical axis). Within each vertical bar, the contribution of each demand component to growth is measured by its vertical length.

Figure 4.11 Demand components of real GDP growth, Malaya, 1900–1939

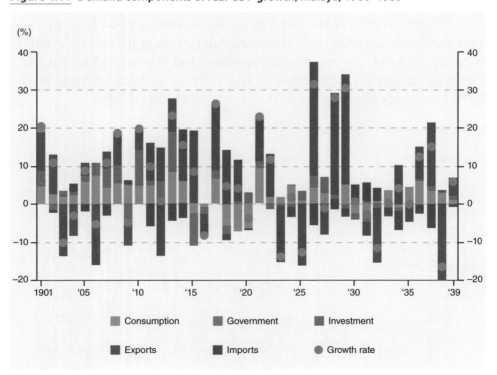

In 1901, consumption contributed about 4 per cent of the 20 per cent overall GDP growth, government spending about 1.5 per cent, investment about 2 per cent, exports 10 per cent, and imports (which shrank) another 2.5 per cent. Aggregate growth is equal to the sum of these components (stock changes, which were small, are not shown). Where a vertical bar lies below the horizontal axis, that expenditure component had contributed negatively to growth in that year. This occured when consumption, government spending, investment or exports contracted, or when imports increased.

The most conspicuous feature that emerges from a review of Figure 4.11 is the dominance of export (dark blue) and import (grey) demand in influencing aggregate growth. It is clear that changes in export and import volumes accounted for the bulk of growth, and so drove much of its volatility. Growth of domestic expenditure components (consumption, government spending and investment) appear to have played only a small role.

Figure 4.12 summarises the same information, but uses a nominal GDP growth metric. The wider range on the growth (vertical) axis reflects the considerable volatility observed in nominal GDP growth. Oscillating nominal export growth accounted for much of this volatility. Prices, as well as volumes, were buffeted by large swings.

Figure 4.12 Demand components of nominal GDP growth, Malaya, 1900–1939

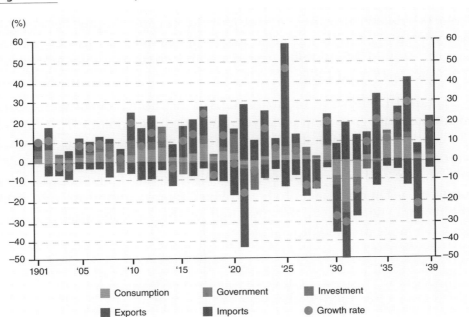

Over the first four decades of the 20th century, Malaya experienced three episodes of large trade gains (World War I, the Roaring Twenties, and recovery from the Great Depression), and two periods of equally steep losses (post-World War I, and the years of the Great Depression).

This analysis suggests that the economy of Malaya rode a commodity roller-coaster between 1900 and 1939. Commodity prices and export volumes veered wildly, and these combined to generate extreme volatility in both the levels and the growth of nominal income.

Although analysts often focus on real GDP metrics when measuring the performance of an economy, nominal measures may better capture the income impacts of terms-of-trade changes. This is why measures of real gross domestic income, which accommodate the real income impacts of terms-of-trade changes, are now generally preferred to narrower measures of GDP in assessing real income growth in small open economies. It is not possible to estimate real gross domestic income for Malaya for the period 1900–1939 given the inadequate data, but it would be expected to bridge the real and nominal estimates shown above.

Decomposition of Export Variations

As observed above, variations in export growth accounted for much of the volatility in annual GDP growth. A decomposition analysis of exports between tin, rubber and other exports can help shed light on the role each played in these variations. As there were hardly any rubber exports from 1900 to 1904, the computation of the decomposition analysis starts from 1905.

Figure 4.13 shows the contributions of tin, rubber and other exports to total export growth in each year in percentage points. The sum of the contributions is identically equal to the percentage change in total exports. Rubber is dominant in accounting for variations in export growth. Tin and other exports played a secondary and comparatively minor role. Tin does seem to have played a more important role after about 1925, whereas in the first half of the sample, other exports played a more prominent role.

Figure 4.13 Components of export growth in real terms, Malaya, 1900–1939

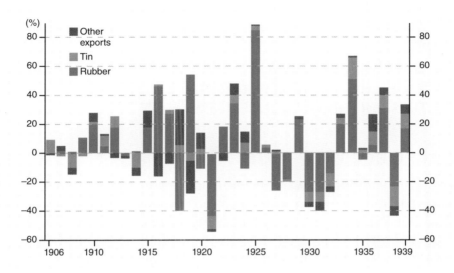

The decomposition analysis confirms the dominant role of rubber (78 per cent) in explaining the variation in exports. Tin, on this calculation, made a minor contribution (4.6 per cent), which was smaller than that of other exports (6.7 per cent). The decomposition of the variance of total exports is described below:

$$\text{Var}\left(\sum_{i=1}^{n} X_i\right) = \sum_{i=1}^{n}\sum_{j=1}^{n}\text{Cov}(X_i, X_j) = \sum_{i=1}^{n}\text{Var}(X_i) + 2\sum_{1 \leq i\ <j\leq n}\text{Cov}(X_i, X_j).$$

Variance decomposition: Sum of the variance of exports = Sum (variances of components) + 2*Covariance of components

- Variance of export growth rate = 970
- Variance of rubber growth rate = 780.7
- Variance of tin growth rate = 46.1
- Variance of other exports growth rate = 67.2
- 2*Covariance = 76

Cyclical Fluctuations from External Shocks

The explanation of cyclical fluctuations in aggregate economic activity is one of the primary concerns of macroeconomics. For early 20th century Malaya, external factors were the main underlying causes of economic downturns and booms. The economy was small and open, and it was highly dependent on its commodity exports. Over the period 1900–1939, three large exogenous shocks to the Malayan economy can be identified:

- World War I, 1914–1918
- The Roaring Twenties, 1920–1929
- The Great Depression, 1929–1932

World War I, 1914–1918

The outbreak of World War I severely interrupted international trade, and restrictions were imposed on some key shipping routes (Chapter 2, Box 2.3). Since world supply had grown considerably by then, prices of rubber initially slumped, negatively impacting the plantations in Malaya. The UK diverted its resources to the manufacture of goods to support the war effort. Communications were difficult, including those between the plantations and the UK. Some plantation managers also returned home for military duty.

This major exogenous shock had serious impacts on Malaya's GDP and its components. The most prominent, and perhaps, unexpected feature of this period is that GDP growth was maintained because of buoyant exports. GDP grew at an average annual rate of 9.4 per cent (Table 4.1). Exports increased, on average, by a remarkable 18 per cent. Malaya's continued impressive export performance was the result of the undisrupted and growing flow of exports to the American economy. World War I was largely fought in Europe, while the US only entered the war in 1917, a year before it ended.

Table 4.1 Annual growth rates of real GDP and its components, Malaya, 1914–1918

	Consumption (C)	Government expenditure (G)	Investment (I)	Exports (X)	Imports (M)	GDP (Y)
1914	8.6	11.1	–14.5	15.0	–12.1	15.5
1915	–4.0	–8.2	–39.3	37.0	–4.3	8.5
1916	–2.0	–4.7	–14.8	–4.3	8.1	–8.0
1917	10.9	–0.4	20.5	18.2	–16.9	26.4
1918	–11.4	–2.4	–17.1	24.2	6.4	4.7
Average	0.4	–0.9	–13.0	18.0	–3.7	9.4

A surprising feature of the World War I period is the low growth in private consumption expenditure and a fall in government expenditure despite the strong GDP growth. Imports also fell by 4 per cent. Under normal circumstances, consumption would be expected to drive imports. However, Table 4.1 indicates that the decline in imports preceded the fall in private consumption. Imports fell 12 per cent in 1914, followed after a lag of one year, by declines of 4 per cent in consumption and 8 per cent in government expenditure. Similarly, imports fell 17 per cent in 1917, followed, after a lag, by declines in consumption (11 per cent) and government expenditure (2 per cent) in 1918.

As the UK was the main source of imports into Malaya, disruptions to imports of consumer goods during World War I were to be expected. It is also probable that adverse consumer sentiment would have affected consumer demand.

Investment declined very sharply during World War I at an average annual rate of 13 per cent. Malayan imports of machinery and equipment were disrupted by the war. As with consumption, adverse consumer sentiment among households, business and government is also likely to have affected investment decisions.

Roaring Twenties, 1920–1929

The Roaring Twenties was a decade of high economic growth and widespread prosperity, driven by recovery from World War I and a catching-up with what might be called postponed spending. Construction boomed and there was rapid growth in demand for consumer goods. The US economy successfully transitioned from wartime to peacetime, and grew rapidly.

Malaya's prosperity during the 1920s can be attributed to the unprecedented growth of the US economy at this time, and especially the phenomenal growth of the country's automobile industry, as mentioned above. By 1930, 60 per cent of American households owned automobiles compared with just 26 per cent a decade earlier. This upsurge in demand was propelled by the reduction in the price of cars due to the new mass production techniques as well as the introduction of consumer credit. The automobile industry created significant forward linkages, with a major expansion in road building and the establishment of gasoline and service stations. It also generated considerable backward linkages by providing a stimulus to industries supplying raw materials such as rubber and others (Willis and Primack, 1989).

The beginning of the Twenties heralded a revival for Malaya's rubber and tin industries, with European shipping restrictions having been lifted. International export quotas were agreed at this time through the Stevenson Rubber Restriction Scheme which remained in place between 1922 and 1928. The intention was to control the build-up of rubber stocks at a time of rising production and declining prices, and to try to ensure a more stable trading environment following the end of World War I (Tate, 1996).[36] The recovery of the automobile industry in the US from 1925 then boosted the demand for rubber, again leading to an increase in its price. Conversely, in the tin sector, high prices resulted from consumption exceeding production due to a short-lived immediate post-war boom in demand for consumer goods. Malaya's exports of rubber and tin experienced substantial growth between 1925–1927 as both their prices and the quantities exported rose.

The 1920s was a period in which Malaya's real GDP generally experienced unprecedented growth, with minor interruptions in three years—1923, 1925 and 1927. This was mainly achieved on the back of the country's unbridled expansion of merchandise exports which more than doubled from Straits$422 million in 1920 to Straits$991 million in 1929.

Malaya's real GDP recorded a significant 32 per cent growth rate in 1926 alone, mainly due to the increase in revenue from rubber exports arising from a sharp increase in the quantity exported from 160,000 tons in 1925 to 241,000 tons a year later, an increase of 51 per cent.

Apart from the contribution of merchandise exports to the growth of GDP in 1926, increased gross fixed capital formation during this year—particularly in construction and machinery—also contributed to this phenomenal increase.

Malaya also recorded high real GDP growth rates of 28 per cent and 31 per cent in 1928 and 1929 respectively (Table 4.2), which again can largely be explained by the remarkable growth of the country's

---

36 While immediate profits were sacrificed, future production in a more stable market was guaranteed by withdrawing a share of output. At the same time, extensive rubber plantations under *Hevea* were being established elsewhere in Asia and beyond (Drabble, 1973; Barlow *et al.*, 1994).

exports (about 37 per cent for both of these years). In 1928, Malaya's total exports of rubber and tin by quantity grew by 37 per cent and 19 per cent respectively, although prices for both these commodities declined. The phenomenal increase in export revenue from rubber in 1929 was mainly fuelled by a sharp increase of about 60 per cent in the quantity of rubber exported, which more than compensated for a 10 per cent drop in its price.

Table 4.2 Annual growth rates of real GDP and its components, Malaya, 1920–1929

	Consumption (C)	Government expenditure (G)	Investment (I)	Exports (X)	Imports (M)	GDP (Y)
1920	–17.3	6.3	36.4	–0.02	2.4	–4.0
1921	29.4	56.9	3.2	4.2	–33.4	22.8
1922	4.6	0.7	–15.7	16.9	–0.3	11.6
1923	4.8	3.2	–10.6	–9.4	66.4	–13.7
1924	12.5	6.6	–10.4	–1.0	8.3	1.6
1925	1.4	3.1	43.2	–10.6	34.8	–12.8
1926	8.4	1.6	30.0	40.4	14.8	31.5
1927	6.7	20.0	32.5	–9.6	1.4	–1.3
1928	2.6	5.2	5.2	37.4	4.4	27.7
1929	13.3	10.5	–10.5	37.1	7.9	30.5
Average	6.6	11.4	10.4	10.5	10.7	9.4

The year 1929 represented the first full year of freedom from restrictions after the removal of the Stevenson Rubber Restriction Scheme. The quantity of rubber exported had by then increased markedly on the back of the frenzied planting activity that had begun in 1925 as a result of high rubber prices in that year (McFadyean, 1944).

Exports and imports overall both grew strongly over the period 1920–1929, with annual average growth rates of 10.5 per cent and 10.7 per cent respectively. The spread of consumerism in the US contributed to growing incomes in Malaya, which in turn generated strong growth in private consumption and in imports.

Beyond trade, Malaya's economy experienced a sudden jump in construction activity beginning in 1927, and continuing into 1928 and 1929. This was attributable in large part to the extensive building works being undertaken by the Public Works Department (PWD). For the Federated Malay States, the PWD Annual Report observed that 'the year was a record one and the expenditure exceeded the former record year of 1921...', and that 'the heavy construction programme for the year taxed the organisation and resources of the department to the utmost...' (Federated Malay States, 1928, pp. 1 and 9). Substantial sums were spent on the construction of buildings, bridges and roads amounting to a total of Straits$12.8 million in 1927 as against a mere Straits$0.2 million a year earlier (Federated Malay States, 1927). In 1928 and 1929, the expenditure on Special Services in the Federated Malay States amounted to Straits$21.7 million and Straits$15.1 million respectively.

The decade of the Roaring Twenties came to a spectacular end with the 1929 Wall Street Crash which resulted in the collapse of many banks and the loss of much of the savings of the middle classes in the US and elsewhere. Investments fell sharply, as did the demand for goods and services. *Laissez-faire* economic policy, which had for so long prevailed, was about to be seriously challenged.

Great Depression, 1929–1932

The period 1929–1932 was marked by the Great Depression during which most countries, and in particular the US, experienced very sharp economic declines. The Depression was triggered by a dramatic and devastating fall in stock prices that started in the US in September 1929 and spread to Europe and beyond. International trade plummeted, and unemployment and poverty rose sharply (Chapter 2, Box 2.3).

The large fall in consumption that resulted could have been caused by the stock market crash. However, some commentators have attributed it to the sharp fall in housing investment. The US residential housing boom in the 1920s was excessive, and once the overbuilding was recognised, the demand for residential buildings fell drastically. Several other events which took place during the Great Depression also reduced consumption expenditure. Politicians at that time were more concerned with balancing the budget than with using fiscal policy to stimulate the economy. The Revenue Act of 1932 increased various taxes, especially for the lower and middle income groups, which had a dampening effect on consumption expenditure (Brunner, 1981). Others, principally Friedman and Schwartz (1963), have placed blame on the

Federal Reserve for allowing the money supply to fall sharply during the Depression.

Malaya, by this time heavily reliant on the US market for its exports, was not spared from the economic crisis (Khoo, 1977). Its real GDP registered large negative growth rates in 1931–1932, mainly due to an unprecedented collapse of its external trade (Table 4.3). In the US, real GNP (in 1958 dollars) fell by an average of 11 per cent between 1930 and 1932 (US Department of Commerce, 1975), with sales of passenger cars declining from 4.5 million in 1929 to 1.1 million in 1932. Largely as a result of this slump, international consumption of rubber fell dramatically to a low point of 690,000 tons in 1931, some 85 per cent below the peak of 1929, and showed little recovery until 1933 (Barlow, 1978). The GDP accounts for the years 1929–1932 show that 1932 represented the worst of Malaya's depression years, with total exports experiencing a negative growth rate of 17.2 per cent.

Table 4.3 Annual growth rates of real GDP and its components, Malaya, 1929–1932

	Consumption (C)	Government expenditure (G)	Investment (I)	Exports (X)	Imports (M)	GDP (Y)
1929	13.3	10.5	−10.5	37.1	7.9	30.5
1930	−9.4	5.4	−18.1	1.8	−14.3	0.6
1931	−13.7	24.9	−21.0	−4.3	−23.9	−3.1
1932	2.0	−1.2	−26.5	−17.2	−22.9	−11.4
Average	−1.9	9.9	−19.0	4.3	−13.3	4.1
Median	−3.7	7.9	−19.6	−1.3	−18.6	−1.3

As a result of the declines in exports, Malaya's overall GDP registered a median decrease of 1.3 per cent over the period (Table 4.3). The median growth rate is a more representative measure for this period as it is not skewed by the very high growth rate of 30.5 per cent in 1929 at the peak of the Roaring Twenties boom. At the nadir of the Great Depression in 1932, GDP had fallen by 11.4 per cent.

Due to the sharp fall in GDP, both consumption and investment also fell substantially in the Great Depression years—consumption saw a median decline of 3.7 per cent and investment fell by 19.6 per cent. Households experienced increasing uncertainty about the future during these times, which also contributed to the fall in consumption.

The fall in consumption and investment brought with it a large drop in imports, with a median decline of 18.6 per cent between 1929 and 1932. This was also partly due to the colonial government's attempt to reduce the widening trade deficit.

Government expenditure increased substantially during these depression years, with a 25 per cent increase in 1931 alone (Table 4.3). A major cause of this was the cost of repatriating large numbers of Chinese and Indian labourers from the plantations and mines who had been laid off as these sectors collapsed.[37] The return passages for a significant number of the foreign workers were paid for by the colonial government.

Other Periods

In trying to explain Malaya's cyclical economic trends during the first four decades of the 20th century, it has been helpful to define this time span based on three external shocks—World War I, the Roaring Twenties, and the Great Depression. These were highly volatile times that markedly affected the welfare and well-being of the people. To complete the story of these four decades, it is also necessary to assess the remaining years, that is, the pre-World War I period of 1900–1913, and the post-Great Depression recovery of 1933–1939. At the centre of the analysis is inevitably the economic situation of Malaya's leading trading partners, the US and the UK, and the role played by Malaya's two major commodities (Box 4.3). A conspicuous feature of these other periods is that, while the external forces were different, their impact on the Malayan economy was predictable. This stable and strong association between external shocks and the performance of the Malayan economy dominated the first half of the 20th century.

The growth of Malaya's real GDP over the period 1900–1939 was thus profoundly influenced by the pattern and movement of Malaya's rubber and tin exports. Given the importance of the export sector, any changes in it had significant spillover effects on other sectors of the economy. A change in export revenues directly affected government

---

37 The deep crisis affecting the Malayan economy in 1931 as a result of the steep fall in rubber prices, combined with the relatively low price for tin, led to widespread unemployment and large-scale emigration of Chinese and Indians workers back to their countries of origin. It is estimated that this outflow amounted to some 400,000 persons between 1931 and 1933 (Del Tufo, 1949).

revenues as well as the incomes of those engaged in the export sector. These changes were transmitted to the rest of the economy through multiplier and accelerator effects. Dawe (1993) has shown how export instability can cause spillovers that affect the structure of relative prices in the economy, which in turn affect investment behaviour and growth. Despite this vulnerability and extreme volatility, Malaya's growth during the first four decades of the 20th century was, nonetheless, impressive.

Box 4.3 **Fluctuations in GDP in 1900–1913 and 1933–1939**

Pre-World War I, 1900–1913

The first decade or so of the 20th century, a period during which the UK was still Malaya's major trading partner, was characterised by growth of real GDP averaging about 8 per cent per year, but with considerable volatility (Box Table 4.2). Annual GDP growth rates were heavily influenced by exports. While tin was still dominant, this period also saw the start of the first big spurt in new rubber planting. Over the period 1900–1913, Malaya's exports grew by an average of 6 per cent.

In 1910, the rubber price was at a peak, having skyrocketed to reach a record of nearly Straits$5.50 per lb. High rubber prices resulted in a rush by Malay smallholders to grow rubber, which had previously been cultivated mainly by the Europeans and the Chinese. New land was cleared and planted with rubber, and, in some cases, fruit trees were cut down and padi fields were cleared and planted with rubber instead (Ooi, 1961). Consequently, new planting in 1910 increased by a phenomenal 146 per cent compared to the previous year. This surge in new planting was sustained over the next few years, and translated into significant growth of gross fixed capital formation in cultivated assets.

In 1910, export revenue from rubber increased by 150 per cent to reach Straits$45 million as a result of an increase in both the quantity exported and the average unit value. The fall in the price of rubber in the three years that followed was more than compensated by significant increases in the quantity of rubber exported. Tin exports also rose, reaching 50,000 tons in 1913. Coupled with the prevailing high prices, this resulted in extremely high revenues. In 1913, Malaya's earnings from these two commodities accounted for three-quarters of the country's total merchandise exports, and contributed to the exceptionally high 23 per cent increase in real GDP in that year (Box Table 4.2).

Box Table 4.2 Annual growth rates of real GDP and its components, Malaya, 1901–1913

	Consumption (C)	Government expenditure (G)	Investment (I)	Exports (X)	Imports (M)	GDP (Y)
1901	5.3	34.8	55.9	16.3	–3.5	20.7
1902	3.4	–15.4	–12.7	18.3	1.3	10.9
1903	2.6	12.5	24.6	–5.4	24.6	–10.0
1904	3.0	9.3	5.4	–12.9	–3.5	–3.0
1905	6.9	10.7	18.2	4.9	3.4	8.7
1906	8.8	–4.3	45.6	–13.9	14.7	–5.1
1907	4.1	1.5	46.1	8.7	4.7	10.7
1908	6.0	9.4	28.1	9.9	–5.6	18.7
1909	5.8	7.2	–26.8	–13.8	–1.8	–4.8
1910	5.4	5.0	71.7	3.9	–8.1	20.0
1911	6.0	1.2	6.9	28.0	15.4	10.2
1912	1.5	3.0	26.3	21.1	33.2	1.1
1913	10.8	10.0	47.0	17.0	8.3	23.2
Average	5.3	6.5	25.9	6.3	6.4	7.8

Also in 1913, gross fixed capital formation in construction expanded markedly, largely due to the expansion of railway construction. Current expenditure on construction rose to Straits$26.9 million in 1913, from Straits$11.1 million a year earlier (Federated Malay States Railways Annual Report, 1913). The construction works undertaken included the laying of permanent ways and sleepers, excavation, earthworks, reclamation works, and the building of bridges, viaducts, tunnels, culverts and living quarters for railway staff.

Post-Great Depression Recovery, 1933–1939

This was a period in which state intervention in economic policy began to be seen by governments as an imperative to combat the misery created by the Great Depression. In March 1933, US President Roosevelt introduced the New Deal as a means to promote economic recovery. It included measures to accelerate public works and create employment as well as social protection transfers, and was funded by deficit spending by the government (Faulkner, 1959). One early effect was a sharp increase in US motor vehicle sales (Carter, *et al.*, 2006). Economic recovery in Malaya began in 1934, and was driven by a resurgence of exports. As the US had long since become the leading destination for Malaya's commodities, this recovery was contingent on the health of the American economy.

Malaya's economy improved over this period, but with the exception of the years 1936 and 1937, growth rates were modest and in some years still negative (Box Table 4.3). The country's real GDP peaked in 1937, when the price and quantity of Malaya's rubber exports rose by 23 per cent and 34 per cent respectively, with exports reaching a record 40-year high of 467,000 tons. In the same year, export revenue from tin increased by 38 per cent to Straits$151 million due to an increase in both the quantity exported and the price. The sudden rise in the demand for tin resulted from an industrial revival, as well as re-stocking.

Both rubber and tin exports were also helped by the implementation of the international tin and rubber agreements that were put in place during the 1930s. These agreements—the International Rubber Restriction Agreement (1931–1941), and the Tin Restriction Agreement (1931–1941)—sought to regulate production, and prevent rapid and severe price oscillations (Yip, 1969). Unlike the earlier Stevenson Rubber Restriction Scheme, the new rubber agreements covered all the major producers, but not the main consuming countries, the US and Japan.

Box Table 4.3 Annual growth rates of GDP and its components at constant 1914 prices, Malaya, 1933–1939

	Consumption (C)	Government expenditure (G)	Investment (I)	Exports (X)	Imports (M)	GDP (Y)
1933	11.9	−0.4	−25.8	−0.7	13.6	−0.1
1934	−3.7	−6.1	9.8	12.7	33.3	3.4
1935	14.6	−2.2	11.5	−4.8	4.5	−0.3
1936	17.2	8.1	11.0	10.6	12.8	12.3
1937	8.6	−0.6	39.3	21.4	31.4	14.6
1938	8.1	13.3	2.7	−24.6	−0.4	−16.9
1939	2.1	5.3	11.7	6.4	3.7	5.6
Average	8.4	2.5	8.6	3.0	14.1	2.6

Malaya's post-Great Depression recovery suffered a jolt in 1938 when real GDP recorded a drop of 17 per cent compared to the previous year (Box Table 4.3). Exports fell by 25 per cent. This was due to falls in the quantity of rubber exported (21 per cent) and in rubber prices (26 per cent), as well as falls in the quantity of tin exported (46 per cent) and in the tin price (22 per cent). The sharp drop in the prices of both commodities occurred despite the operation of the restriction schemes, which were aimed at preventing just such severe fluctuations.

In the US, factory sales of passenger cars almost halved in 1938, the biggest one-year drop in 40 years. The Great Depression of the 1930s is thus seen by some as actually comprising two back-to-back recessions, one that lasted 43 months from August 1929 to March 1933, and a second that lasted 13 months from May 1937 to June 1938 (Carter et al., 2006). Two explanations have been advanced for the second recession. One attributes it to the premature reduction of fiscal stimulus, and the other to wrong monetary policy. When Roosevelt became president in 1933, he initiated a programme of heavy government spending which resulted in a small deficit. The economy turned, and GNP rose 7.7 per cent. When in 1936 GNP rose by 14 per cent, Roosevelt feared an unbalanced budget and reduced spending for 1937. This caused the economy to fall back into recession in 1938, when real GNP fell by 5 per cent. However, Friedman and Schwartz (1963) maintain that the policy of the Federal Reserve to offset the expansionary effect of the continuing influx of gold into the US by raising the deposit-reserve ratio was also a factor leading to the decline in money supply, and consequently of the economy.

In 1939, Malaya experienced an economic recovery from the brief recession with real GDP growth of 6 per cent. At the outset of World War II, US tin stocks were abnormally low and there was a scramble to buy. Export quotas were raised, leading to an increase in Malaya's tin exports (Yip, 1969).

International Comparisons

In this final section, trends in Malaya's 1900–1939 GDP growth rates and its two major components of private consumption expenditure and gross exports are compared with those of its two major trading partners, the US and the UK, together with four Asian countries so as to provide an international perspective. Such comparisons can help to improve understanding of Malaya's economic trends.

GDP Growth Rates

The largest shocks to the international economy in the period 1900–1939 originated mainly in Europe and North America: World War I and the Great Depression. These shocks reverberated in Malaya and throughout the economies of Asia.

Fluctuations in GDP growth in the US had a clear and strong influence on Malaya's export-driven economy (Figure 4.14). Particularly conspicuous is the fact that the magnitude of the downturn in Malaya's economy during the Great Depression was even larger than that of the US. Other Asian countries, while seriously affected by the Great Depression, did not experience as great a shock as did Malaya or the US

(Figure 4.15) (Boomgaard and Brown, 2000). Growth in Malaya during this period was thus positively correlated with that in the US. The links between growth in the US economy and growth in Malaya's economy are shown to be significantly stronger than those between Malaya and the UK.

Figure 4.14 Trends and cross plots of Malaya's nominal GDP growth rates and those of the US and UK, 1900–1939

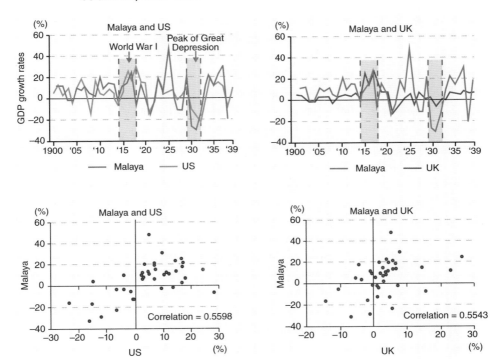

Source of data for US:
Carter, et al. (2006). Historical Statistics of the United States, Millennial Edition, Volume 3, Economic Structure and Performance, New York: Cambridge University Press, Series Ca 10, pp. 3–25.

Source of data for UK:
Feinstein (1972). National Income, Expenditure and Output of The United Kingdom, 1855–1965, Cambridge: Cambridge University Press, T. 8–11.

Figure 4.15 Cross plots of nominal GDP growth rates of selected Asian countries against the US and UK, 1900–1939

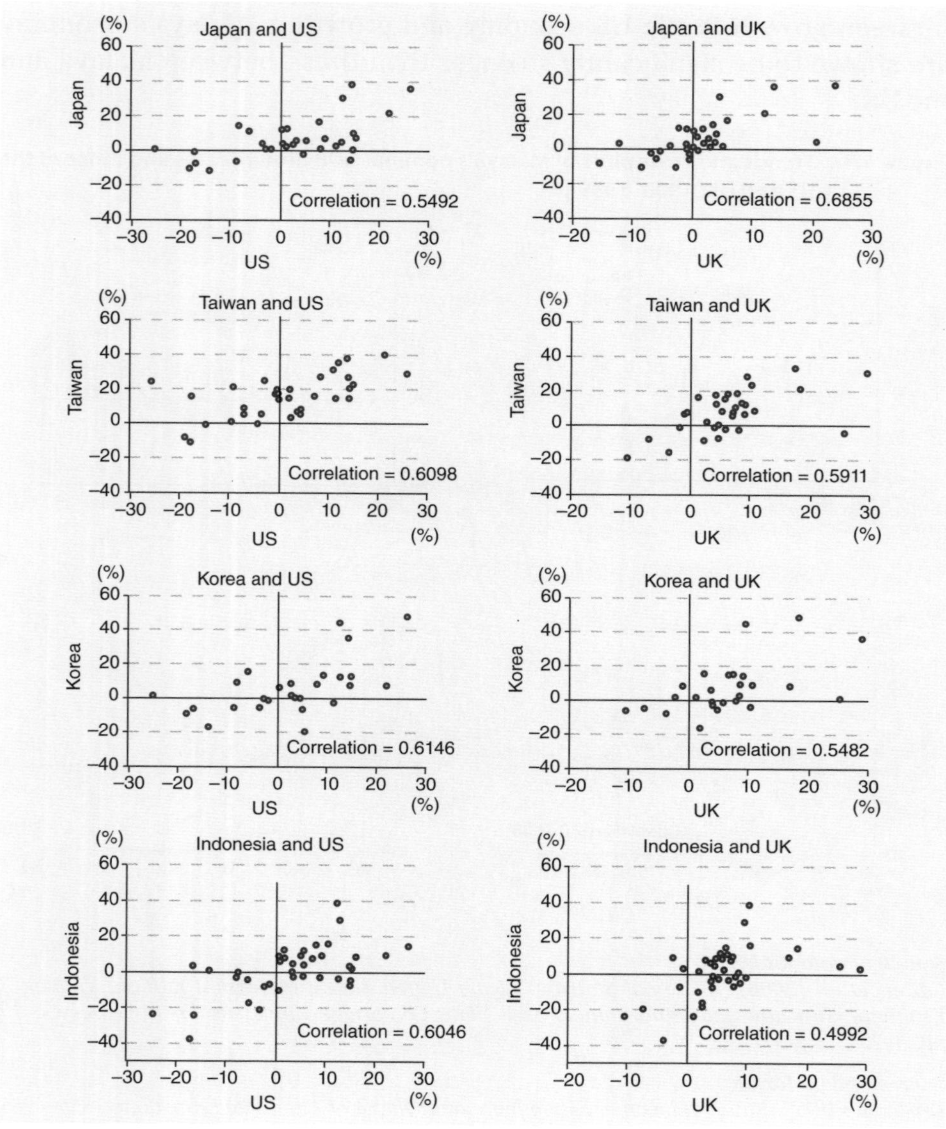

Source of data for US:

Carter, et al. (2006). *Historical Statistics of the United States, Millennial Edition, Volume 3, Economic Structure and Performance,* New York: Cambridge University Press, Series Ca 10, pp. 3–25.

Source of data for UK:

Feinstein (1972). *National Income, Expenditure and Output of the United Kingdom, 1855–1965,* Cambridge: Cambridge University Press, T. 8–11.

Sources of data for Japan Korea and Taiwan:

Mizoguchi and Umemura (eds.) (1988). *Basic Economic Statistics of Former Japanese Colonies, 1895–1938, Estimates and Findings,* Tokyo: Toyo Keizai Shinposha, pp. 228, 232 and 236.

Source of data for Indonesia:

Van der Eng (2001). *'Long-term Trends in Gross Domestic Expenditure in Indonesia'. International Workshop on Modern Economic Growth and Distribution in Asia, Latin America and the European Periphery:* A Historical National Accounts Approach. Tokyo, March 2001.

As an indication of the dominant role played by the US in Malaya's growth, in a simple regression of Malaya's nominal GDP growth rate on those of the US and the UK, the latter was statistically insignificant whereas that of the US had an important influence. On average, over the whole period, a 1 percentage point change in the US growth rate led to a 0.68 percentage point change in the growth rate of Malaya. The effect was even stronger in the Great Depression years (Figure 4.14).

Given its increasing dependence on rubber and tin exports, the question arises as to whether Malaya was more sensitive to cycles in the international economy than other Asian countries. The Great Depression does seem to have had a more dramatic effect on Malaya's growth than it did on that of the benchmark countries considered here. Figure 4.15 displays cross-plots of the nominal GDP growth rates in Japan, Taiwan, Korea and Indonesia against GDP growth rates in the US and the UK. The simple correlations of growth rates are reported in each cross-plot.

Interestingly, all four Asian countries were significantly affected by GDP growth in the US and, to a lesser extent, the UK. For Indonesia and Japan, like Malaya, the link to the US economy was direct – severe depression in the US had an immediate and direct impact on their exports. For Korea and Taiwan, the link was more indirect. It operated via their trade with Japan, the major trading partner of both during the period, which was itself strongly affected by any downturn in the US economy.

Figure 4.16 shows the annual nominal GDP growth rates of Malaya alongside those of the four Asian countries—Indonesia, Japan, Korea and Taiwan. Volatility in growth rates is a salient characteristic in all five economies, but is particularly conspicuous for Malaya and Indonesia.

Consumption Expenditure

The share of private consumption expenditure in nominal GDP was by far the lowest in Malaya in comparison with the six international benchmark countries (Figure 4.17). Industrialised countries such as the US and UK, with their much greater per capita income, would be expected to have had high consumption rates. The share of consumption in Malaya was closest to that of Japan, a country known to have an unusually high savings rate.

Figure 4.16 Comparisons of trends of Malaya's nominal GDP growth rates with those of selected Asian countries, 1900–1939

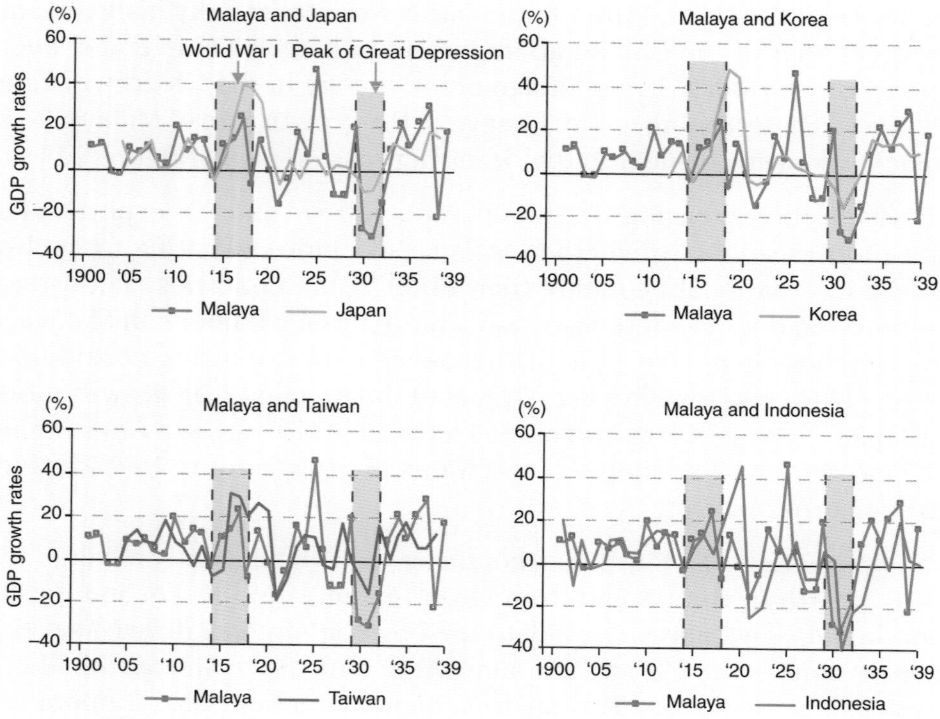

Sources of data for Japan Korea and Taiwan:
Mizoguchi and Umemura (eds.) (1988). Basic Economic Statistics of Former Japanese Colonies, 1895–1938, Estimates and Findings, Tokyo: Toyo Keizai Shinposha, pp. 228, 232 and 236.

Source of data for Indonesia:
Van der Eng (2001). 'Long-term Trends in Gross Domestic Expenditure in Indonesia'. International Workshop on Modern Economic Growth and Distribution in Asia, Latin America and the European Periphery: A Historical National Accounts Approach. Tokyo, March 2001.

Figure 4.17 highlights the very high level of consumption expenditure in Korea as compared with Malaya. This may reflect Korea's very low income during this period, while Malaya's much higher proportion of exports to GDP would have reduced its proportion of consumption expenditure.

Gross Exports

In the first four decades of the twentieth century, Malaya had one of the most trade-dependent economies in the world. The export share of its GDP was much higher than all the six benchmark countries, and

Figure 4.17 Comparisons of Malaya's trends in shares of private consumption in nominal GDP with those of selected countries, 1900–1939

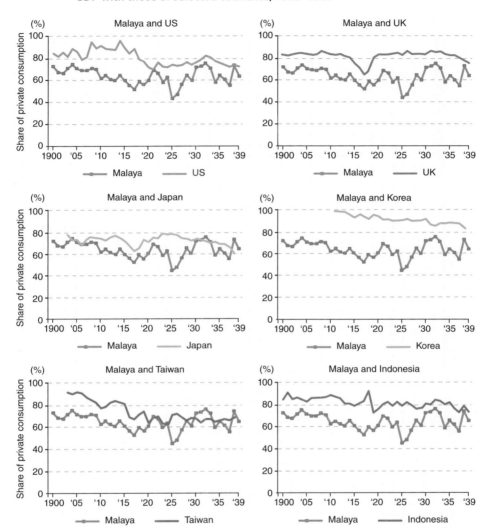

Source of data for US:
Carter, et al. (2006). Historical Statistics of the United States, Millennial Edition, Volume 3, Economic Structure and Performance, New York: Cambridge University Press (GDP), Series Ca10 (PFCE) (1900–1929), pp. 3–25, Series Cd 1 (1929–1939), pp. 3–230, Series Cd 153, pp. 3–243.

Source of data for UK:
Feinstein (1972). National Income, Expenditure and Output of The United Kingdom, 1855–1965, Cambridge: Cambridge University Press, T8–11.

Sources of data for Japan Korea and Taiwan:
Mizoguchi and Umemura (eds.) (1988). Basic Economic Statistics of Former Japanese Colonies, 1895–1938, Estimates and Findings, Tokyo: Toyo Keizai Shinposha, pp. 228, 232 and 236.

Source of data for Indonesia:
Van der Eng (2001). 'Long-term Trends in Gross Domestic Expenditure in Indonesia'. International Workshop on Modern Economic Growth and Distribution in Asia, Latin America and the European Periphery: A Historical National Accounts Approach. Tokyo, March 2001.

Figure 4.18 Comparisons of Malaya's trends in shares of exports of goods and services of nominal GDP with those of selected countries, 1900–1939

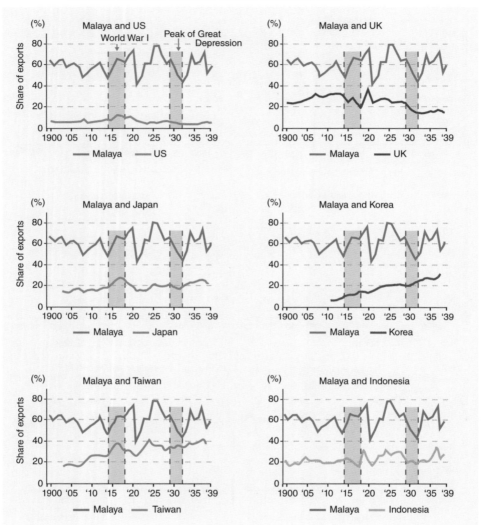

Source of data for US:
Carter, et al. (2006). *Historical Statistics of the United States, Millennial Edition, Volume 3, Economic Structure and Performance,* New York: Cambridge University Press (GDP), Series Ca10 (Exports of goods and services) (1900–1928), pp. 3–25, Series Ee365 (1929–1939), pp. 5–500, Series Ca 77, pp. 3–40.

Source of data for UK:
Feinstein (1972). *National Income, Expenditure and Output of The United Kingdom, 1855–1965,* Cambridge: Cambridge University Press, T8–11.

Sources of data for Japan Korea and Taiwan:
Mizoguchi and Umemura (eds.) (1988). *Basic Economic Statistics of Former Japanese Colonies, 1895–1938, Estimates and Findings,* Tokyo: Toyo Keizai Shinposha, pp. 228, 232 and 236.

Source of data for Indonesia:
Van der Eng (2001). *'Long-term Trends in Gross Domestic Expenditure in Indonesia'.* International Workshop on Modern Economic Growth and Distribution in Asia, Latin America and the European Periphery: A Historical National Accounts Approach. Tokyo, March 2001.

was 10 times that of the US (Figure 4.18). The export share of GDP was also far more volatile in Malaya than in the other countries due to the considerable fluctuations in the prices of its major exports.

Malaya's resource-based economy was thus highly vulnerable to the vicissitudes of the US economy, and especially to fluctuations in the international prices of, and demand for, its primary export commodities. During the first four decades of the 20th century, three external shocks—World War I, the Roaring Twenties, and the Great Depression—had a major impact on growth performance. Economic diversification, moving away from the high export dependence on the basic commodities of rubber and tin, was thus an imperative for Malaysian policy makers after the end of colonial rule.

*   *   *

The next chapter employs econometric techniques to assess the volatility and sources of economic growth in Malaya during the period 1900–1939, and contrasts these with economic growth in contemporary Malaysia during the period 1970–2009.

CHAPTER

5

Production of rubber sheets from latex for export,
predominantly for US industries

Volatility and Sources of Growth in Historical and Contemporary GDP

In Chapter 4, a detailed account was given of trends in Malaya's GDP and its components for the period 1900–1939, together with an analysis of short-term fluctuations, including the impact of external shocks on the economy. An assessment was also made of the annual variations in the growth of the GDP components, and it was observed that variations in export growth accounted for much of the volatility in GDP growth. A decomposition analysis of annual growth in exports among tin, rubber and other exports further showed that variations in exports of rubber were the dominant factor.

In this chapter, economic volatility and its impact on economic growth in Malaya are assessed over the period 1900–1939, and contrasted with post-independence Malaysia over the period 1970–2009. Economic volatility is identified with short-term fluctuations in real GDP around its longer-term trend. Variations in export and GDP volatility are modelled to examine their effects on economic performance, and an assessment is made of how they might have affected growth and development. The impact of volatility on long-run growth performance is then analysed by examining variations in volatility using regression techniques, including cross-country studies.

The sources of economic growth are estimated using a standard growth accounting approach. Economic growth is attributed to two sources: the use of more inputs (the primary factors of capital and labour) in production processes, and improvements in the productivity of those inputs. Having identified the contribution that additional inputs make to growth, what is left over, or the residual, is attributed to changes in total factor productivity (TFP). In principle, TFP might reflect increases in efficiency given existing technology, the adoption of new and better technologies, or institutional innovations that yield more output per unit of input.

Volatility and Growth

Trend Growth, Residual Growth and Economic Volatility

The large swings in the levels of GDP, and the see-saw pattern seen in its rate of growth from 1900–1939, suggest that Malaya's economy was buffeted by a high level of volatility. Questions arise as to precisely how much volatility was experienced, and what its probable impacts were.

The concept of volatility and its measurement are explained below. In the next section, selected volatility metrics are applied to Malaya for the period 1900–1939 and compared with the same metrics for post-independence Malaysia for the period 1970–2009. Following that analysis, an assessment is made of the channels through which volatility might have influenced the country's economic growth and development in both periods, including its impact on consumption. The final section attempts to quantify the depressing effect of volatility on long-run growth.

Statistically, volatility is identified with values that are highly changeable, or fluctuate widely, around some reference point. Measuring volatility thus first requires the identification of such reference values. When considering real GDP, such reference values are typically identified with *trend* GDP. The residual differences (the *cyclical* component) between observed GDP and trend GDP then generate measures of volatility.

In the simplest model, the residual or cyclical component of GDP is assumed to be additive:

$$GDP\ (t) = Trend\ GDP\ (t) + Cyclical\ GDP\ (Residual)\ (t)$$

where (t) dates observations. In many applications, however, the residual component is assumed to be multiplicative:

$$GDP\ (t) = Trend\ GDP\ (t) * Cyclical\ Factor\ (Residual\ Factor)\ (t)$$

where observed and trend GDP coincide only when the cyclical or residual factor is equal to 1. The multiplicative form has the advantage that the cyclical factors are directly linked to the percentage deviation of the trend from the observed values. The tendency for GDP to drift up over time also lends some technical statistical advantages to this model. Malaya's real GDP followed a distinctive upward trajectory from 1900 to 1939, albeit with considerable irregularity. The value of real GDP in 1939 was nearly nine times its value in 1900. To accommodate this aspect of the data, the measures of volatility calculated here are all based on the multiplicative form or, equivalently, in natural logarithm (LN) terms:

$$LN\ (GDP\ (t)) = LN\ (Trend\ GDP\ (t)) + LN\ (Cyclical\ GDP\ (t))$$

From this, the output gap is:

$$LN\ (Cyclical\ GDP\ (t)) = LN\ (GDP\ (t)) - LN\ (Trend\ GDP\ (t))$$

There is, however, no single correct approach to identifying trend GDP and a wide variety of methods can be used. Perhaps the simplest method is to use centered moving average values. When considering trends in annual GDP, a 5-year moving average is often used. A span of five years is considered long enough to encapsulate a regular economic cycle, but short enough to register possible changes in the underlying trend over time. The 5-year moving average is defined as:

$$MA(X(t)) = (X(t-2) + X(t-1) + X(t) + X(t+1) + X(t+2))/5$$

In Figure 5.1, the trajectory of the LN of real GDP, its 5-year moving average values and the percentage deviation of this moving average from observed GDP levels are shown. Note that in calculating moving average values, it is necessary to drop two observations at the start of the sample, 1900 and 1901, and two observations at the end of the sample, 1938 and 1939. The moving average values, like the LN of GDP values, follow a non-linear trend, and the deviations of actual from trend values (right side axis) are often more than ±5% in size (represented by the broken horizontal lines). The chart also shows that the deviations get larger in later years.

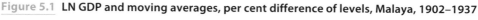

Figure 5.1 **LN GDP and moving averages, per cent difference of levels, Malaya, 1902–1937**

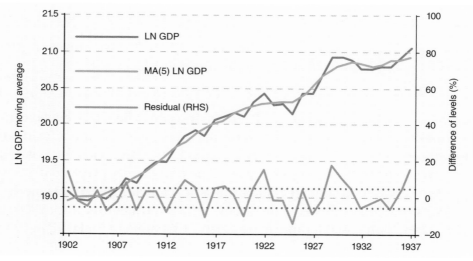

A more complex method of filtering out trends seeks to minimise observed deviations from observed values, but also penalises any changes in the trend growth rate. The most popular such filter is the Hodrick-Prescott (HP) filter. The choice of trend method is particularly important when used to estimate capacity output and the output gap. [38]

Application of the HP filter to GDP for the years 1930–1939 is shown in Figure 5.2.

Figure 5.2 **HP filter and residuals of GDP, Malaya, 1900–1939**

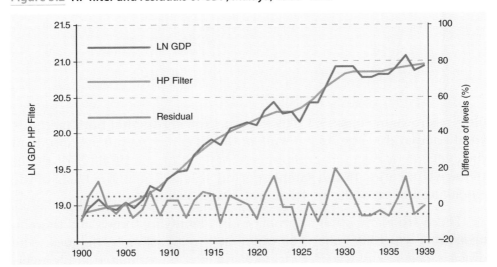

Note:
A weighting value of 7 is used in this application of the HP filter as recommended for annual data by Pesaran and Pesaran (1997). Other authors have advocated use of larger weights, often 100, but Ravn and Uhlig (2002) show that an optimal value for annual observations is much closer to 7.

The results of the application of the HP filter again suggest the frequent presence of large residuals (cyclical components), and indicate that the per cent deviations of trend from observed GDP growth get larger in later years. A comparison of the residuals generated by the application of the moving average method and HP

---

38 A recent illustration of this was the debate between James Bullard (President of the St. Louis Federal Reserve) and Nobel laureate Paul Krugman concerning the size of the output gap in the US in 2012. Bullard (2012) thought the HP appropriate, arguing that a linear trend would exaggerate the output gap as it assumes that the economy's capacity was unaffected by the cyclical downturn. Krugman (2012) challenged the use of the HP filter as a measure of potential output, arguing that 'the use of the HP filter presumes that deviations from potential output are relatively short-term, and tend to be corrected fairly quickly,' but 'in any protracted slump gets interpreted as a decline in potential output.' According to Phillips and Jin (2015), the Krugman view has merit, but the relatively short-lived deviations from trend in the case of Malaya suggest the HP filter is a suitable statistical approach to measuring potential output and the output gap.

Figure 5.3 Moving average and HP differences (per cent from trend), Malaya, 1900–1939

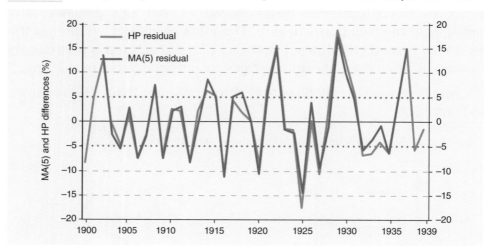

filter is shown in Figure 5.3. This comparison shows that both methods yield comparable results in terms of the sign and overall magnitude of the cyclical, or residual, components of GDP. As the HP filter does not require truncation of the sample period, this will form the basis of the calculation of volatility metrics in the next section.

There are many other approaches to identifying trends and thereby measuring volatility, many of which use regression techniques. The precise forms employed vary widely and may be estimated in LN levels or differences in LNs (growth rates), and may consist of a variety of explanatory variables, including polynomials in time and lagged values of the LN of GDP, or growth rates (Dabušinskas *et al.*, 2012).

Economic Volatility: Malaya 1900–1939 Compared with Malaysia 1970–2009

In this section, a widely used metric of economic volatility is explained and is used to compare volatility in Malaya during the period 1900–1939 with that in post-independence Malaysia over the 1970–2009 period. Throughout, trend growth is obtained from an HP filter applied to the LN of real GDP, and the cyclical component is measured as the per cent deviation of the implied trend level of GDP from its actual, or observed, value.

In Figure 5.4, the trend and cyclical components of real GDP are shown for post-independence Malaysia over the period 1970–2009. The residuals are the per cent differences between the level of HP trend of real GDP and the observed value of real GDP.

Figure 5.4 HP trend of LN GDP and residuals (per cent difference from trend), Malaysia, 1970–2009

Figure 5.4 suggests that the measured cyclical component of GDP is much smaller in post-independence Malaysia (1970–2009) than in colonial Malaya (1900–1939). This is confirmed in Figure 5.5, where the residual, or cyclical, components of each de-trended series are compared side by side. Whereas the vast majority of the trend values from the later period are contained within a ±5 per cent interval of the actual values, in 22 out of the 40 years from 1900–1939, the cyclical components (observed less trend values) fall outside the ±5 per cent interval.

Figure 5.5 HP residuals (per cent difference from trend), Malaya, 1900–1939 and Malaysia, 1970–2009

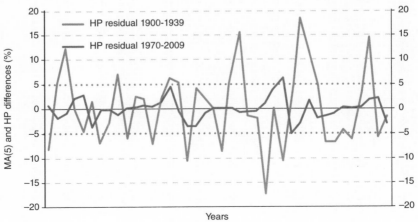

A useful and often-used metric of volatility is the standard deviation of the residual, or cyclical, components of GDP. The standard deviation is a statistical parameter which measures the dispersion of values from the mean or average. The larger the standard deviation, the greater the dispersion of values around the average. The simple average of the volatility measures should, by construction, be small as trend estimates smooth out positive and negative cyclical components. From 1900–1939, the average percentage residual was just –0.3 per cent. The average value for the period 1970–2009 was even smaller (in absolute terms) at –0.025 per cent.

Although the averages of the raw volatility measures are similar and are both close to zero as the positive and negative residuals self-cancel, their standard deviations differ enormously. The standard deviation of the percentage deviation of trend from actual GDP for the period 1930–1939 was 3.5 times larger than the same measure for the period 1970–2009.

The differences within different sample periods show similar startling variations. Figures 5.6 and 5.7 show the recursive, or rolling, averages for five- and 10-year measures of the standard deviation over each period. These measures calculate the standard deviations at the end point of each overlapping interval of five and 10 years, starting with a comparison of 1900–1905 (1900–1909) with 1970–1975 (1970–1979), and then moving the five- and 10-year windows forward by one year. This allows peaks in volatility as well as periods of comparative tranquility to be easily identified.

Figure 5.6 Rolling 5-year standard deviations of trend from observed levels of GDP, Malaya, 1900–1939 and Malaysia, 1970–2009

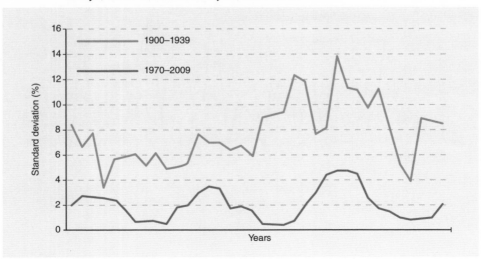

Figure 5.7 **Rolling 10-year standard deviations of trend from observed levels of GDP, Malaya, 1900–1939 and Malaysia, 1970–2009**

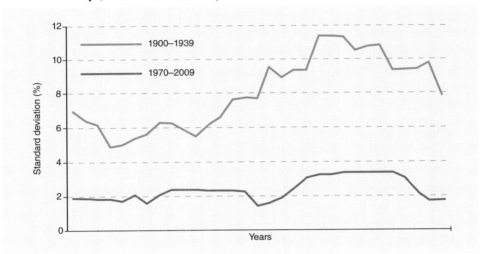

In comparison to volatility experienced in other places and at other times, volatility in pre-war Malaya was intense. Year-to-year swings in real GDP growth of 10 percentage points or more were not unusual. In fact, they were the norm. There were 21 such events between 1900 and 1939. To put this tumultuous history in context, during the Great Recession of 2008–2009, growth in the US veered from a pre-crisis peak of just above 2 per cent to a low of −4 per cent, a swing of 6 percentage points. In the subsequent upswing, growth rose by 7 percentage points.

Assessment of the Impact of Volatility on Development and Growth

The volatility experienced in pre-war colonial Malaya, in terms of both the frequency and the magnitude of shocks, is probably without modern precedent. It would be surprising if volatility of this intensity did not have wider economic consequences.

The impact of volatility on long-run growth is the subject of much discussion. If volatility is associated with high risk and high returns, with waves of creative destruction as posited by Schumpeter's theory of economic development, or with higher levels of precautionary savings, it may contribute to long-term growth. There is also evidence at a sectoral level that fast-growing sectors tend to be more volatile (Imbs, 2007).

If, however, volatility dampens the appetite for investment in built and human capital, distorts the allocation of resources, or leads to policy errors, it can have adverse effects on growth (Timmer, 1989). The negative impacts of volatility can be expected to be more acute when the shock-absorbing capacity of an economy is low. Countries with an undiversified export base and weak institutional capacities, and in which financial market development is at a low level might, therefore, be more vulnerable to negative impacts than others.

While evidence concerning the existence of the so-called *resource curse*—in which long-run growth prospects are damaged by natural resource abundance—is mixed (Sachs and Warner, 1995), there is an emerging consensus that the export price (or terms-of-trade) volatility experienced by countries that are dependent on a narrow basket of resources is harmful. Indeed, the harmful effects of volatility, particularly in terms of reduced investment in built and human capital, have been found to outweigh any benefits from resource booms (Cavalcanti *et al.,* 2012). Some supporting evidence for Malaya is available. The exponential growth rate of real GDP for the period 1900–1919 was 7 per cent when volatility was lower. Conversely, growth was lower at 4 per cent during the period 1920–1939 when there was higher volatility. In sum, higher volatility may have contributed to lower growth in colonial Malaya.

Identifying the specific effects of volatility on economic growth requires data points that capture variations both across countries and across time. Before making a quantitative assessment of the impact of volatility on growth, it is instructive to ask what a comparison of pre-war Malaya with post-independence Malaysia might reveal.

A number of stylised facts can be identified:

■ First, macroeconomic volatility in post-independence Malaysia, despite the sharp recession of the mid-1980s and the severity of the Asian Financial Crisis in the late 1990s, has never matched the extent of the volatility experienced in pre-World War II Malaya.

■ Second, investment rates in pre-World War II Malaya were anaemic compared to the high investment rates in post-independence Malaysia that have been associated with substantial advances in per capita income and reduced poverty levels (Figure 5.8).

■ Third, rapid progress in educational achievements across the population did not occur until after independence. In pre-World War II Malaya, educational advances affecting the majority of the population were for the most part negligible, and there was a high dependence on a largely unskilled, low-wage migrant labour force.

■ Fourth, greater macroeconomic stability after independence was, in part, due to the diversification of the country's productive base. With an independent sovereign government and institutional development, fiscal and monetary policies also became tools for macroeconomic management.

Unfortunately, the comprehensive data that would be needed to identify the initial sources of volatility and to track the mechanisms through which they eventually influence long-run growth prospects are not available.[39] Consequently, the income impacts of terms-of-trade changes cannot be accounted for using measures such as gross national income (Chapter 3, Box 3.1). The focus here, therefore, remains on simple metrics of real GDP growth volatility and its investment component.

Figure 5.8 **Share of real investment rates in GDP, Malaya, 1900–1939 and Malaysia, 1970–2009**

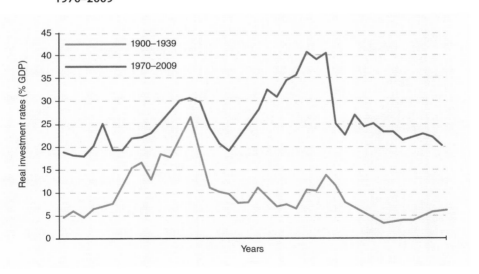

---

39 For example, although it is clear that variations in the prices of rubber (and to a lesser extent, tin) had profound influences on local income and government revenue (Thoburn, 1977), it is not possible to construct comprehensive terms-of-trade measures (that would weigh all export prices against the price of Malaya's import basket) to quantify the shocks.

Figure 5.8 shows that investment in pre-war Malaya had two main phases. Investment rates rose from 1900 through to 1913, reaching a peak in that year of 26 per cent of real GDP. It is likely that this first phase was associated with significant investments in land cultivation for rubber plantations, and in the built assets and equipment that were the backbone of Malaya's rubber industry. But once this initial capital expansion phase was completed, investment rates collapsed, reviving only for a short period in the 1920s and then languishing at low levels.

Figure 5.9 compares volatility in investment with volatility in real GDP (which might be considered as a proxy for unanticipated shocks to real GDP). This investment volatility metric is derived in the same way that volatility is measured for GDP. Investment was even more volatile than GDP. Extreme volatility in exports, particularly rubber, and the consequent volatility in real income was associated with even more pronounced volatility in investment (Box 5.1). These low and highly volatile investment rates would probably have held back economic diversification, which in turn would have further weakened the country's defenses against volatility and entrenched its commodity dependence.

Figure 5.9 **Per cent differences of investment and GDP from trend, Malaya, 1900–1939**

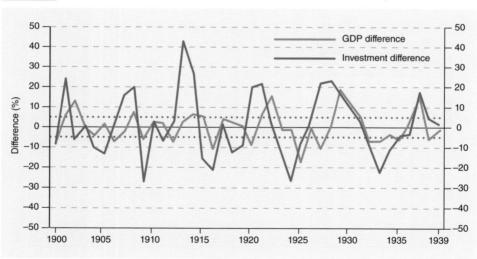

Box 5.1 20th century evolution of Malaysia's rubber and tin exports

The distinctive supply and demand characteristics of rubber and tin led to extreme volatility. Rubber and tin have low price elasticities of supply and demand (Wharton, 1963; Mohamed Ariff, 1972; Lim, 1973), while their income elasticities of demand are high (Balassa, 1964). Low price elasticities and frequent short-run changes in demand explain their volatility (MacBean, 1966). Rubber and tin prices fluctuated particularly severely during the interwar years and continued to do so in the post-World War II era (Box Figures 5.1 and 5.2). For rubber, the average standard deviation was 0.274 for the period 1905–1938, compared with 0.177 for the period 1947–1995, whereas for tin the corresponding figures were 0.163 and 0.151. A similar declining trend in volatility is evident for export volume. Although rubber and tin prices have remained volatile since 1995, as Malaysia's exports are now much more diversified, any impact on the economy is greatly diminished.

Box Figure 5.1 **Rubber and tin prices, Malaysia, 1900–2010**

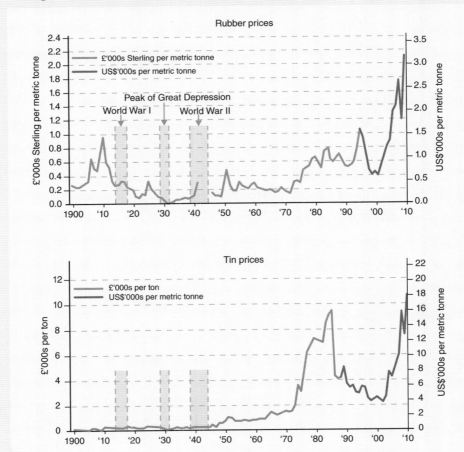

Box Figure 5.2 Rubber and tin production in Malaysia as a percentage of world total, 1900–2007

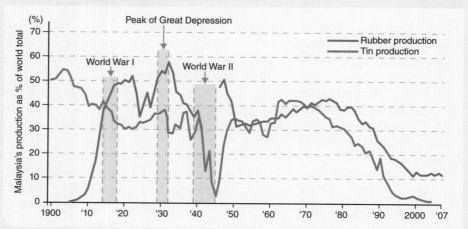

Throughout the 20th century, growth rates in Malaya's rubber production were positively correlated with growth rates in US rubber consumption (Box Figure 5.3).

Box Figure 5.3 Cross plot of Malaysia's annual growth rates of rubber production with growth rates of US rubber consumption, 1914–1995

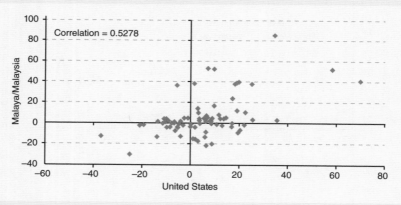

Note:
Data before 1914 are not shown because of the small quantity of Malaya's rubber production. No data are available for 1942–1945.

By 1919, Malaya's exports of rubber exceeded those of the rest of the world combined. Apart from the period under Japanese rule, Malaya's share of world supply of rubber did not fall below 30 per cent until the late 1980s (Box Figure 5.4). In 1990, Malaysia still accounted for 25 per cent of world natural rubber output, but by then rubber's contribution to the country's export earnings was less than 4 per cent compared to 55 per cent 30 years earlier. By the end of the century, rubber accounted for less than 1 per cent of Malaysia's total export earnings.

Malayan tin production continued to grow steadily, reaching a peak of 52,000 tons in 1904 and levelling thereafter (Thoburn, 1994). Production declined during World War I as a result of export controls and shipping disruptions. There were further falls in tin exports in the years 1921–1923 when the Federated Malay States and the Dutch East Indies withheld tin from the market in the face of reduced post-war demand. With economic recovery, tin output expanded. Growth of output in other tin-producing countries, particularly in Bolivia and also in the Dutch East Indies, Thailand and China contributed to a decline in Malaya's share of world output. Although this share remained significant, it had fallen to 37 per cent by 1930 compared to over 50 per cent at the turn of the century (Box Figure 5.4).

World War II severely disrupted Malaya's tin industry, but a massive post-war rehabilitation programme brought production back up to 55,000 tons in 1949. It increased further in the 1950s and 1960s, reaching a peak of 77,000 tons in 1972 (Jomo, 1990a). However, during the last 30 years of the 20th century, tin production declined markedly to well below the level it had been a hundred years earlier, and tin's relative importance to the country's economy steadily declined. Tin exports accounted for about 20 per cent of gross export earnings in 1970. This fell to less than 10 per cent in 1980, and by the late 1990s tin contributed less than 1 per cent.

Box Figure 5.4 Share of global natural rubber and tin production, Malaysia, 1900–2007

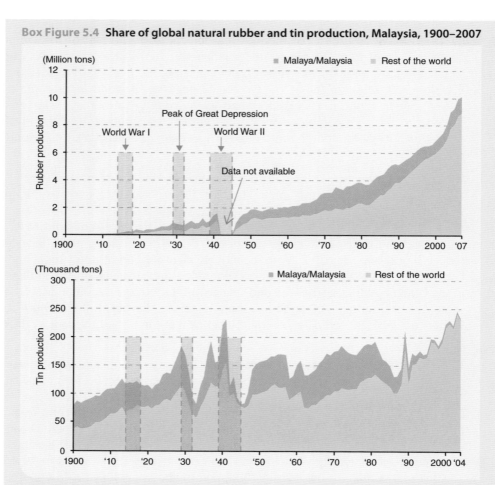

Note:

Data for years before 1963 relate to Malaya.

Sources of data for figures in this box are:

1. *Malayan rubber figure for 1905 refers to exports and was obtained from Tate (1996), pp. 210.*
2. *Figures for 1942–44 were obtained from Kratoska (1998), Table 8.3, pp. 227.*
3. *International Rubber Study Group, Rubber Statistical Bulletin, (various years).*
4. *For tin, Lim (1967), Appendix 2.1.*
5. *International Tin Council, Statistical Year Book, 1968, T.1, pp. 23.*
6. *Annual Report, International Tin Council, 1967–68, Appendix C, pp. 22; 1969–70, Appendices B & C. pp. 19–20; 1982–83, Appendices B & C, pp. 30, 31.*
7. *International Tin Council, Tin Statistics, 1970–80, pp. 19, 63; 1976–86, pp. 19, 66.*
8. *International Tin Statistics, Bulletin No. 1, June 1991, pp.1, No. 16–17, January 1996, pp.1 and 3.*
9. *United Nations Statistics Division, UN Comtrade database website http://comtrade.un.org*
10. *United Nations database website http://data.un.org , Food and Agriculture Organization*

While investment rates in post-independence Malaysia were also highly uneven (Figure 5.10), they were several orders of magnitude greater than those in the colonial era, averaging well above 20 per cent of GDP and peaking at over 40 per cent on the cusp of the Asian Financial Crisis in 1997. While there may even have been *over-investment* and waste in some years, particularly in the mid-1990s, stronger investment performance in the post-independence period occurred in circumstances in which growth was much less volatile. A comparison of the colonial and post-independence periods shows that, while investment was volatile in both, it was significantly more volatile in the colonial period, with a standard deviation 50 per cent higher than that recorded in the post-independence period.

Figure 5.10 **Per cent differences of investment trends from observed trend, Malaya, 1900–1939 and Malaysia, 1970–2009**

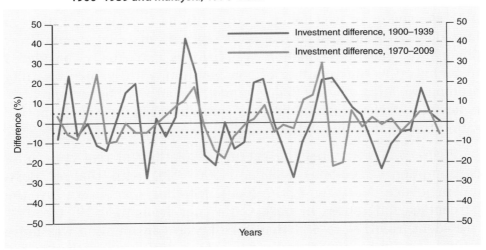

The observations about physical capital probably also apply to human capital, but there are unfortunately no readily available data to compare human capital accumulation in the colonial period with that in post-independence Malaysia. However, greater uncertainty, the low incomes of the bulk of the population, a lack of relatively secure employment opportunities outside plantation agriculture, and under-developed credit markets seem likely to have limited private incentives to invest in children's education during the colonial period.

Other factors, too, probably affected human and physical capital accumulation. Since a government's ability to invest and deliver services depends on its ability to pay for them, the volatility in revenues that were increasingly sourced from taxes on rubber and tin would have prevented sustained commitments to much-needed investments in social and economic infrastructure, and to essential service delivery. The experience of colonial Malaya seems to resonate with a much wider body of evidence which shows the debilitating effects of volatility on investment and economic advance (Cavalcanti *et al.*, 2012).

It was only with the raft of post-independence policy reforms, including measures relating to land, and concerted efforts to invest in health, ensure universal access to education and develop infrastructure, that the conditions were reset, and structural buffers against volatility effectively built.

Volatility in Consumption Trends

As an indicator of well-being, real per capita consumption, though imperfect, is of interest insofar as it registers material standards of living of the general population. Well-being is also usually considered to be linked to the volatility of consumption, with greater volatility eroding welfare, all else being equal. Essentially, households are believed to prefer predictability and smoothness in their consumption rather than erratic fluctuations.

Figure 5.11 compares the extent of volatility of real per capita consumption in colonial Malaya (1900–1939) with that of post-independence Malaysia (1970–2009). Volatility is shown by the percentage differences of observed values from their HP trend. It is evident from Figure 5.11 that volatility in consumption was more pronounced in the first four decades of the 20th century than in the period between 1970 and 2009. In the earlier period, the standard deviation of the residual, or cyclical, component of consumption was 1.6 times greater than that for the later period. Nevertheless, consumption volatility in colonial Malaya was substantially lower than the volatility seen in GDP.

The higher volatility during the colonial period can be attributed to the greater dependence at that time of employment and income on exports of tin and rubber, which themselves demonstrated extreme volatility, as discussed above. Following independence, the successful efforts to diversify the economy created more and varied employment opportunities.

Figure 5.11 **Consumption per capita, HP trend and percentage residuals, Malaya, 1900–1939 and Malaysia, 1970–2009**

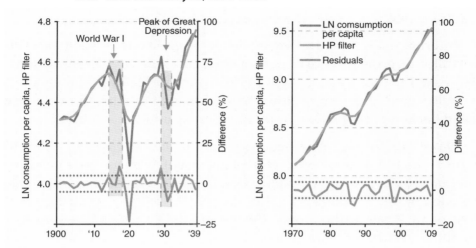

Source:
Data for Malaysia are from the World Bank, World Development Indicators downloaded from http://databank.worldbank.org/data/reports.aspx?source=2&country=MYS&series=&period= on 30 March 2016.

The higher volatility is also likely to have contributed to the slower growth of consumption during the earlier period of just 1 per cent, as compared to the 3.5 per cent experienced in the 1970–2009 period (Chapter 6). The prevailing volatility of income would have created high levels of uncertainty, and thus would have influenced savings and consumption behaviour. When future incomes are uncertain, individuals or households may choose to save more to create a buffer to support future consumption. Such precautionary savings behavior can temporarily arrest current consumption growth, with the main impact being to reduce levels of consumption (Deaton, 1991; Carroll, 1997).

Impact of Volatility on Growth

Malaya's growth rates of GDP and of exports were particularly erratic in the first four decades of the 20th century. For example, real GDP grew at 26.4 per cent in 1917 following a decline of 8 per cent in the previous year, and growth rates reached around 30 per cent in 1926, 1928 and 1929. Export growth exhibited similarly acute volatility (Chapter 4).

There are sound theoretical reasons as to why such volatility is likely to have affected Malaya's long-run growth potential. Imperfect insurance and capital markets make it difficult to smooth out fluctuations in demand, which can lead to lower investment and growth. Conversely, volatility in incomes can encourage precautionary savings, which would raise investment. The issue is, therefore, an empirical one: what does the evidence support?

International comparative evidence suggests that such marked volatility in growth of GDP per capita and exports is likely to have depressed the long-run growth performance of Malaya. The effect of volatility can be analysed either by examining variations in volatility using decade-average data, or by using cross-country studies.

Dawe (1996) used cross-country data to investigate the effect of export volatility on growth, regressing country mean growth rates, *inter alia*, on a measure of export volatility. His dependent variable is, for each of the 85 countries in his sample, the average annual growth rate of GDP per worker over the period 1970–1985. Dawe's export volatility variable is defined as:

$$V_Y = \frac{1}{T} \sum_{j=1}^{T} \frac{|X_j - \bar{X}_j|}{Y_j}$$

where T is the number of time periods (16 years), X is constant-price exports, $\bar{X}$ is a centred five-year moving average of exports and Y is constant-price GDP. The absolute deviation of exports from the moving-average trend is normalised by GDP, and averaged over time. He concluded that export volatility depressed growth.

Using a cross-section sample of 92 countries, Ramey and Ramey (1995) also found that volatility in the growth of GDP per capita (as measured by its standard deviation) depressed the average growth of GDP per capita.

Variations in Export and GDP Volatility – Decadal Means

A meaningful measure to investigate whether average GDP per capita has been affected by export volatility over a decade-long period can be obtained by taking the means of growth and volatility over a series of ten annual observations. The export volatility measure employed is similar to that adopted by Dawe, but the trend for exports is given by its HP filter rather than its moving average. It is defined for decade i as:

$$V_{iY} = \frac{1}{T_i} \sum_{j=1}^{T_i} \frac{|X_j - \hat{X}_j|}{Y_j}$$

where T_i is the time period for decade i (usually 10 years, but 9 for the first), X is constant-price exports, $\hat{X}$ is the HP trend for exports (smoothing parameter set at 6.25) and Y is constant-price GDP.

The decade means of growth and two measures of volatility are given in Table 5.1. Measures of volatility are shown in columns three (the standard deviation of growth of GDP per capita over the decade) and four (Dawe's measure of export volatility as defined above). The figures confirm the substantial volatility in GDP growth and exports over the first four decades of the 20th century, and also show that these were considerably lower in post-independence Malaysia, when volatility was markedly less pronounced.

Table 5.1 **Decade means of real GDP growth and volatility**

Period	GDP per capita growth (%)	Standard deviation (%)	Vi_Y (%)
Malaya 1900–1939			
1901–1909	1.301	10.686	3.329
1910–1919	7.140	9.545	3.168
1920–1929	5.398	16.081	6.295
1930–1939	−2.274	8.994	6.224
Malaysia 1970–2009			
1971–1979	5.609	3.113	1.292
1980–1989	2.988	3.312	1.018
1990–1999	4.278	5.209	1.879
2000–2009	2.602	2.886	4.229

Figure 5.12 shows a cross-plot of export volatility and growth. A regression of decade-mean growth rates on decade-mean export volatility suggests that growth was somewhat subdued in decades with high export volatility. The coefficient on volatility (0.563) was not statistically significant, however (standard error of 0.540). From the decade averages, it is thus not possible to reject the null hypothesis that growth was unaffected by volatility. Meanwhile, cross-plots and regressions of decade-mean GDP per capita growth against GDP volatility (its standard deviation over the decade) suggest there is little or no effect of GDP volatility on growth.

Figure 5.12 **Cross plots of variations in GDP and export volatility against GDP per capita growth rates, Malaya, 1900–1939 and Malaysia, 1970–2009**

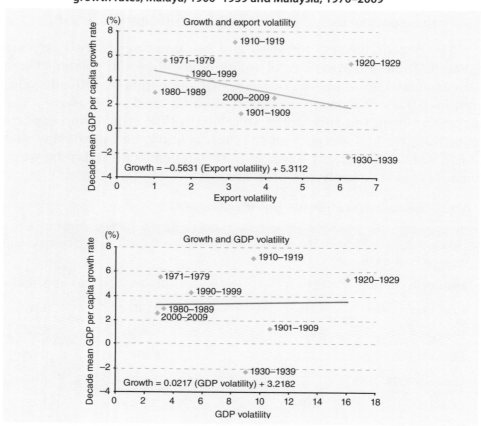

Cross-country Studies – Dawe's Model

An alternative approach for assessing the effects of volatility on growth is to use estimated coefficients derived from cross-country studies—namely, those of Dawe (1996), and Ramey and Ramey (1995).

By applying Dawe's coefficient on export volatility to Malaya's and Malaysia's V_Y, it is possible to estimate how much real GDP per capita growth was depressed by the volatility of exports. Based on Dawe's coefficient on volatility (–0.325), Table 5.2 reports predicted mean GDP growth rates in pre-1940 Malaya and post-1970 Malaysia had exports been more stable.

Table 5.2 **Cross-country model estimates of real GDP growth and volatility**

	Dawe's model	Ramey and Ramey's model
Coefficient on volatility	–0.325	–0.154
Sample mean volatility	2.04%	5.25%
Malaya 1900–1939		
Mean growth 1901–1939*	2.93%	2.93%
Volatility*	5.54%	11.83%
Growth with zero volatility	4.73%	4.75%
Growth with mean volatility	4.07%	3.95%
Malaysia 1970–2009		
Mean growth 1971–2009*	3.82%	3.82%
Volatility*	2.36%	3.80%
Growth with zero volatility	4.59%	4.41%
Growth with mean volatility	3.93%	3.60%

* Observed values.
Note:
Volatility in the Dawe model is given by $\bar{V}_Y$. Volatility in the Ramey/Ramey model is the standard deviation of GDP per capita growth.

Exports were far less volatile in Malaysia post-1970—V_Y = 2.36 per cent compared with V_Y = 5.54 per cent in the earlier period—so volatility would be expected to have had a less severe effect on growth. According to Dawe's model, in the complete absence of export volatility, mean growth in Malaya over the period 1901–1939 would have been 4.73 per cent, or 1.8 percentage points higher than actual. For Malaysia between 1971 and 2009, mean growth in the absence of volatility would have been 4.59 per cent, or 0.77 percentage points higher than actual.

The counter-factual of zero volatility is obviously unreasonable—there would inevitably have been some degree of export volatility. In the row labelled 'Growth with mean volatility' in Table 5.2, an estimate is given of mean growth had Malaya's and Malaysia's export volatility been equal to the country-mean values of export volatility in Dawe's sample (cross-country mean $\bar{V}_Y$ = 2.04 per cent). In this case, mean growth would have been 4.07 per cent over the period 1901–1939 (a gain of 1.14 percentage points compared to the actual value of 2.93 per cent), and 3.93 per cent over the period 1971–2009 (compared to the actual value of 3.82 per cent). The post-1970 effect is less marked because Malaysia's export volatility in this period (2.36 per cent) was only marginally above the mean value from Dawe's sample (2.04 per cent). According to Dawe's model, therefore, export volatility in the colonial period had a substantial negative impact on growth.

Cross-country Studies – Ramey and Ramey's Model

In their simplest model, Ramey and Ramey (1995) regressed mean GDP per capita growth across countries on its standard deviation. They obtained a statistically significant coefficient of –0.154, with a standard error of 0.067.

The standard deviation of Malaya's real GDP per capita growth over the period 1901–1939 was 11.83 per cent, but was substantially lower in the later period at 3.80 per cent (Table 5.2). Had GDP per capita been growing at its trend rate each year, its standard deviation would have been zero. According to Ramey and Ramey's simplest model, Malaya's mean growth over the earlier period was reduced by 1.82 per cent (4.75 minus 2.93 per cent), very close to the amount implied by Dawe's model. The counter-factual of zero GDP volatility is again unlikely. Had Malaya's growth been as erratic as the average value recorded across countries in Ramey and Ramey's sample (5.25 per cent), the average growth rate would have been 3.95 per cent, around 1 percentage point higher than the actual rate. The international evidence thus suggests that mean GDP per capita growth in Malaya would have been between 1 and 2 percentage points higher had the country's exports been less volatile.

Over the post-1970 period, GDP volatility reduced growth by only 0.58 percentage points (4.41 minus 3.82 per cent, Table 5.2). The standard deviation of Malaysia's growth rate (3.80 per cent) was lower than the mean volatility over the countries in Ramey and Ramey's sample (5.25 per cent). Had Malaysian growth been as volatile as that of the average country, growth would have been a little lower (3.60 per cent) than that actually experienced (3.82 per cent).

Concluding Observations

The implications of the international cross-country studies, and especially that of Dawe, may be compared with those from the decade-average results reported above. Malaya's average annual growth in GDP per capita over the period 1900–1939 was 2.93 per cent, while the predicted growth rate for this period from the decade-average regression is a little lower at 2.25 per cent.

Given the point estimates from the decade-average regression, average annual growth in GDP per capita would have been 5.31 per cent with zero export volatility, and 4.16 per cent had volatility in Malaya been equal to the cross-country mean of Dawe's sample (2.04

per cent). Assuming a more typical level of export volatility, Dawe's international study predicts a mean growth rate of 4.07 per cent, while the decade-average regressions predict a mean growth rate of 4.16 per cent. The two approaches thus arrive at very similar conclusions.

Export volatility and erratic economic growth were more conspicuous in the first four decades of the 20th century and could, therefore, be expected to have had a depressing effect on Malaya's average growth performance. Had export volatility been lower and, as a consequence, had annual GDP growth been less erratic, Malaya's growth performance would have been far stronger. Export volatility and uneven growth were much reduced in the four decades after 1970, and economic growth could be expected to have been stronger as a result.

Sources of Growth

Interest in the factors that underpin the wealth of nations is as old as the discipline of economic inquiry itself. Adam Smith, the father of modern economics, stressed the importance of capital accumulation and increasing specialisation in creating the foundations of wealth.

While these ideas and those of other classical economists remain relevant, more contemporary perspectives on economic growth stress the importance of policy; trade and investment; education and health; macroeconomic management and institutions (property rights and economic governance); and technological change in explaining growth. Factors such as location, access to markets or to major trading routes, and resource endowments (including the resource curse) also feature in many explanations. And conditional on other relevant determining factors, a tendency has been observed for poorer countries to grow more quickly than those that are wealthier—the conditional convergence hypothesis.

An expansive empirical literature has emerged that examines economic growth.[40] One strand applies modern econometric methods

---

40 Since the early 1990s, a large number of growth accounting studies, especially for the newly industrialised economies of East Asia, have accumulated (Young, 1992, 1995; World Bank, 1993; Kim and Lau, 1994; Krugman, 1994; Bosworth et al., 1995; Bosworth, 1997; Ghesquiere, 2007; Eichengreen, et al. 2012). However, the results of these studies have been inconclusive and highly variable. They tend to be sensitive to the specifications of each individual study, which makes them difficult to interpret and use in understanding East Asia's economic growth. It is even more difficult to derive policy implications from the results (Felipe, 1998).

to large panel data sets to test theoretical ideas, and to explain the broad determinants of growth across countries and time (for example, Mankiw, Romer and Weil, 1992). Another strand looks at growth within countries, and seeks to *account* for the sources of that growth (for example, Bosworth and Collins, 2003). These latter growth accounting exercises are more concerned with measurement than explanation.

Growth accounting begins with the idea that the flow of aggregate output in an economy is related to the flows of services provided by capital and labour inputs. How much output is produced for a set level of inputs is determined by the level of technology in the economy. More sophisticated variants disaggregate the inputs into different types of physical capital and human capital as well as labour services. As capital and labour services expand, or the level of technology advances, output grows. This basic idea is captured in the relationship:

Growth of aggregate output = Growth of capital × Weight of capital + Growth of labour × Weight of labour + Growth of total factor productivity

Under certain technical conditions, it can be shown that the weights of capital and labour equate to their shares in national income. The sources of growth framework is outlined in Box 5.2.

The application of this growth accounting relationship proceeds by putting in observed values for output growth on the left hand side and those for growth of capital and labour on the right hand side, weighted by their allocated value shares in national income. The growth of total factor productivity is then obtained as the residual difference between aggregate output growth and the weighted growth of factor inputs. A growth accounting exercise for colonial Malaya is set out below.

The capital stock data used here were calculated using the *perpetual inventory method* (Albers, 2002), drawing on estimates of capital expenditure derived from the new series of investment data provided by this study. Unfortunately, there were no independent observations for employment over the years 1900–1939. Population was used as a proxy. This proxy is valid in circumstances in which the share of employment in the total population is stable, a condition that is more likely to be satisfied over longer than shorter intervals of time. Measurement errors in calculating the capital stock, in approximating employment and the value shares of capital and labour in national

Box
5.2 **Sources of growth analysis**

Early efforts to quantify the contribution of each of the proximate causes of increased output to economic growth—capital accumulation, labour accumulation and productivity gains—were pioneered by Nobel laureate Robert Solow (1957). The accounting framework derived from his ideas seeks to measure the proportions of economic growth that can be attributed to growth of the capital stock, growth of the labour force and changes in overall productivity.

The growth accounting, or sources of growth, analysis starts with a standard production function relating the contribution of labour and capital to aggregate production, and then adds a term to capture total factor productivity (TFP). TFP measures the contribution to production of efficiency, technology and other influences on productivity such as governance, institutions and policies. In practice, what is termed TFP is a combination of data errors and omissions of other factors that should be included in the growth equation as well as efficiency gains and technological change (Perkins et al., 2013).

This production function is then converted into a form that can be used to measure the contribution of changes in each term—expansion of the labour force, additions to the capital stock and growth in TFP—to overall growth as follows:

$$g_Y = (W_K \times g_K) + (W_L \times g_L) + a$$

where g_Y stands for growth of total income or GDP; that is, g_Y is the rate of aggregate economic growth. Similarly, g_K and g_L are the growth rates of the capital stock (K) and the labour force (L) respectively. W_L and W_K represent, respectively, the shares in total income of wages and of returns on capital. The final term, a, is the rate of change in TFP. It shows how the growth in output depends on the growth in inputs (K and L) and the growth in the productivity of those inputs (a).

income will have been carried over into the estimates of total factor productivity growth reported below.

Looking at the entire 4-decade period of 1900–1939, the growth accounting exercise suggests that, of the annual average 5.5 per cent exponential GDP growth in real terms, growth of the capital stock accounted for 1.7 percentage points, and growth of employment another 1.8 percentage points, implying total factor productivity (TFP) growth of 2.0 percentage points (Table 5.3). The corresponding estimates for the first half of the period, from 1900–1919, are that growth of the capital stock accounted for 2.6 percentage points, and labour for 1.9 percentage points of GDP growth, which averaged 7.2 per cent anually over this period. This implies TFP growth of 2.6 percentage points.

The analogous estimates for the period 1920–1939, in which growth rates were lower, suggest markedly reduced capital investment and TFP growth.

Table 5.3 **Sources of economic growth (per cent), Malaya, 1900–1939**

Total output growth	1900–1919	1920–1939	1900–1939
Real GDP exponential growth	7.2	4.3	5.5
Contribution of:			
Physical capital	2.6	0.8	1.7
Labour	1.9	1.6	1.8
Total factor productivity	2.6	1.8	2.0

These calculations point to the possibility of gains in TFP during the colonial period. If these estimates prove to be robust, establishing the sources of productivity advance would require further in-depth investigation.

Figure 5.13 presents TFP calculations for successive 10-year intervals, starting in 1909 (the first nine years' data are used to seed the calculation) and ending in 1939. TFP growth is shown alongside the contributions of the growth of capital and labour, and total GDP growth. These calculations show that the rolling 10-year averages of capital and labour are considerably smoother than GDP growth itself, and that the residual TFP growth estimates move more or less in step

Figure 5.13 **GDP growth, capital, labour and total factor productivity, 10-year moving averages at constant 1914 prices, Malaya, 1909–1939**

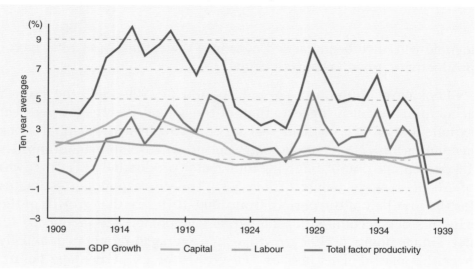

with the variations in growth. This suggests that the estimates of TFP growth may be susceptible to the same factors that generate volatility in the fortunes of exporting industries, particularly rubber. It is also noteworthy that far lower year-to-year volatility is observed in relation to the measurement of capital stock as compared to investment rates (Figure 5.9). The measurement of capital stock involves accumulating investment flows over long periods, and so will have averaged out any high frequency movements occurring over shorter intervals.

A number of caveats should be mentioned regarding the use of growth accounting methods to measure TFP. Of these, the most important is the likely presence of unknown and possibly large measurement errors which are then conflated with the TFP estimates. Both labour and capital measures should reflect the inputs actually employed in production. One possible source of measurement error in the study's estimates arises from the use of population growth as a proxy for employment growth. This is because changes in labour force participation and actual employment, both of which affect the amount of labour used in production, will not have been captured. The measurement of capital employed used here is also open to error, as it has not taken account of variations in capital utilisation. Equipment and machinery would very likely have lain idle periodically due to recession and declining export demand, especially that used in the production of rubber and tin. So the growth rates of labour and capital *used in production* are likely to have been different from those used in the growth accounting exercise.

A deeper existential question also exists concerning the theoretical validity of the aggregate production function relationship on which growth accounting exercises are based. The argument is that the growth accounting relationship *works* only because it is anchored in the national income accounting identity that relates GDP to the sum of factor incomes. From this perspective, the residual also captures the weighted growth of wages and profits.

Perhaps the most telling criticism of growth accounting exercises is that they reveal little about the causes of growth. Say, for example, it is discovered that growth of capital and TFP account for the bulk of GDP growth in a country. One possible explanation is that an investment push has supported this growth in TFP. It could also be the case that a positive productivity shock has lifted expected profits and encouraged investment in capital. Alternatively, a third common factor, such as an improvement in the quality of institutions could have stimulated both capital investment and productivity advances.

While a growth accounting exercise might reveal the proximate *sources* of growth, it cannot without further inquiry identify the primary *causes* of growth. As Rodrik (2008) has observed, the *discovery* that East Asia's growth miracle was driven by the accumulation of inputs (capital and labour) rather than by gains in productivity deflects attention from the real issue of how these countries were able to raise their savings and investment rates (in both built and human capital) over a sustained period. Rodrik (2014, pp. 54) also highlighted the role of government in Malaysia's post-independence growth record—Malaysia (and Thailand) 'were particularly well endowed with natural resources and would have remained resource-based economies had their governments not emphasized industrialization.'

Studies on productivity growth in East Asia have nevertheless yielded some interesting results. The intense debate about the sources of growth has directed researchers to learn more about growth processes. It has also made countries more conscious of the importance of the role of productivity in the process of economic growth. An example is Malaysia, which since the mid-1990s, has been focusing on enhancing innovation and productivity to transform itself from being an input-driven economy to a knowledge-based one. However, productivity levels are still wanting, and the economy remains highly dependent on traditional factor inputs of labour and capital.

*   *   *

The final chapter brings together the main strands of the statistical and econometric analyses made in Chapters 4 and 5 to draw some conclusions about the legacy of British colonial economic management. It contrasts this with the outcome of 40 years of economic performance in the post-independence era.

CHAPTER 6

Colonial commerce in a Malayan town in the early 20th century

From Colonial Control to National Economic Management

This study of the Malayan economy, conducted with the objective of filling the gap in the existing historical series, has generated a new series of GDP estimates for the first 40 years of the 20th century. With these new estimates, students of Malaysia's economic history will be able to form a better understanding of the country's performance during this period, and of the factors which contributed to what was, by any standards, seemingly impressive GDP growth, albeit with the cyclical shocks that characterized those years.

The study has also demonstrated the use of an innovative methodological approach to estimating GDP from very limited data. There were many challenges involved in aggregating data of variable quality from the geographical areas of Malaya under the differing administrations of the Straits Settlements, the Federated Malay States and the Unfederated Malay States. Some discussion of the methods used and the treatment of data have been included as a reference for researchers interested in this process of developing historical GDP estimates (Chapter 3). The new series enables fresh analyses to be made of long-term trends in Malaya's economic development.

The results of the GDP estimation have been situated in the context of the geo-political, economic and socio-demographic circumstances of that time, and some perspectives and conclusions about Malaya's economic development have been provided. The study has emphasised the intense volatility and highly erratic growth of the country's major exports during the study period, and the depressing effect this had on its average growth performance. Export volatility and uneven growth were much reduced in the four decades after 1970, and economic growth could be expected to have been stronger as a result.

This final chapter provides a broad macro assessment of growth and consumption trends over the period 1900–1939 under *laissez-faire* colonialism, and compares this with the country's performance under national economic management during the period from 1970 to 2009. The year 1970 is taken as the starting point for the comparison because the period between independence in 1957 and 1969 was essentially a transitional one in which the new government maintained the existing *laissez-faire* approach to a large extent. It was only after the racial riots of 1969, which may be understood in part as a response to the failures of *laissez-faire*, that a comprehensive interventionist approach was adopted towards economic management.

Forty Years of Roller-coaster Economic Growth

The first four decades of the 20th century were highly significant for the development of the Malayan economy and were characterized by trade openness, with exports of goods and services accounting on average for 60 per cent of nominal GDP. There was a manifold increase in the real value of exports, from just Straits$85 million in 1900 to Straits$1.16 billion in 1937, while real GDP increased over the same period from Straits$143 million to Straits$1.4 billion, reflecting the close association between the two.

One major conclusion of the study concerns the influential role of exports in determining GDP growth, and within exports, the role of rubber and tin as the two main drivers of the economy. Given the dominance of these two commodities in GDP growth, any shocks affecting them such as a fall in prices, would be expected to have indirect ripple effects on other sectors of the economy, and on the revenue-earning and spending capacity of the government. This is in addition to the direct impacts on wages and incomes in the rubber and tin sectors themselves. The major oscillations in the international prices of rubber and tin, and their impact on Malaya's export earnings, government revenues and the incomes of producers represent a classic illustration of commodity instability.

Comparison of Malaya's experience with that of several international and regional countries has shown that it was the most dependent on trade in terms of the share of exports in GDP (Chapter 4). The major implication for Malaya's economy of this dependence on only two primary commodities with highly changeable prices was the volatility and instability reflected in the extreme fluctuations of GDP over the 40-year period. While all the comparator countries also experienced economic volatility, the Malayan economy had the widest range of economic swings and instability. The annual growth rate of GDP in Malaya ranged from a peak of 46.2 per cent in 1925 to a trough of −30.7 per cent in 1931, a swing of 77 percentage points. Similarly excessive volatility can be observed in the prices of the country's major exports. In a comparison of several raw materials, rubber was found to be the most susceptible to price fluctuations during the period 1921–1928 (Bauer, 1961). Average annual variations in rubber prices were 47 per cent, while the lowest price as a share of the highest price was just 3 per cent (Jomo, 1986).

Another conclusion relating to Malaya's trade dependence that emerges from this study is the considerable influence of the US market and, to a lesser extent, that of the UK on the pattern of fluctuations in the country's annual GDP. Given that the US was the main destination of Malaya's rubber and tin, any economic boom or slowdown in the US economy seriously affected the demand for these commodities, resulting in tremendous volatility in the Malayan economy.

The decomposition analysis of aggregate GDP growth also highlighted the significant role of the export sector (Chapter 4). Changes in export and import volumes accounted for the bulk of growth, and also drove much of its volatility. Growth of the domestic expenditure components of GDP—private consumption, government spending and investment—played a lesser role. This analysis suggests that the economy of Malaya rode a commodity roller-coaster between 1900 and 1939. Three large exogenous shocks to the economy— World War I (1914–1918), the Roaring Twenties (1920–1929), and the Great Depression (1929–1932)—were the main underlying causes of economic booms and busts. Malaya's commodity-dependent economy was thus highly vulnerable to the vicissitudes in the demand for, and international prices of, rubber and tin.

Colonial Support for British Business

European, and predominantly British, investments increased substantially in the Malay Peninsula over the course of the late 19th century and during the first few decades of the 20th century. The bulk of these investments were in the mining and plantation sectors, and were intended to exploit the comparative advantages of the Peninsula—its tropical climate, fertile soils and proximity to major maritime routes. By 1931, British firms accounted for more than two thirds of total tin production, having displaced the earlier dominance of Chinese owners. Similarly in the case of rubber, European plantation companies, again largely British, were the dominant players. This was due to their ability to mobilise large amounts of capital through joint stock companies on the London stock market. These foreign-owned businesses reaped huge profits and dividends, which, it seems safe to assume, were mostly repatriated to their foreign shareholders, and only to a lesser extent were reinvested in Malaya.

Great emphasis was placed by the colonial authorities on the maintenance of a market-driven or *laissez-faire* economic system, with the objective of facilitating the exploitation of tin and rubber for profit by British businesses. The private sector, including plantation and mining companies, agency houses, banks and middlemen, were given free reign to operate and maximise profits. The colonial administration protected and promoted the interests of the commodity companies by providing a supportive legislative and institutional environment. Other forms of government support included the provision of choice land for plantations with minimal restrictions and at nominal prices, low export duties and taxes, and the subsidisation of the immigration of low-cost labour from India. Local manufacturing was embryonic at this time and there was little downstream processing of rubber or tin. There was a heavy reliance on imports, mainly from the UK, to meet consumer needs.

This pattern of asset accumulation by the UK and its private sector was similar to the practice in other colonies. By the eve of World War I, the UK presided over the world's pre-eminent colonial empire, owning foreign assets equivalent to nearly two years of its own national income. By the turn of the 20th century, capital invested abroad was yielding around 5 per cent a year in dividends, so the UK's national income was around 10 per cent higher than its domestic product (Piketty, 2014).

As a result of its large net positive position in foreign assets, the UK was able to run structural trade deficits in the late 19th and early 20th centuries. It received considerably more in goods and services from the rest of the world than it exported. But it had a large surplus on its income account due to remittances, which resulted in an overall surplus that then further strengthened its net foreign investment position. This strongly positive balance of payments position enabled the UK to increase its holdings of foreign assets year after year. In contrast, for Malaya and other colonies in which capital assets were mainly owned by foreigners, it was possible to have a high domestic product but a much lower national income, once profits and rents flowing abroad were deducted from the total. As long as the UK remained the colonial power with political and military control, it was able to manage the inequality that inevitably arose in this situation. However, in the wake of the cumulative shocks of World War I and the Great Depression, and later, World War II and decolonisation, the UK's foreign assets dwindled considerably (Piketty, 2014).

Inequality and Unbalanced Development

One consequence of such *laissez-faire* practices was uneven development, with economic growth and prosperity concentrated in the west coast states of the Peninsula where most of the tin mines and rubber plantations were located. These states had better physical and social infrastructure, established to serve the commercial interests of the colonial government and the export-oriented private sector, as well as a significant population base. Even within the Federated Malay States, there were disparities between the socio-economic development of Perak and Selangor, and that of Pahang and Negri Sembilan. In the east coast states, where the predominantly Malay population were mainly engaged in low-productivity subsistence agriculture and fishing, development lagged markedly.

Another consequence of *laissez-faire* was the sharp inequalities that developed in relation to ownership and control of the economy (Puthucheary, 1960; Hirschman, 1988; Curtis, 2003).[41] At the time of independence and up to 1970, foreigners still owned over 60 per cent of the share capital in limited companies overall, with 75 per cent in the agricultural sector and 73 per cent in the mining sector. Revenues from these two sectors still accounted for the bulk of export earnings (Economic Planning Unit-Malaysia, 1974). This situation reflected the legacy of British colonial economic policy which sought to protect and preserve its long-established business interests in the newly emerging nation state of Malaysia.

Despite the dearth of data on income inequality during the pre-World War II period, the mechanisms that promoted the interests of some groups at the expense of others can be clearly identified. The big commercial agency houses (including Guthrie and Company, Edward Boustead and Co., Harrisons and Crosfield, Sime Darby, and Barlow and Co.), supported by the joint stock companies and with

---

41 By 1950, 70 per cent of the acreage of rubber estates was owned by European (primarily British) companies, compared to 29 per cent Asian ownership (Curtis, 2003).

major financial backing from London and the British banks (some with branches in Malaya), enjoyed privileged access to land, facilitated by the colonial administration. This system worked particularly well for the agency houses and other independent companies. Given their capital, technology and enterprise, and the minimal deductions for taxation, there was a strong economic rationale for them to maximise their profits.

The inevitably imbalanced nature of colonial economic development in Malaya is highlighted by the large differences in consumption levels among different groups. Six different consumption standards were utilised in this study to show the different expenditure patterns as part of the methodology for estimating private consumption expenditure. These were Malay labour, Chinese labour, Indian labour, Asiatic clerical, Eurasian clerical and European (Chapter 3). These standards reflected differences in consumption levels and expenditure patterns among ethnic and occupational groups, and between rural and urban areas.

Figure 6.1 shows the share of Malaya's population assigned to each of these six standards in 1931 as well as the ratio of per capita expenditure in each standard relative to the overall weighted per capita expenditure. Expenditure here relates only to that captured through the indirect estimation approach described in detail in Chapter 3, which should not significantly affect comparisons of differentials.

Figure 6.1 **Shares of population by consumption standards at constant 1914 prices and inequalities in expenditure, Malaya, 1931**

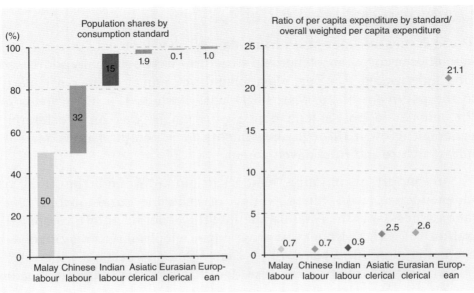

The inequality in consumption standards is striking. For those persons spending according to the European consumption standard, comprising just 1 per cent of the population, expenditure levels were more than 21 times higher than the overall average. Conversely, for the overwhelming majority of the population living according to the Malay, Chinese and Indian labour standards, collectively comprising 97 per cent of the population, expenditure was 24 per cent below the weighted average for all groups combined. This broad pattern of inequality in consumption remained much the same throughout the first four decades of the 20th century.

Investment growth rates in real terms—averaging less than 10 per cent per annum—were also very low, as was government expenditure, suggesting that little of the production surplus was being reinvested in the domestic economy. Wages of workers in rubber plantations and tin mines were also relatively low, and while they were responsive to declines in prices, they were more sticky when commodity prices were on the upswing.

It was clear that the colonial government had no strategic vision for economic transformation or for the social development of the local population. The overriding principle of colonial policy was rather to maximise profits from the rubber and tin industries, primarily for the benefit of British businesses. Colonial economic development thus created stark imbalances and inequalities.

Development Disparities

These issues of uneven and unbalanced development, poverty and inequities in corporate ownership structures were eventually addressed after independence as part of national development plans, particularly in the aftermath of the May 1969 racial clashes. The initial focus of the immediate post-independence government was on accelerating economic growth through investments in agricultural development, infrastructure and rural development.

An important initiative embarked upon around the time of independence, with the objective of reducing rural poverty and landlessness, was the establishment of the Federal Land Development Authority (FELDA). Under this programme, which increasingly involved the cultivation of oil palm rather than rubber as originally intended, poor landless farmers were resettled in large government schemes throughout the country. The land, which was cleared at government expense, was initially leased to rural families, but with an option for purchase using the proceeds of the produce. Settlers were provided with employment and incomes while the trees were maturing and until they became income-generating. The FELDA programme is widely seen as a highly successful land reform model which contributed over time to significant reductions in rural poverty and the creation of a rural middle class. It did face challenges in later years, however, as many of the more educated children of the early settlers were no longer interested in living in rural areas or working on their parents' farm holdings, creating a labour shortage that has since been filled by migrant workers.

Tackling the structural weakness of the country's open economy—of over-dependence on its two primary commodity exports—became a major policy imperative after independence in order to help address widespread poverty among the predominantly rural population. Between 1957 and 1970, the diversification of production and income away from rubber and tin was the major strategic policy thrust, especially given the continuing effects of market uncertainty and commodity price volatility. The rise of synthetic rubber created further challenges. When natural rubber prices increased sharply, industrial users abroad were able to substitute synthetic for natural rubber, thereby reducing demand for Malayan/Malaysian rubber. Fluctuating prices, problems of market structure and international politics placed natural rubber at a considerable disadvantage (Barlow, 1978). These factors underlined the need not only to reduce costs and improve quality, but also pointed to the importance of diversification of the economy.

Much was achieved during this immediate post-independence period in terms of growth, the expansion of infrastructure across the country and rural development, and there were also some increases in living standards. Less, however, was achieved in terms of overall poverty reduction, employment creation and addressing the economic imbalances among Malaysia's people, states and regions. Most large companies were still foreign-owned, while small urban businesses were predominantly Chinese and the Malays were overwhelmingly engaged in farming. The May 1969 racial conflict, which arose in part out of dissatisfaction with these disparities, then led to a radical shift in the direction of national development policy.

The New Economic Policy (NEP)—announced in 1971 with the aim of creating national unity—had two fundamental goals: ending poverty among all communities, and restructuring Malaysian society so as to remove the association of ethnicity with occupation and location. The broader objective was growth with equity, involving aggressive affirmative action policies and programmes that have been directly or indirectly maintained ever since within national development planning (Jomo, 1990b).

The NEP reflected a more interventionist government concerned with rectifying the inequalities created during the colonial era, and it heralded a sharp break from the *laissez-faire* approach of the past. One primary aim was to reduce foreign ownership of corporate capital from 70 per cent in 1970 to 30 per cent by 1990. Foreign companies trading in Malaysia's natural resources were restructured through equity buyouts by public-sector enterprises and were placed initially under government control and management.[42] Resource revenues were then used by the government to redistribute income and reduce absolute poverty through multiple economic and social pathways. Government expenditure as a share of GDP grew so sharply that it imposed a strain on its financial resources.

Dependence on a limited number of primary commodities with highly volatile prices had been recognised as being an unsustainable economic strategy, especially since tin is a non-renewable resource and natural rubber is substitutable (Lim, 2011). The focus of the first stage of economic diversification was thus the diversification of agriculture away from rubber to oil palm and other crops, as well as the export of timber. This process had already started in the 1960s, and had been a thrust of both the Second Five-year Federation of Malaya Plan, 1961–1965 (Federation of Malaya, 1961) and the First Malaysia Plan, 1966–1970 (Economic Planning Unit-Malaysia, 1966). During the second stage, which began in the 1970s and gathered pace in the 1980s, there was further diversification away from the primary sectors to the secondary sectors, especially labour-intensive manufacturing and later heavy industries as well (Zainal Aznam Yusof and Bhattasali, 2008).[43]

---

42 By 1990, foreign ownership of share capital had been reduced to just 25 per cent of the total, compared to 67 per cent in 1970 (Zainal Aznam Yusof, 2011).

43 During the decades of very rapid economic growth of the 1970s and 1980s, strong government intervention had also helped to propel rapid export-led industrialisation in South Korea, Taiwan and Singapore (Perkins, 2013).

The commercial planting of oil palm had begun in the 1920s, but it was not until after World War II that the area under cultivation increased greatly and the crop became a major export earner. Rubber and tin have remained significant commodity exports, but in terms of value they have been greatly eclipsed by palm oil (Figure 6.2).[44] Increasingly, however, hydrocarbons—both oil and gas—have dominated Malaysia's earnings from natural resource exports and have contributed substantially to government development expenditure. Between 1990 and 2015, natural resources (renewables and non-renewables) accounted for some 28 per cent of the country's export revenues, albeit with considerable year-to-year variations.

Figure 6.2 Trends in exports of rubber, tin and palm oil, Malaysia, 1964–2014

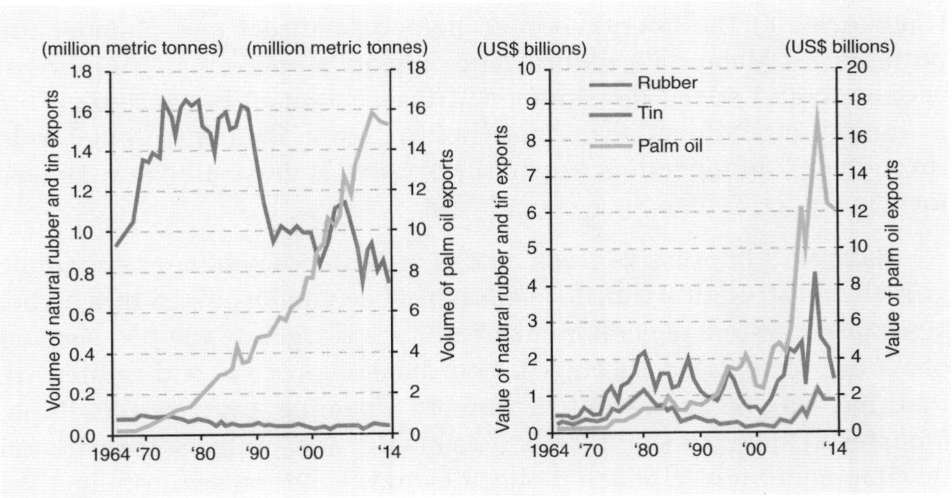

Source of data:
*United Nations Statistics Division, UN Comtrade website https://*comtrade.un.org/data/ accessed 28 June 2016.

Industrial development, first for import substitution and later for exports, was another route promoted by the Malaysian government to generate wage employment and reduce absolute poverty. Free Trade Zones were established in which industrial land was made available at low prices together with fiscal incentives, and this proved to be an effective means of encouraging foreign and local companies to begin manufacturing activities in the country. These Free Trade Zones were situated relatively close to local labour supply as well as to port

---

44 Malaysia's world ranking in rubber exports was first in 1965 and 1990, and fourth in 2014; in tin exports, it was first in 1965 and 1990, and second in 2014; in palm oil, it was first in 1965 and 1990, and second in 2014.

facilities. This industrial development strategy was also aimed at the development of industrial skills much needed for a new nation. The scale of structural transformation of the economy was such that by 1987 the manufacturing sector had became the country's main economic driver, overtaking the agricultural sector in terms of its contribution to GDP (Zainal Aznam Yusof, 2011).

Broad-based development post-independence, and in particular after 1970, was facilitated by an approach to development planning that was no longer primarily concerned only with economic growth, but now also encompassed social dimensions such as distribution as well as emerging environmental concerns. A sequence of 11 five-year national development plans and four Outline Perspective Plans—which provide longer-term perspectives on the intended development trajectories of the country—have helped to direct and channel the potential of Malaysia's natural and human resources in support of economic and social development (Hassan Osman Rani, 2007). This evolution of national economic policy, from British colonial rule through post-independence up to the present, is illustrated in summary form in Figure 6.3.

Malaysia's impressive track record of post-independence economic growth and structural transformation has been underpinned by a highly centralised system of economic governance. Target-driven policies and plans are formulated through a coordinated process and framework that has as its centre the Economic Planning Unit in the Prime Minister's Office. This unit is responsible for, and controls, the national development budget, which it allocates to the federal sector ministries and a network of State Economic Planning Units and State Economic Development Corporations which handle project implementation.

Malaysia's relatively high-quality public administration has supported the effective implementation of many of the programmes set out in the five-year development plans. Well-executed and well-resourced programmes have in turn helped to transform Malaysia's economic and social development standing. From being a low-income agrarian economy dependent on a few primary commodities, it has become a modern diversified one, on the verge of achieving high-income status. As part of this process, Malaysia has established several internationally-renowned institutions to provide support for sectoral research and development. These have focused on improving the standard of the export products developed in the country's

Figure 6.3 Evolution of Malaysia's economic policy

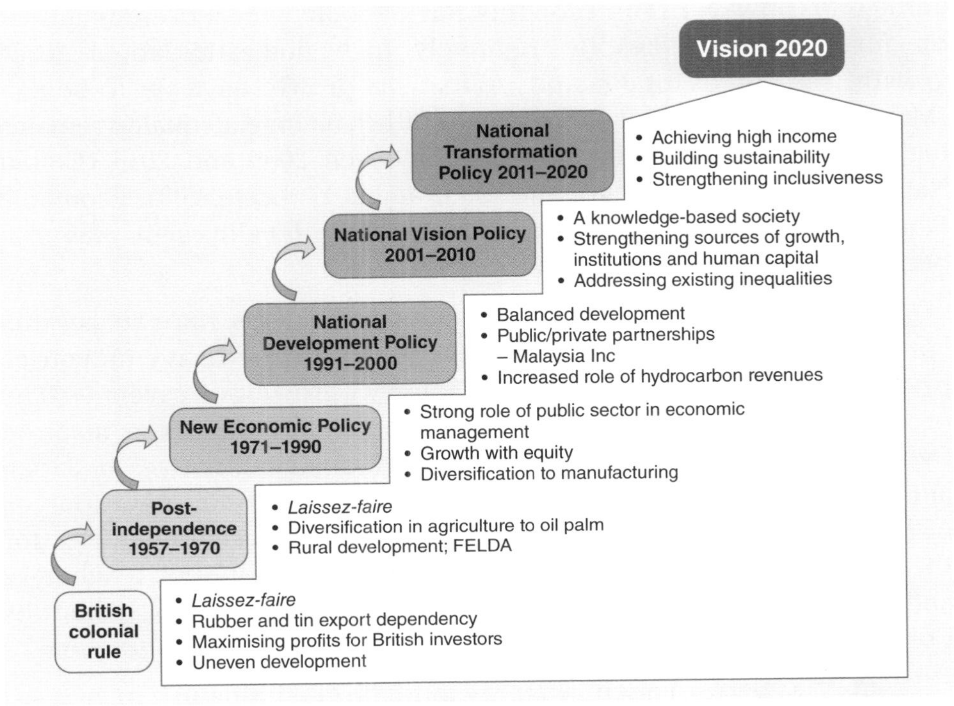

natural resource-based industries and, more recently, on advancing technological development in the electronics sector.[45]

Foreign direct investment, especially from the US and Japan, has continued to play an important role in the country's economic development (Tan, 2014). Domestic players have also become increasingly significant (Jomo and Tan, 2011). Substantial social investments in health, and especially in education, have helped to build the human capital necessary to support economic growth. With national control over economic management came a greater moral consciousness and a long-term vision for the creation of a more unified, socially just and cohesive nation, underpinned by a system of parliamentary democracy based on that of the British.

---

45 These include the Palm Oil Research Institute of Malaysia (PORIM); the Malaysia Agricultural Research and Development Institute (MARDI); the Forest Research Institute of Malaysia (FRIM); and the Standards and Industrial Research Institute of Malaysia (SIRIM). Some of these institutes have also established commercial arms to promote Malaysia's exports. Moreover, the Federal Industrial Development Authority (FIDA), renamed the Malaysian Industrial Development Authority (MIDA) in 1987, was set up to coordinate and promote industrial activities and attract foreign direct investment (Tan and Mohamed Ariff, 2001). In the electronics sector, the Malaysian Institute of Microelectronic Systems (MIMOS) was established in 1985 to assist local firms in design and technological development.

These impressive achievements have not been without cost and ambiguity, however. The economy has become ever more dependent on foreign labour despite relatively high domestic labour force growth. Targets for total factor productivity growth have yet to be met (Mahadevan, 2007; Zainal Aznam Yusof, 2011). Income inequality remains high, albeit with some improvement between 2009 and 2014 (United Nations Development Programme, 2007 and 2014; Leete, 2007; Economic Planning Unit-Malaysia, 2015), and regional development has not benefited all states equally.

Moreover, not all of the major planning initiatives were successful. For example, the early 1980s saw the launch of the heavy industries programme, initially financed by the country's growing oil revenues. The programme was influenced by the Look East Policy which was inspired by the economic successes of the heavy industry initiatives of Japan and South Korea. The primary rationale was to develop new sources of economic growth and reduce dependence on foreign countries for the supply of industrial raw materials, intermediate inputs, machinery and capital goods. The government established the Heavy Industries Corporation of Malaysia (HICOM) in 1981 to manage the programme.

HICOM's performance was, by and large, uninspiring. Several projects under this programme had high production costs and suffered heavy financial losses due to sluggish demand and an inability to compete in international markets (Economic Planning Unit-Malaysia, 1989; Mohamed Ariff, 1991). As the fiscal costs and strains on Malaysia's financial system mounted, the government scaled back the promotion of heavy industries. The programme did not lead to the establishment of internationally competitive industries as had been expected.

Changing Demographics

This narrative of Malaya's economy would be incomplete if it did not touch on the critical role played by international labour migration in the Peninsula's economic development. The mining and plantation industries would have faced severe labour shortages and would not have developed as they did without the inputs and skills of foreign workers. The total population of all the Peninsula's states at the turn of the century was just 1.7 million. Natural increase, or the difference between births and deaths, was negligible. Net inflows of labour migrants to the west coast states accounted for almost all of the Peninsula's rapid population growth in these decades (Chapter 2).

Inflows of overseas labour from a number of sources, especially from China and India, changed the Peninsula's ethnic composition. [46] Malaysia's multi-ethnic, multi-cultural and multi-lingual character stems to a large extent from this period of British colonial rule. Although there had been a history of earlier migration of Malays, Chinese and Indians to the Malay Peninsula over centuries, labour migration—especially from southern China and southern India where there was abundant supply—peaked during the first four decades of the 20th century. The flows slowed due to the Great Depression and, somewhat later, as a result of a tightening of immigration regulations.

The share of Malays in the population (including those born in the Dutch East Indies), which was close to two-thirds in 1901, had fallen to slightly less than half by 1931 and remained at this level until independence. The share of the Chinese, which had remained at around 29 per cent between 1901 and 1921, rose markedly to reach 38 per cent by 1947. The Indian share increased to 15 per cent in 1921, but subsequently declined to 11 per cent in 1947. Fast-forwarding to the middle of the second decade of the 21st century, the population of Peninsular Malaysia remains ethnically mixed, although the shares have changed significantly. The Malay share has increased the most, to more than 60 per cent of the total population due to higher fertility rates, while the shares of the Chinese and Indians have decreased and are likely to decline further as a result of their relatively lower fertility rates. The changing demographic profile of the Peninsula's population will continue to have important political and social implications.

Similarities and Divergences in Historical and Contemporary GDP

Similarities in Per Capita GDP Growth

Real per capita GDP in the states of the Malay Peninsula was, by 1939, over three times larger than it had been in 1900. This equates to a real per capita exponential growth rate of 2.9 per cent which, taken at face value, is an impressive achievement (Figure 6.4).

---

46 While population numbers and balance have been of enduring political, economic and social focus, and although national integration is a continuing challenge, apart from the May 1969 ethnic riots, the country has avoided the violent conflicts that have been a feature of several other ethnically-diverse societies.

Figure 6.4 Real GDP per capita, Malaya, 1900–1939 and Malaysia, 1970–2009

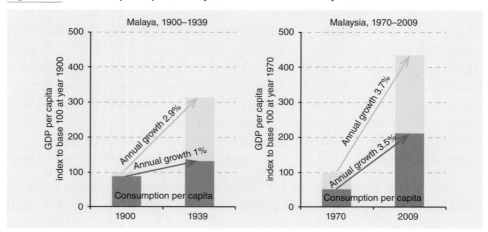

Source of data:
Data for Malaysia are from the World Bank, World Development Indicators downloaded from http://databank.worldbank.org/data/reports.aspx?source=2&country=MYS&series=&period= on 30 March 2016.

To put this in perspective, real per capita GDP growth over the 40-year period from 1970–2009 was 3.7 per cent. This period includes the celebrated years of the Asian Miracle (Birdsall *et al.*, 1993) when Malaysia, along with other countries in East and Southeast Asia, was rapidly closing the gap with high-income countries. It also includes the Asian Financial Crisis (Hunter *et al.*, 1999) which flared in the late 1990s and lingered into the early years of the 21st century (Asian Development Bank, 1999), and the Great Recession of 2008–2009.[47] The earlier period of 1900–1939 was, likewise, scarred by the Great Depression of the early 1930s. Indeed, nominal and real per capita GDP in the Malay Peninsula were lower in 1939 than they had been in 1929 on the cusp of the Great Depression.

It may appear from this simple comparison that Malaysia's outstanding economic achievements following independence were almost matched by those of the Malay states 70 years earlier. Closer examination, however, reveals a stark divergence.

---

47 The Great Recession (2008–2009) also had widespread international repercussions, with financial and real effects felt world-wide (Llaudes *et al.*, 2010; Jawaharlal, 2011). Indeed, Krugman (2008) has argued that these dynamics closely parallel the events and consequences of the Great Depression. But the effects on Malaysian growth in 2009 were far less severe and more short-lived. Real GDP fell by 1.6 per cent in 2009, and rose by 7.2 per cent in 2010.

Divergence in Per Capita Consumption Growth

There is little doubt that the first four decades of the 20th century saw some economic improvements in Malaya, especially along the west coast. There were investments in essential and long-lived economic infrastructure connecting major population centres and nodes of production to ports as well as in electrification. There was also some limited investment in social infrastructure. Primary and extractive industries—estate agriculture (primarily rubber) and tin production—created jobs and provided incomes, both directly and through payment of taxes.

By 1939, consumption per capita in real terms among the settled population of Malaya was 51 per cent higher than it had been in 1900. While this improvement was undoubtedly welcome, the question remains as to why advances in the general standard of living, equivalent to growth of just 1 per cent per year, lagged so far behind real per capita GDP growth, which, as mentioned, averaged 2.9 per cent per year between 1900 and 1939.

Further comparison with post-independence Malaysia is illuminating (Figure 6.5). Over the 40 years spanning 1970 to 2009, per capita consumption advanced at an average rate of 3.5 per cent, only marginally less than average income growth of 3.7 per cent.[48] It seems that growth in the miracle years delivered rapid advances in the average standard of living as well as large reductions in the incidence of absolute poverty. By contrast, the consumption dividend from growth in the earlier period (1900–1939) was far less.

Two possible explanations could account for this divergent experience. The first lies in the differences that exist between measures of gross domestic product (GDP) and measures of gross national income (GNI), the latter of which subtracts net primary income paid abroad (Chapter 3, Box 3.1). As indicated earlier, between 1900 and 1939, while GNI might have been somewhat less than GDP, it might also have grown much more slowly. No such difference is seen in the data covering the 1970–2009 period.

---

48 While Malaysia achieved remarkable economic growth in the post-independence period, this growth was largely the result of huge investments from both the public and private sectors. Investments were initially financed from national savings, but by the early 1990s, they were increasingly driven by large inflows of foreign capital (Rasiah, 1995). Due to the increasing investments, the savings-investment gap fell and eventually turned negative, and a trade deficit resulted. The high growth of the 1990s, resulting largely from extraordinary investments, turned out to be unsustainable. Improvements in total factor productivity, or technological progress, are essential for long-run economic growth.

Figure 6.5 Growth of real GDP and consumption per capita, Malaya, 1900–1939 and Malaysia, 1970–2009

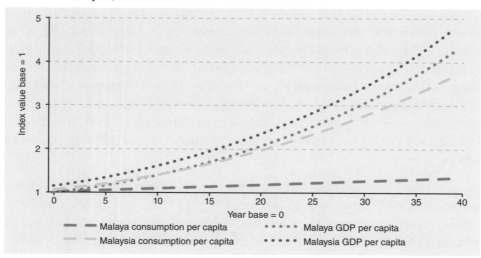

Note:
The lines have been fitted using exponential trends in GDP per capita and consumption per capita with data expressed as indices, with base = 1.
Malaya trends refer to the 40-year period 1900–1939. Malaysia trends refer to the 40-year period 1970–2009.

Source of data:
Data for Malaysia are from the World Bank, World Development Indicators downloaded from http://databank.worldbank.org/data/reports.aspx?source=2&country=MYS&series=&period= on 30 March 2016.

Unfortunately, the balance of payments data for net primary income required to validate this conjecture are not available. As the bulk of investment in large-scale estate agriculture and tin mining was foreign investment, often facilitated through joint stock companies in London and elsewhere, it seems safe to assume that much of the income from such production was repatriated. The large trade surpluses of Malaya were likely to have been accompanied by significant outward remittances of income, primarily surpluses from estate agriculture and tin production, but also including any money repatriated by workers.

This alone, however, cannot explain the divergence between growth of consumption and national income in the earlier period (Figure 6.5). The gap that existed between consumption and income growth also seems to imply a decline in the share of labour in value added, and/or that an increasing share of income had been captured by households with lower propensities to consume (or, less likely, high propensities to remit earnings overseas). Here too, there are gaps in the data, but fragmentary evidence confirms the plausibility of this hypothesis.

The availability of a very large pool of unskilled migrant labour from China and India to work on the plantations, and earlier in the tin mines, suggests that upward pressure on wages would have been limited (Chapter 3, Figure 3.3), and that windfalls from the boom years would have been almost entirely reaped by investors and the owners of land.

The indirect evidence on wages and prices gathered as part of this study indicates that real wages of agricultural and non-agricultural workers were 46 per cent higher in 1939 than in 1900, but it also shows that there were episodic declines in real wages. Indeed, throughout most of the 1920s, a period when Malaya benefited from rising export prices, real wages languished far below their level in 1900.

The first four decades of Malaya's economic growth offer an interesting and distinctive illustration of Piketty's (2014) characterisation of the *'Belle Époque'* or 'Gilded Age' . This term refers to the period from the 1870s until the outbreak of World War I in the US, UK and France during which the return on capital exceeded the growth rate of the economy. This resulted in an increase in the share of capital income (profits, dividends, rents) in the overall economy at the expense of earned income (wages and salaries).

During the Gilded Age, income inequality widened for two reasons. First, capital ownership was more unequally distributed and the rising income from capital went to fewer and richer households. Second, wages were largely stagnant, so the gap between rich and poor widened. From what we now know about the Malayan economy, real wages were more or less stagnant between 1900 and 1939, growing on average at only around 1.6 per cent per annum. As GDP per capita grew at almost twice this rate, the return on capital must also have exceeded the growth rate of the economy, just as during the Gilded Age—but with one important difference. In Malaya, much of the capital was owned by foreign individuals and companies, and the income flows from it would largely have been remitted overseas. Owners of land and capital in Malaya would also have shared the benefits, and this would have widened income distribution among the local population.

By contrast, the post-independence miracle years were characterised by diversification into labour-intensive manufacturing activities that were integrated into global supply chains, and in which workers' wages grew as capital, built and human, deepened. This export-led growth was built on the foundations of earlier investments in education and health, and in economic and social infrastructure. Such trade liberalisation and export-led development may not always be as effective as once thought, however. The 'fallacy of composition' argument suggests that, if many developing countries adopted such policies at the same time, this could create general equilibrium effects that would then weaken or even undo the favourable effects of the policy. One such mechanism works through a deterioration in the terms of trade. Certainly, Malaysia was not alone in pursuing outward-looking policies. In reviewing the evidence, Mayer (2002, pp. 18) concluded that 'countries with the lowest proportion of skill- and technology-intensive manufactures and the greatest proportion of labour-intensive products in their manufactured exports have faced declining manufactures terms of trade' that have weakened the benefits of export-led development. By shifting their exports into manufactured goods of a higher skill- and technology-intensity, other countries, including Malaysia, have been more successful.

Savings and investment rates were also considerably higher in post-independence Malaysia, often above 20 per cent of GDP, compared to pre-independence Malaya, when they were often below 10 per cent. Malaysia's sustained economic growth contributed to significant reductions in poverty throughout the country. Whereas more than half of Malaya's households were living in absolute poverty at independence, by the middle of the second decade of the 21st century, this figure had fallen to negligible proportions, while hardcore poverty had been almost eradicated (United Nations Development Programme-Malaysia, 2007; Economic Planning Unit-Malaysia, 2016).

In the late 19th century and early part of the 20th century, Malaya was undoubtedly a wealthy country. It was this inherent wealth, as represented by its abundance of land, its tin and rubber, and the economic promise of these natural resources that motivated the British to intervene in Malaya and to move progressively towards complete political control. Once security had been established, substantial European investments in the mining and plantation industries followed. Despite extreme economic volatility and commodity price fluctuations, profits and dividends were high and British commercial interests in Malaya flourished.

At independence, Malaya was still an underdeveloped country, as evidenced by multiple social and economic indicators. While GDP was relatively high, GNI was probably much lower in view of the large leakages that flowed back overseas as profits and rents.

Even so, the British had put in place institutions and systems that provided significant support for economic growth and social development after independence. These included a national civil service with capacity for planning and programme implementation, a system of rudimentary education for the masses and premier schools for the elite, a criminal justice system, social and physical infrastructure, and institutes that contributed to productivity gains, such as the Rubber Research Institute. The country's infrastructure endowment in terms of electricity, railways and roads, while skewed to support British commercial interests, as was also the practice in other colonies, compared favourably with other countries in Southeast Asia (Booth, 2016).

The British colonial administration also ensured the maintenance of law and order. This would have benefited the population more broadly, and may partly help explain the large influxes of foreign labour. While many endured great hardship and exploitation, the chance to live in a secure environment with multiple economic opportunities would have been attractive. The British did not engage in the egregious excesses and intolerant behaviour displayed by some of the other colonial powers such as the repression of existing cultural identities or the use of forced cultivation (Kwang and Roemer, 1981; Cole *et al.*, 1989; Booth, 2016). The British colonial power did, however, lack a development vision for the country's people and, accordingly, it failed to make strategic investments in the interests of the local population or balanced regional development. These became pressing political imperatives that had to be addressed after independence by the government, national policy makers and development planners.

*   *   *

Broadening Knowledge

Several areas of research interest have emerged in the course of this case study that would further enrich the findings presented here. These are shared below.

A Century of GDP Estimates

Several attempts have been made to develop GDP estimates for Malaya (Malaysia) that cover the period before the Department of Statistics-

Malaysia began producing regular annual official national income accounts (Chapter 1). These include the work of the Retrenchment Commission covering the Federated Malay States for the period 1932–1937, Benham's estimates for the years 1947–1949, the World Bank's for the years 1949–1953, and Wilson's for 1954. The latter three sets of estimates covered British Malaya—the Federation of Malaya and the Crown Colony of Singapore. Subsequently, Lim (1967) and Lee (1968) converted these earlier British Malayan estimates to Peninsular Malaysian estimates, while Walters (1960) prepared the first set of national accounts for Peninsular Malaysia for the years 1955–1959. Abraham and Gill (1969a) covered the period 1956–1966 before the exercise of developing official national accounts became the responsibility of the Department of Statistics-Malaysia.

Drawing on all the earlier estimates, Rao (1976) assembled the national accounts of Peninsular Malaysia for the 25-year period from 1947–1971 at current and constant 1959 prices. He also attempted to revise the national accounts data of the late 1940s and 1950s to achieve consistency with the 1960–1971 official estimates.

Given the new series of expenditure-based GDP estimates that has been produced by this study, it would be useful for researchers not only to evaluate and further refine this work, but to use it as part of the basis for the development of a coherent and consistent set of estimates covering the entire 20th century. One challenge in doing this is the dearth of information about the Malayan economy during the period of Japanese occupation. If estimates for this period could be made, it would allow a reconciliation of the new estimates for the period 1900–1939 with those produced by Rao (1976) for the period 1947–1971. A second challenge would be to develop GDP estimates for Sabah and Sarawak for the period before Malaysia was formed in 1963. A third challenge would be to bring these various estimates together in a user-friendly format on a publicly-accessible website.

Remittance Flows, Financial Leakages and International Comparisons

The mobility of people, particularly though not exclusively, between Malaya and China as well as between Malaya and India was a remarkable feature of the pre-World War II period (Chapter 2). Remittances flowed from the Chinese and Indian workers, and also possibly from the Javanese and Sumatran workers, to their families in their countries of origin. Although there is a very substantial research literature covering the demographic and socio-cultural characteristics of migrant workers in Malaya as well as their contributions, living conditions and the hardships that they encountered, there has been hardly any research on the magnitude of remittance flows by foreign workers to their home countries during this period of Malaya's colonial history.

In the same vein, it would be insightful to study the magnitude of the outflows of funds to the UK from Malaya during the colonial period. The UK was the major source of foreign investment during this period, through independence and up until 1970. At independence in 1957, the UK owned more than 90 per cent of the stock of foreign direct investment in Malaya (Athukorala and Menon, 1996), most of which was in the primary sector, mainly in tin mining and rubber plantations. A systematic collation of information on the nature and amounts of profits, rent, and other funds repatriated by the colonial government and the private agency houses to the UK during the colonial period would be very interesting.

A comparison of Malaya's economic growth under British colonial rule, and the institutions put in place to support that growth, with the experience of other colonies in the Asia region—such as Ceylon (Sri Lanka), the Dutch East Indies (Indonesia) and Korea—could shed light on the reasons for the observed differences in patterns of growth and development in these countries, both during colonial rule and after independence.

Inequality

The unbalanced and uneven development of Malaya in the pre-World War II period must have been reflected in some level of income and asset inequality between and within ethnic communities, and between the east and west coast states. There is very limited published data and analysis on the scale and consequences of disparities in the early decades of the 20th century, with much of the official data on employment, income and asset ownership beginning only after independence.

It would be interesting to determine whether and how the patterns of inequality changed during the course of the 20th century transition from a subsistence to a modern economy (Van Zanden, 2004). Given the continuing public policy concern about creating a fairer and more equitable society, the historical information gap on this topic is a critical area for research.

APPENDICES

Water transport connecting communities across and along rivers
in early 20th century Malaya

Appendix 1

Data Sources for Estimating GDP Components and Their Limitations

The data sources used to derive the four components of GDP for the study period (1900–1939) are described in the boxes below, along with some of their limitations and the challenges faced. These components are private final consumption expenditure (PFCE); government final consumption expenditure (GFCE); gross fixed capital formation (GFCF); and exports and imports of goods and services. The publications referred to here are listed in the bibliography under Historical Administrative and Annual Reports (pp.221–227).

Appendix Box 1.1	Data sources for estimating PFCE and their limitations

Constructing a series on PFCE for pre-war Malaya was very challenging because of the lack of available data on actual consumption expenditure. As a result, a combination of direct and indirect approaches was used depending on the availability of the data.

Data on PFCE are usually obtained through household expenditure surveys, but the first Household Budget Survey for the Federation of Malaya was conducted only in 1957–1958 (Federation of Malaya 1959). An earlier Cost of Living Pilot Survey had been carried out in Singapore from mid-August to mid-September 1948 (Department of Statistics-Singapore, 1950). That survey was of limited use to this study, however, as it did not capture the significantly broader rural, agricultural and mining base of Malaya's economy. It also only covered the expenditure behavior of Europeans and higher-income Asiatic groups.

Direct data on private consumption were available only for expenditures on transport, utilities, health, education and opium/*chandu*. Consumption of other items had to be calculated indirectly using a variety of data sets and sources. These data were categorised according to six consumption standards to reflect the very different expenditure patterns of different population groups. The main basis for estimating the consumption expenditures for the European, Eurasian and Asiatic sectors of the population was a study on living expenses conducted in 1930 and contained in *The Report of the Commission on the Temporary Allowances*

1931 relating to Singapore (Miller, 1931). For the Malays and Chinese, food consumption patterns were sourced from the *Diet Scales of Government Hospitals 1936*. The *Johore Annual Report, Labourer's Specimen Monthly Budget 1933* provided the basis for estimating the consumption expenditure of Indians.

Data on population, disaggregated by ethnicity and occupation, were used to estimate the size of these six consumption standards. These data were obtained from the population census reports of 1901, 1911, 1921, 1931 and 1947, while data on natural population increase were drawn from the *Annual Report on Registration of Births and Deaths*. Apart from these sources, other reference materials used included the *Annual Administrative Reports* of various states as well as the annual series of the *Straits Settlements Blue Book*.

While these data sources formed the basis of the calculation of the indirect consumption expenditures of the six population groups, some data on direct expenditures were available. Expenditure data on health, education and utilities were obtained from the *Annual Reports of the Medical, Education and Electrical Departments* respectively, and data on rail transport came from the *Annual Report, Federated Malay States Railways*.

In order to derive PFCE at constant prices, it was necessary to construct a consumer price index series. As no data were available for pre-war Malaya, this was based instead on the annual cost-of-living indices for Singapore. These were published in the *Average Prices, Declared Trade Values, Exchange and Currency for the year 1939, Malaya*, and in the *Average Prices, Declared Trade Values, Exchange and Currency, Volume and Average Values of Imports and Exports, Market Prices, and Cost of Living for the year 1951, Malaya*.

Appendix Box 1.2 — **Data sources for estimating GFCE and their limitations**

Since Malaya did not exist as an administrative unit during the study period, statistical information on government output, or expenditure, was obtained separately for the Straits Settlements, the Federated Malay States and the Unfederated Malay States. The most complete and comprehensive time series data were available for the Straits Settlements, followed by the Federated Malay States, with only broad expenditure figures available for the Unfederated Malay States.

Straits Settlements
Government expenditure in the Straits Settlements included that incurred by the states of Penang and Malacca, by the municipalities of George Town and Malacca, and by the Rural Boards of Penang and Province Wellesley, as well as expenditure by other government bodies including the Education Board and the Hospital Board. Data for Singapore were excluded from the study.

States of Penang and Malacca
Government expenditure data for the Straits Settlements for the period 1900–1938 were contained in the *Blue Book, Straits Settlements*. Data for the year 1939 were published in the *Financial Statements, Straits Settlements*. Detailed expenditure data by heads of department were available for the entire study period. For the period from 1910–1939, however, personal emoluments and other expenditure items were not shown individually for Penang and Malacca, but were given on a consolidated basis for the Straits Settlements overall.

Municipalities of George Town and Malacca
Data on expenditures incurred by the municipalities of George Town and Malacca were also contained in the *Blue Book, Straits Settlements*. For the municipality of George Town, data were available by both class of account and heads of department for the years 1900–1906, 1929, and 1937–1938. Data for the years 1929 and 1937–1938 were obtained from the *Administration Report of the Municipality of George Town, Penang*.

Only very basic expenditure data were available for the remaining years, with the exception of 1939. These data appeared as one-line figures with no disaggregation by class of account or heads of department. For the municipality of Malacca, detailed expenditure information by both class of account and heads of department was available only for the period 1900–1910, with data for the period 1911–1938 given as one-line expenditure totals. No expenditure data were available for either municipality for the year 1939, even as total figures.

Rural boards
The four rural boards covered were the Penang Island Rural Board, Province Wellesley Rural Board, Dindings Rural Board and Malacca Rural Board. The Penang Rural Board was established in 1909, followed by the other three. By 1911, the total expenditure incurred by each Board was published in the *Blue Book, Straits Settlements* series, but without any detailed information by class of account. This continued until 1938, with no expenditure figures available for 1939 for any of the Rural Boards.

Other government bodies (education and hospital boards)
Data on expenditure by the Education and Hospital Boards of the Straits Settlements appeared in the *Return of all Municipalities, Local Boards and any other Public Bodies in the Colony*. This was published in the *Blue Book, Straits Settlements* annual series for the period 1911–1939. The expenditure data of the Education Board were given at an aggregated level only, with no disaggregation by class of account, or by the individual settlements. The data provided by the Hospital Board similarly gave only total expenditures, but these were at least given separately for Singapore, Penang and Malacca. This was a considerable improvement on the consolidated figures for the Straits Settlements provided by the Education Board.

Federated Malay States

For the Federated Malay States, the availability and level of detail of the data on government expenditure published in official documents differed between the three periods of 1900–1921, 1922–1929 and 1930–1939.

For 1900–1921, the only information available was for total government expenditure on a consolidated basis, covering various broad types of expenditure. This was published in the *Annual Report, Federated Malay States*. Hardly any data were available at the departmental level for this early period. For the years 1922–1929, information on GFCE was generally available at departmental level, but only as total amounts without breakdown by class of account. Data for these years were obtained from the annual Federated Malay States Reports with varying titles: (i) *Report on the Accounts of the Federated Malay States* (1922, 1923, 1924); (ii) *Report on the Public Accounts of the Federated Malay States* (1925); (iii) *Auditor-General's Report on the Public Accounts for the Federated Malay States* (1926, 1927); and (iv) *Report by the Auditor-General of the Federated Malay States on the Revenue and Expenditure* (1928, 1929).

The information available for the period 1930–1939 was the most comprehensive, and was contained in the government's financial statements. These statements identified expenditure by heads of department at the federal level, as well as separately for Perak, Selangor, Negri Sembilan and Pahang. Other source documents, including the *Annual Report, Federated Malay States*, contained relatively long time series expenditure data, although the figures were generally aggregated and only gave total expenditure.

Unfederated Malay States

Of Malaya's three administrative units, the Unfederated Malay States had the weakest data on government expenditure. Financial records for the earlier years were practically non-existent, with record-keeping only introduced after the States were brought under British protection. Data were subsequently published in the respective States' *Annual Reports*, but with varying levels of coverage and detail. Departmental data were available for specific years for Kedah, Perlis and Trengganu. For Johore and Kelantan, the annual reports gave government expenditure data at the aggregate level only, with no expenditure information by heads of department.

Data limitations

Five challenging issues were faced in computing Malaya's GFCE.

Firstly, the unavailability of government statistics for the entity of Malaya meant that data had to be constructed from its constituent administrative units, for which information had been acquired with varying degrees of accuracy and completeness. The total government expenditure figures that have been obtained by summing up these figures are thus only as accurate as the estimates for the constituent units.

Secondly, the challenge of estimating government expenditure was compounded by the changing number and names of heads of department. The procedure for reporting expenditures changed over time, including in terms of which expenditures were reported by the different heads of department. As the administration evolved, the list of heads of department itself changed as needs changed, with some departments being abolished, others being integrated and still more being newly created. The financial obligations of these heads of department also changed over time, reflecting their evolving relative importance.

Thirdly, the detailed expenditure data in the official financial records were collected for administrative rather than for research purposes, so expenditure by detailed categories of consumption was not available. One-line statements on expenditure items such as 'electric light, water and conservancy', as given in the *Financial Statement for the Federated Malay States' Medical (Federal) Department* in 1930, for example, did not distinguish between expenditure on electricity, water and so on. Various adjustments were necessary to ensure that the expenditure data conformed to the requirements of national accounting.

Fourthly, the financial statements of various government bodies included not only expenditures related to the producers of government services, but also those related to industries or trading departments, which should be excluded from estimates of GFCE.

Fifthly, the government expenditure records from the different constituent units of Malaya were compiled using different calendar systems. While the Straits Settlements and the Federated Malay States used the Gregorian calendar in the presentation of government expenditure statistics, the Unfederated Malay States used the Islamic calendar in their published financial records. No attempt was made to adjust the data for the Unfederated Malay States in order to make them consistent with the Gregorian calendar. Since the expenditure of these States represented a small proportion of Malaya's total expenditure, any resulting errors would have been small.

Appendix Box 1.3 **Data sources for estimating GFCF and their limitations**

Cultivated assets

The calculation of the value of cultivated assets in Malaya also faced considerable challenges due to data limitations. Data on annual new planting of rubber trees were unavailable before 1918, when figures were given for the total planted area only. A census was conducted in 1921 to determine the area planted with rubber, and this provided data on annual new planting for the period from 1917 to 1921, disaggregated according to smallholdings and estates (Figart, 1921). From 1922 onwards, figures were given in official publications for both total planted and newly planted acreages, separately for smallholdings and estates. Higher-yielding bud-grafted rubber plants were first planted in the early 1920s. Time series data on annual new plantings of bud-grafted trees were available in official publications for the period 1922–1939, while figures for total planted acreages of bud-grafted trees were available for the period 1935–1939, given separately for smallholdings and estates.

Ordinary rubber trees took about six years to mature and start producing, as compared to five years for the bud-grafted rubber trees. The cost-structure of bringing an acre of rubber to maturity also varied between the two types. Data on maturity cost were obtained for as many years as possible in order to take account of the changes in cost over time. Five cost-per-acre estimates were used, including three for estates (with 1913, 1924 and 1935 as base years), one for smallholdings (1924) and another for bud-grafted trees (1935) (Figart, 1925; Akers, 1914 and Grist, 1950).

No direct data were available on annual new planting acreage for coconuts. Although there was some information on total planted acreage by state, there were gaps for a number of years, and the data did not generally differentiate between estates and smallholdings. Where data on annual newly planted coconut acreage were lacking, they were approximated by taking the year-to-year changes in total planted acreage. There was little information on the cost-per-acre of bringing coconut to maturity, which generally takes around five years. Data on smallholdings were available for only one year out of the 40-year study period (1931), and for estates for only two years (1908 and 1935) (Federated Malay States, 1932b; *Agricultural Bulletin*, Straits Settlements and Federated Malay States, 1909, and Grist, 1950).

Other perennial crops planted in Malaya before the 20th century included arecanut, coffee and gambier. Their cultivation experienced a downturn in the first two decades of the century due to the emergence of rubber. As direct data on the annual newly planted acreage for these crops were not available in official records, these again had to be approximated by taking year-to-year changes in the total planted acreage. The time to maturity varied with each of these crops— four years for arecanut, three for coffee, and one and a half for gambier. The cost per acre of bringing arecanut to maturity was based on information given in the *Report of Proceedings of the Third Inter-Departmental Agricultural Conference* (Federated Malay States, 1932b, Appendix 19), while cost-per-acre estimates of bringing coffee and gambier to maturity for the reference year 1935 were provided by Grist (1950).

Malaya's cultivation of other perennial crops—oil palm, tea and pineapple—only began in the second and third decades of the 20th century. Oil palm cultivation on a commercial scale started in 1917, and was concentrated mainly in Johore and Selangor, while tea cultivation was relatively insignificant prior to 1928. Direct data on annual new planting areas for all these crops were often not available, and these had to be approximated instead by taking the year-to-year changes in total planted area, for which data could be obtained from official publications.

Unlike other perennial crops, pineapple plants have a relatively short life of around five years, after which they are removed. Estimates of annual newly planted acreage of pineapple were therefore based not only on year-to-year changes in total planted acreage as with the other crops, but also took into account acreage that would no longer be productive after five years. The gestation period to bring these crops to maturity again varied, from three years for oil palm and tea, to 18 months for pineapple. The estimated cost-per-acre was based on information available for 1932 for tea, and for 1935 for pineapple and oil palm (Ministry of Agriculture and Cooperatives, 1966 and Grist, 1950).

Data limitations
A first major limitation common to all of the crops, apart from rubber, in the second half of the study period was the lack of statistics on annual newly planted acreage. Instead, these had to be calculated indirectly based on year-to-year changes in the total planted acreage of each of these crops. This proxy method should have given a fairly accurate picture of annual newly planted acreage as long as there was limited replanting activity, and as long as abandoned areas were taken into account in the published figures on total acreage. Historical records indicate that there was no significant replanting activity of these crops during the period, with the possible exception of rubber, and then only after 1933–1934 (Straits Settlement and Federated Malay States, 1941). Where total planted acreage for a particular crop in any given year was shown in the official data as lower than in the preceding year, it was assumed that there had been no new planting of that crop in that year.

Secondly, only limited information was available to distinguish total planted acreage for estates from that of smallholdings, again apart from for rubber. Differentiation between smallholdings and estate cultivation was necessary because the cost-structure of the latter was considerably higher, meaning that different cost-per-acre estimates were required. Where estate and smallholding figures were not directly available, they were estimated using a two-step approach. Estate acreage was first estimated based on the assumption that its share of the total planted acreage was the same as the nearest year for which data on both total acreage and estate acreage were available. Smallholding acreage was then obtained as a residual by subtracting estate acreage from total planted acreage.

A third challenge related to the availability of cost-per-acre estimates. Ideally, contemporary cost-per-acre estimates should have been used for different time periods in order to take account of changes in costs over time. But the availability of such estimates varied from crop to crop.

Fourthly, the cost-per-acre estimates are indicative only, being based on generalisations. They did not take into account the varying conditions under which crops were cultivated, such as geographical location, topography, terrain and type of land. The cost-per-acre of bringing rubber to maturity, for example, would have varied according to whether the crop was planted on hilly land which required terracing, or on gently undulating land. Rubber planted in heavy coastal clay soils or in low-lying or swampy areas requiring drainage would also have had a higher cost-per-acre (Grist, 1950).

Construction

Data on construction output for the period were sparse, with the first survey conducted only in 1963. The only information about outlays on construction for the period 1900–1939 was incorporated into the financial statements of the government accounts relating to general government departments and trading departments. Data on building permits approved for dwelling construction were also of some use. As colonial records on dwelling construction based on building permits were kept by the municipalities as well as by town and sanitary boards, they rarely included construction that was done without building permits or approval from the authorities, however. This meant that large numbers of dwellings in rural areas belonging to the poorer classes were excluded (*Report of a Committee Appointed to Consider the Alleged Shortage of Houses*, Federated Malay States, 1923).

One approach to putting together a series on fixed capital formation for construction would be to estimate construction output by inflating the value of the basic materials required—cement, sawn timber, plywood, mild steel bars and rods, floor and roofing tiles, and bricks—using coefficients from input-output studies. The gross output of the construction industry, which included maintenance and repairs, would then have to be excluded in order to arrive at GFCF in construction. With the exception of cement figures for the Federated Malay States, this approach was limited by lack of data.

Machinery and equipment
GFCF for machinery and equipment was based on statistics on foreign trade and domestic production. There was very little manufacturing activity in Malaya during the study period, and minimal domestic production of machinery and equipment, so estimates of GFCF in this area was based on foreign trade statistics.

Data challenges relating to the estimation of net imports of machinery and equipment into Malaya included the fact that official trade statistics were for the Straits Settlements as an entity, the Straits Settlements as a part of British Malaya, and the entity of British Malaya rather than for Malaya alone. Machinery and equipment entering Malaya from Singapore should ideally have been treated as imports, but it was not possible to distinguish trade between Singapore and the other constituent units of Malaya from the official published trade statistics.

Only limited data were available for net imports of machinery and equipment for the different time periods, and for Malaya's various administrative units. The Federated Malay States had by far the longest time series, followed by the

Unfederated Malay States (with the exception of Kedah and Perlis). The data series for Penang and Malacca started in 1912, with the data presented initially as part of the Straits Settlements (1913–1927), and later as part of British Malaya (1928–1939). While in some cases machinery and equipment items were given in detail in the trade statistics with as many as 172 items listed, in many others the trade data showed only abbreviated categories ranging from as few as four to as many as 28. Additionally, the net imports of machinery and equipment shown in the trade statistics were given in basic prices, which had to be converted into market prices by adding trade and transport margins. No commodity taxes were levied on these imports.

Not all the net imports of machinery and equipment could be capitalized. Some items would have doubled up for use by households, such as motorcars, motorcycles, tools, furniture and fixtures, or have had multiple uses. Yet other items would have been used as inputs for construction activities, or for intermediate consumption (for repairs and maintenance), with a portion also used for current consumption (in the case of military expenditure). Only after the proportion of net imports used for such purposes had been estimated could the remaining value of net imports of machinery and equipment be capitalised at market prices.

Appendix Box 1.4 **Data sources for estimating exports and imports of goods and services and their limitations**

Trade data were available for the different administrative units, with the Straits Settlements having the most comprehensive time series. In order to derive exports and imports for Malaya, the external trade figures of the constituent units were summed, excluding inter-settlement and inter-regional trade. The external trade of Malaya was analysed according to trade with the Rest of the World (ROW) excluding Singapore, and trade with Singapore. This rather unique approach of treating Singapore separately and not as part of the ROW was made possible by the existence of a strong database on Singapore's external trade statistics.

Trade data for Penang and Malacca with the ROW were available for the entire 40-year period, while their trade data with Singapore were available only for the years 1900–1927. These data were given in official publications including the *Straits Settlements Blue Book*, *Statistical Tables Relating to British Colonies*, *Appendices to Report on Trade of Straits Settlements*, and *Return of Foreign Imports and Exports, British Malaya and the Foreign Trade of Malaya*. Data on trade between the Federated Malay States and the ROW and Singapore were available for the years 1905–1939, and were obtained mainly from the *Report on the Trade* and *Customs Department, Federated Malay States,* as well as from the yearly series entitled *Annual Report of the Federated Malay States.* For the Unfederated Malay States, trade data with the ROW were available from 1921 in the *Return of Foreign Imports and Exports, British Malaya* and the *Foreign Trade of Malaya.* There were almost no data available on their trade with Singapore during the period.

Data limitations
The data series on foreign trade for pre-war Malaya had several limitations, including the varying levels of completeness and accuracy of the data for the constituent entities. Data for the Unfederated Malay States were the most deficient, and estimates had to be made. As their share in Malaya's total trade was the lowest of all the entities, any errors introduced as a result of these estimation procedures would have been small.

Another limitation was the uncertainty as to whether or not parcel post data had been included in the published statistics, as no explicit mention was made of this. Once it was established that these figures had been excluded, estimates were made using certain assumptions and the results obtained were added. Estimates for coins and bullion posed a similar challenge—while figures were shown for some years, this category was not mentioned at all in other years. For these years, it was assumed that their values had been included in the total trade figures, and separate estimates were made. These amounts were then subtracted from the total, as coins and bullion do not form part of merchandise imports and exports.

A further challenge concerned trade data for the Straits Settlements, which for some years were presented on a consolidated basis only (consisting of estimates for Singapore, Penang, Malacca, Dindings, Labuan, Christmas Island and Cocos-Keeling Islands), without any disaggregation to reflect inter-settlement trade. In these cases, separate estimates were made for Penang and Malacca.

Services
As there were no data available on the exports and imports of services for Malaya for the study period, these were estimated based on statistical evidence from post-war Malaya.

Appendix 2

Appendix Tables of GDP and Its Components, Malaya, 1900–1939

Table A1.1 Major components of GDP in purchasers' values at current prices in Straits$ millions

Year	PFCE	GFCE	Gross capital formation*		
			Cultivated assets	Construction	Machinery and equipment
1	2	3	4	5	6
1900	115.6	6.5	0.4	5.3	2.5
1901	119.2	8.6	0.6	8.8	2.9
1902	130.8	7.8	0.8	7.9	2.2
1903	135.9	8.8	1.0	9.2	2.8
1904	139.6	9.6	1.4	10.6	1.6
1905	144.8	10.3	1.7	12.7	1.4
1906	152.1	9.6	3.6	10.9	4.1
1907	166.7	10.2	5.5	15.1	8.0
1908	178.1	11.3	8.2	22.0	7.9
1909	179.6	11.5	9.4	12.3	4.2
1910	189.0	12.1	17.2	20.4	5.8
1911	212.9	13.0	22.6	16.8	8.6
1912	231.3	14.4	26.6	25.0	10.1
1913	257.4	15.9	29.0	52.2	18.0
1914	266.9	16.8	23.2	38.5	17.8
1915	274.4	16.6	26.0	18.8	6.8
1916	289.9	17.1	25.6	15.1	8.0
1917	333.2	17.6	36.5	28.1	7.3
1918	351.0	20.6	36.7	20.0	5.7
1919	377.5	25.7	33.6	26.4	12.7
1920	401.3	35.5	33.0	66.2	30.8
1921	385.7	40.8	31.0	56.2	29.6
1922	355.8	36.1	30.5	23.4	14.2
1923	364.4	36.5	22.7	21.4	12.9
1924	410.6	38.8	25.4	19.6	11.1
1925	428.5	41.2	24.5	32.0	21.7
1926	482.7	43.6	29.7	40.6	31.8
1927	503.1	51.3	44.8	60.1	31.8
1928	511.0	53.2	41.0	71.9	31.0
1929	568.9	57.8	42.1	64.6	28.2
1930	487.6	57.5	40.8	40.0	19.1
1931	342.6	58.1	22.7	31.1	11.1
1932	300.7	49.3	19.8	19.1	6.1
1933	310.8	45.2	14.9	12.8	4.9
1934	308.0	43.7	13.5	11.5	8.4
1935	376.9	45.6	12.8	15.0	11.0
1936	432.4	48.3	14.6	17.5	12.8
1937	507.1	51.9	16.3	26.8	21.0
1938	524.5	56.2	15.3	31.7	23.5
1939	541.4	59.8	28.7	33.6	20.6

Table A1.1 (Cont'd) **Major components of GDP in purchasers' values at current prices in Straits$ millions**

GFCF**	Exports of goods and services	Imports of goods and services	GDP in purchasers' values at current prices	Year
7=4+5+6	8	9	10=2+3+7+8−9	
8.2	102.7	73.8	159.2	1900
12.3	105.6	70.2	175.5	1901
10.9	125.1	79.5	195.1	1902
12.9	123.3	89.7	191.3	1903
13.6	108.2	84.1	187.0	1904
15.9	123.2	90.2	204.0	1905
18.6	133.9	95.5	218.8	1906
28.6	138.2	103.6	240.1	1907
38.0	120.0	97.3	250.0	1908
26.0	131.0	93.1	255.0	1909
43.4	167.9	107.7	304.7	1910
48.0	190.2	135.1	329.0	1911
61.7	233.2	164.8	375.8	1912
99.2	225.7	174.0	424.1	1913
79.5	194.7	147.8	410.1	1914
51.7	252.5	141.0	454.2	1915
48.7	332.5	171.7	516.4	1916
71.9	406.4	191.1	638.0	1917
62.4	369.4	209.4	593.8	1918
72.8	466.5	270.4	672.1	1919
130.0	484.8	387.9	663.7	1920
116.8	224.3	210.7	556.9	1921
68.2	255.0	184.6	530.4	1922
57.0	378.1	218.7	617.2	1923
56.1	396.9	246.7	655.9	1924
78.1	742.2	331.3	958.7	1925
102.1	789.8	406.7	1,011.5	1926
136.6	606.9	409.7	888.1	1927
143.9	483.2	408.9	782.4	1928
134.9	604.8	429.6	936.8	1929
99.9	382.9	351.9	676.1	1930
65.0	229.0	226.0	468.7	1931
45.0	168.8	166.9	396.8	1932
32.6	214.6	169.3	433.9	1933
33.4	358.2	219.3	524.0	1934
38.8	352.2	231.3	582.3	1935
44.9	443.5	260.0	709.1	1936
64.1	643.3	351.8	914.7	1937
70.5	366.8	305.4	712.6	1938
82.9	489.4	336.4	837.1	1939

Notes: * The 'increase in stocks' component of gross capital formation was deemed to be negligible during this period.
  ** Excludes land improvement, breeding stock, draught animals, daily cattle, and the like, which is deemed to be negligible or is conceivably zero.

Table A1.2 Major components of GDP in purchasers' values at constant 1914 prices in Straits$ millions

Year	PFCE	GFCE	Gross capital formation*		
			Cultivated assets	Construction	Machinery and equipment
1	2	3	4	5	6
1900	125.3	7.1	0.4	3.5	2.5
1901	132.0	9.6	0.8	6.3	3.0
1902	136.5	8.1	1.0	5.5	2.4
1903	140.1	9.1	1.2	6.8	3.0
1904	144.2	10.0	1.7	8.1	1.8
1905	154.1	11.0	2.1	10.0	1.5
1906	167.7	10.6	4.3	11.0	4.5
1907	174.6	10.7	6.3	14.3	8.5
1908	185.0	11.7	8.6	20.6	8.1
1909	195.8	12.6	9.9	12.9	4.5
1910	206.3	13.2	18.0	22.7	6.1
1911	218.7	13.4	23.7	17.5	8.9
1912	222.0	13.8	27.9	25.3	10.0
1913	245.8	15.1	29.3	46.5	17.2
1914	266.9	16.8	23.2	38.5	17.8
1915	256.2	15.4	26.0	16.9	5.4
1916	251.2	14.7	25.6	10.2	5.3
1917	278.5	14.7	31.2	14.5	3.7
1918	246.7	14.3	30.9	7.5	2.6
1919	208.2	13.9	27.3	10.6	5.1
1920	172.1	14.8	26.8	19.7	12.1
1921	222.6	23.2	24.6	19.4	16.6
1922	232.8	23.4	25.7	14.9	10.5
1923	244.1	24.1	19.1	16.5	10.0
1924	274.5	25.7	17.7	14.8	8.5
1925	278.3	26.5	17.0	25.0	16.6
1926	301.6	26.9	19.0	32.3	24.9
1927	321.7	32.3	28.7	47.9	24.4
1928	330.1	34.0	26.3	56.4	23.5
1929	374.1	37.5	23.2	51.0	20.8
1930	338.9	39.5	27.8	34.7	15.4
1931	292.6	49.4	21.1	30.8	9.6
1932	298.4	48.8	20.8	19.1	5.3
1933	334.0	48.6	14.5	14.6	4.4
1934	321.6	45.6	13.8	15.9	7.1
1935	368.6	44.6	10.6	21.3	9.2
1936	431.9	48.2	10.6	25.0	10.0
1937	468.8	48.0	10.5	38.7	14.3
1938	506.8	54.4	9.9	39.5	15.9
1939	517.5	57.2	18.5	41.0	13.3

Table A1.2 (cont'd) **Major components of GDP in purchasers' values at constant 1914 prices in Straits$ millions**

GFCF**	Exports of goods and services	Imports of goods and services	GDP in purchasers' values at current prices	Year
7=4+5+6	8	9	10=2+3+7+8–9	
6.5	85.3	81.2	143.0	1900
10.1	99.2	78.3	172.6	1901
8.8	117.3	79.4	191.3	1902
11.0	110.9	98.9	172.2	1903
11.6	96.7	95.4	167.0	1904
13.7	101.4	98.7	181.6	1905
19.9	87.3	113.2	172.3	1906
29.1	94.9	118.5	190.8	1907
37.3	104.3	111.9	226.4	1908
27.3	89.8	109.9	215.6	1909
46.8	93.3	101.0	258.6	1910
50.0	119.4	116.6	285.0	1911
63.2	144.6	155.3	288.2	1912
92.9	169.3	168.1	355.0	1913
79.5	194.7	147.8	410.1	1914
48.2	266.7	141.5	445.0	1915
41.1	255.3	153.0	409.3	1916
49.5	301.7	127.2	517.2	1917
41.0	374.9	135.4	541.5	1918
43.0	429.5	130.6	564.0	1919
58.6	429.4	133.8	541.2	1920
60.5	447.4	89.1	664.6	1921
51.0	523.0	88.9	741.4	1922
45.7	473.9	147.8	639.9	1923
40.9	469.4	160.2	650.3	1924
58.6	419.7	215.8	567.3	1925
76.2	589.1	247.8	746.1	1926
100.9	532.4	251.2	736.2	1927
106.2	731.6	262.1	939.8	1928
95.1	1,002.7	282.8	1226.6	1929
77.9	1,020.4	242.5	1234.1	1930
61.5	976.8	184.5	1195.7	1931
45.2	808.9	142.3	1058.9	1932
33.5	803.4	161.7	1057.8	1933
36.8	905.3	215.5	1093.9	1934
41.1	861.6	225.1	1090.8	1935
45.6	952.9	253.9	1224.8	1936
63.5	1156.5	333.5	1403.3	1937
65.3	871.7	332.0	1166.1	1938
72.9	927.7	344.5	1230.8	1939

Notes: * The 'increase in stocks' component of gross capital formation was deemed to be negligible during this period.
** Excludes land improvement, breeding stock, draught animals, daily cattle, and the like, which is deemed to be negligible or is conceivably zero.

Table A1.3 **Value and annual growth rate of components of GDP in purchasers' values at constant 1914 prices in Straits$ millions**

Year	Population (millions)	PFCE Value	PFCE Annual growth (%)	GFCE Value	GFCE Annual growth (%)	Total gross fixed capital formation* Value	Total gross fixed capital formation* Annual growth (%)
1	2	3	4	5	6	7	8
1900	1.67	125.3	na	7.1	na	6.5	na
1901	1.73	132.0	5.3	9.6	34.8	10.1	55.9
1902	1.79	136.5	3.4	8.1	−15.4	8.8	−12.7
1903	1.87	140.1	2.6	9.1	12.5	11.0	24.6
1904	1.94	144.2	3.0	10.0	9.3	11.6	5.4
1905	2.01	154.1	6.9	11.0	10.7	13.7	18.2
1906	2.07	167.7	8.8	10.6	−4.3	19.9	45.6
1907	2.14	174.6	4.1	10.7	1.5	29.1	46.1
1908	2.20	185.0	6.0	11.7	9.4	37.3	28.1
1909	2.24	195.8	5.8	12.6	7.2	27.3	−26.8
1910	2.30	206.3	5.4	13.2	5.0	46.8	71.7
1911	2.40	218.7	6.0	13.4	1.2	50.0	6.9
1912	2.52	222.0	1.5	13.8	3.0	63.2	26.3
1913	2.63	245.8	10.8	15.1	10.0	92.9	47.0
1914	2.71	266.9	8.6	16.8	11.1	79.5	−14.5
1915	2.76	256.2	−4.0	15.4	−8.2	48.2	−39.3
1916	2.82	251.2	−2.0	14.7	−4.7	41.1	−14.8
1917	2.88	278.5	10.9	14.7	−0.4	49.5	20.5
1918	2.88	246.7	−11.4	14.3	−2.4	41.0	−17.1
1919	2.87	208.2	−15.6	13.9	−2.7	43.0	4.7
1920	2.89	172.1	−17.3	14.8	6.3	58.6	36.4
1921	2.92	222.6	29.4	23.2	56.9	60.5	3.2
1922	2.95	232.8	4.6	23.4	0.7	51.0	−15.7
1923	2.98	244.1	4.8	24.1	3.2	45.7	−10.6
1924	3.04	274.5	12.5	25.7	6.6	40.9	−10.4
1925	3.13	278.3	1.4	26.5	3.1	58.6	43.2
1926	3.27	301.6	8.4	26.9	1.6	76.2	30.0
1927	3.43	321.7	6.7	32.3	20.0	100.9	32.5
1928	3.54	330.1	2.6	34.0	5.2	106.2	5.2
1929	3.64	374.1	13.3	37.5	10.5	95.1	−10.5
1930	3.75	338.9	−9.4	39.5	5.4	77.9	−18.1
1931	3.72	292.6	−13.7	49.4	24.9	61.5	−21.0
1932	3.62	298.4	2.0	48.8	−1.2	45.2	−26.5
1933	3.62	334.0	11.9	48.6	−0.4	33.5	−25.8
1934	3.73	321.6	−3.7	45.6	−6.1	36.8	9.8
1935	3.88	368.6	14.6	44.6	−2.2	41.1	11.5
1936	4.03	431.9	17.2	48.2	8.1	45.6	11.0
1937	4.24	468.8	8.6	48.0	−0.6	63.5	39.3
1938	4.43	506.8	8.1	54.4	13.3	65.3	2.7
1939	4.58	517.5	2.1	57.2	5.3	72.9	11.7

Table A1.3 (cont'd) **Value and annual growth rate of components of GDP in purchasers'**
values at constant 1914 prices in Straits$ millions

Malaya's exports		Malaya's imports		GDP in purchasers' values at constant prices		Per capita GDP		
Value	Annual growth (%)	Value	Annual growth (%)	Value	Annual growth (%)	Value (Strats$)	Annual growth (%)	Year
9	10	11	12	13=3+5+ 7+9−11	14	15	16	
85.3	na	81.2	na	143.0	na	85.6	na	1900
99.2	16.3	78.3	−3.5	172.6	20.7	99.5	16.3	1901
117.3	18.3	79.4	1.3	191.3	10.9	106.6	7.1	1902
110.9	−5.4	98.9	24.6	172.2	−10.0	92.3	−13.4	1903
96.7	−12.9	95.4	−3.5	167.0	−3.0	86.1	−6.7	1904
101.4	4.9	98.7	3.4	181.6	8.7	90.4	5.0	1905
87.3	−13.9	113.2	14.7	172.3	−5.1	83.2	−8.0	1906
94.9	8.7	118.5	4.7	190.8	10.7	89.2	7.2	1907
104.3	9.9	111.9	−5.6	226.4	18.7	103.0	15.5	1908
89.8	−13.8	109.9	−1.8	215.6	−4.8	96.2	−6.6	1909
93.3	3.9	101.0	−8.1	258.6	20.0	112.4	16.8	1910
119.4	28.0	116.6	15.4	285.0	10.2	118.7	5.7	1911
144.6	21.1	155.3	33.2	288.2	1.1	114.5	−3.6	1912
169.3	17.0	168.1	8.3	355.0	23.2	134.9	17.8	1913
194.7	15.0	147.8	−12.1	410.1	15.5	151.3	12.2	1914
266.7	37.0	141.5	−4.3	445.0	8.5	161.4	6.7	1915
255.3	−4.3	153.0	8.1	409.3	−8.0	145.4	−9.9	1916
301.7	18.2	127.2	−16.9	517.2	26.4	179.9	23.7	1917
374.9	24.2	135.4	6.4	541.5	4.7	187.9	4.5	1918
429.5	14.6	130.6	−3.6	564.0	4.2	196.5	4.5	1919
429.4	0.0	133.8	2.4	541.2	−4.0	187.0	−4.8	1920
447.4	4.2	89.1	−33.4	664.6	22.8	227.4	21.6	1921
523.0	16.9	88.9	−0.3	741.4	11.6	251.7	10.7	1922
473.9	−9.4	147.8	66.4	639.9	−13.7	214.8	−14.6	1923
469.4	−1.0	160.2	8.3	650.3	1.6	214.0	−0.4	1924
419.7	−10.6	215.8	34.8	567.3	−12.8	181.4	−15.2	1925
589.1	40.4	247.8	14.8	746.1	31.5	228.1	25.7	1926
532.4	−9.6	251.2	1.4	736.2	−1.3	214.5	−6.0	1927
731.6	37.4	262.1	4.4	939.8	27.7	265.6	23.8	1928
1,002.7	37.1	282.8	7.9	1,226.6	30.5	337.1	26.9	1929
1,020.4	1.8	242.5	−14.3	1,234.1	0.6	329.5	−2.2	1930
976.8	−4.3	184.5	−23.9	1,195.7	−3.1	321.6	−2.4	1931
808.9	−17.2	142.3	−22.9	1,058.9	−11.4	292.3	−9.1	1932
803.4	−0.7	161.7	13.6	1,057.8	−0.1	292.1	−0.1	1933
905.3	12.7	215.5	33.3	1,093.9	3.4	293.7	0.5	1934
861.6	−4.8	225.1	4.5	1,090.8	−0.3	281.4	−4.2	1935
952.9	10.6	253.9	12.8	1,224.8	12.3	304.2	8.1	1936
1,156.5	21.4	333.5	31.4	1,403.3	14.6	331.0	8.8	1937
871.7	−24.6	332.0	−0.4	1,166.1	−16.9	263.3	−20.5	1938
927.7	6.4	344.5	3.7	1,230.8	5.6	268.5	2.0	1939

Note: * *Excludes land improvement, breeding stock, draught animals, daily cattle, and the like, which*
is deemed to be negligible or is conceivably zero.
na denotes not applicable.

Table A1.4 **PFCE by major consumption categories at current prices in Straits$ millions**

		Major consumption categories			
Year	Food	Beverages and tobacco	Clothing	Rent	Domestic servants
1	2	3	4	5	6
1900	75.4	2.6	9.6	3.4	2.9
1901	75.2	2.5	12.3	3.7	3.0
1902	82.3	3.0	14.0	3.9	3.5
1903	86.2	3.3	13.9	4.1	3.6
1904	86.2	3.1	15.8	4.2	3.5
1905	89.2	2.8	15.8	4.5	3.7
1906	92.8	3.3	16.3	5.0	4.3
1907	103.2	3.2	18.1	5.4	5.0
1908	111.3	3.3	19.4	5.8	5.4
1909	112.7	3.4	18.6	6.1	5.7
1910	114.5	4.1	19.6	6.2	5.9
1911	127.3	5.2	20.5	7.0	8.0
1912	139.5	5.4	20.9	7.2	8.8
1913	152.5	7.3	22.6	8.8	10.6
1914	153.5	8.3	25.5	10.5	14.0
1915	153.7	7.6	33.4	10.2	13.8
1916	155.4	10.9	36.8	10.1	13.0
1917	184.9	10.8	37.0	11.2	16.0
1918	194.2	12.5	41.7	11.1	14.1
1919	223.1	11.8	41.2	10.3	11.5
1920	243.0	11.1	40.5	10.3	11.9
1921	219.7	15.4	45.9	14.4	16.8
1922	199.8	16.2	37.5	17.2	17.9
1923	205.2	14.1	34.7	20.4	18.4
1924	234.3	15.4	38.8	24.3	21.5
1925	244.2	15.3	39.1	25.5	21.5
1926	274.2	16.6	41.5	28.5	22.9
1927	283.7	17.1	43.8	33.1	24.5
1928	288.3	17.9	44.7	37.7	25.6
1929	324.8	20.6	48.6	43.4	29.9
1930	278.7	17.3	42.8	36.6	26.2
1931	184.2	15.3	35.6	25.3	19.7
1932	159.0	15.3	31.3	21.1	18.5
1933	162.7	15.8	34.7	20.7	19.7
1934	163.0	14.8	30.3	19.6	19.5
1935	209.9	16.2	35.7	22.6	23.8
1936	240.1	19.6	42.9	26.7	28.5
1937	290.0	21.4	49.7	29.4	32.2
1938	290.5	23.4	55.3	33.6	34.7
1939	293.7	25.8	61.5	37.5	35.6

Table A1.4 (cont'd) PFCE by major consumption categories at current prices in Straits$ millions

Major consumption categories					
Transport*	Clubs	Opium / chandu	Miscellaneous**	PFCE	Year
7	8	9	10	11=2+3+4+5+ 6+7+8+9+10	
4.6	1.1	9.1	7.0	115.6	1900
4.9	1.2	9.2	7.2	119.2	1901
5.3	1.2	9.8	7.9	130.8	1902
5.9	1.3	9.4	8.2	135.9	1903
5.9	1.2	11.2	8.5	139.6	1904
6.3	1.3	12.4	8.8	144.8	1905
7.1	1.3	12.7	9.3	152.1	1906
7.6	1.4	12.5	10.3	166.7	1907
7.8	1.5	12.6	11.1	178.1	1908
8.1	1.5	12.3	11.2	179.6	1909
8.8	1.7	16.7	11.6	189.0	1910
11.4	2.5	18.0	13.1	212.9	1911
12.7	2.9	19.7	14.1	231.3	1912
14.4	3.7	21.8	15.7	257.4	1913
15.5	4.3	18.8	16.6	266.9	1914
14.9	3.7	20.1	17.0	274.4	1915
16.3	4.0	25.7	17.7	289.9	1916
18.3	4.9	29.8	20.4	333.2	1917
17.2	5.0	33.9	21.4	351.0	1918
17.3	4.5	35.0	23.0	377.5	1919
17.4	3.8	39.0	24.4	401.3	1920
18.0	5.9	25.1	24.5	385.7	1921
16.1	6.3	22.0	22.9	355.8	1922
15.3	6.2	26.6	23.6	364.4	1923
17.0	7.0	25.5	26.8	410.6	1924
18.7	7.0	29.1	28.2	428.5	1925
21.4	7.3	38.6	31.7	482.7	1926
21.4	7.7	38.1	33.6	503.1	1927
20.8	8.1	33.1	34.8	511.0	1928
22.4	9.2	31.0	39.2	568.9	1929
19.0	8.2	24.1	34.8	487.6	1930
14.1	7.5	15.1	25.7	342.6	1931
12.4	7.8	12.5	22.9	300.7	1932
12.8	8.8	12.4	23.4	310.8	1933
12.9	8.3	16.3	23.2	308.0	1934
14.7	9.7	15.9	28.6	376.9	1935
16.6	11.7	13.7	32.7	432.4	1936
19.2	12.8	14.2	38.1	507.1	1937
20.0	14.2	13.2	39.6	524.5	1938
20.4	13.9	11.9	41.0	541.4	1939

Notes: * Includes coaching, ferry, and motoring services provided by railways.
      ** Includes health, education, utilities, furniture, furnishings and household equipment and operation, cultural and personal services, and other goods and services not included elsewhere.

Table A1.5 **PFCE by major consumption categories at constant 1914 prices in Straits$ millions**

Year	Food	Beverages and tobacco	Clothing	Rent	Domestic servants
1	2	3	4	5	6
1900	78.6	3.5	11.9	4.5	3.9
1901	82.9	3.7	12.6	4.8	4.1
1902	85.7	3.9	13.0	4.9	4.3
1903	88.2	4.0	13.4	5.1	4.4
1904	89.8	4.0	13.5	5.2	4.4
1905	95.3	4.3	14.4	5.5	4.7
1906	103.4	4.7	15.9	6.0	5.2
1907	108.4	4.9	16.7	6.2	5.5
1908	115.4	5.3	17.9	6.6	5.9
1909	122.3	5.7	19.2	7.0	6.3
1910	125.7	5.8	19.7	7.2	6.5
1911	129.5	6.3	20.3	8.2	8.8
1912	129.5	6.5	20.3	8.4	9.7
1913	141.0	7.3	22.7	9.4	11.7
1914	153.5	8.3	25.5	10.5	14.0
1915	147.6	7.9	24.1	10.1	13.2
1916	141.7	7.4	22.8	9.7	12.5
1917	156.7	8.4	25.7	10.7	14.1
1918	138.6	7.2	22.0	9.5	12.1
1919	118.0	5.8	17.9	8.1	9.8
1920	97.0	4.5	13.9	6.6	7.6
1921	131.0	6.4	19.3	8.9	10.8
1922	137.7	6.8	20.5	9.3	11.5
1923	141.5	7.0	21.2	9.6	11.8
1924	160.9	8.2	24.7	10.9	13.8
1925	161.8	8.2	24.7	11.0	13.8
1926	171.7	8.7	26.3	11.6	14.7
1927	183.2	9.4	28.2	12.4	15.8
1928	190.8	9.8	29.4	12.9	16.5
1929	217.8	11.4	34.4	14.8	19.3
1930	199.6	10.2	30.6	13.5	17.1
1931	178.1	8.8	26.4	10.9	14.3
1932	182.2	9.1	27.4	11.1	14.8
1933	203.8	10.5	31.4	12.4	17.0
1934	193.4	9.8	29.2	11.8	15.8
1935	222.9	11.5	34.5	13.6	18.6
1936	262.9	14.0	41.9	16.0	22.6
1937	285.5	15.3	45.8	17.4	24.8
1938	309.5	16.8	50.1	18.9	27.1
1939	317.5	17.1	51.3	19.4	27.7

Table A1.5 (cont'd) **PFCE by major consumption categories at constant 1914 prices in Straits$ millions**

Major consumption categories					
Transport*	Clubs	Opium / chandu	Miscellaneous**	PFCE	Year
7	8	9	10	11=2+3+4+5+ 6+7+8+9+10	
4.2	1.1	9.9	7.6	125.3	1900
4.5	1.2	10.2	8.0	132.0	1901
4.9	1.2	10.2	8.3	136.5	1902
5.5	1.3	9.7	8.5	140.1	1903
5.5	1.3	11.6	8.9	144.2	1904
5.9	1.4	13.2	9.4	154.1	1905
6.6	1.5	14.1	10.3	167.7	1906
7.3	1.6	13.1	10.8	174.6	1907
7.4	1.7	13.1	11.6	185.0	1908
7.8	1.8	13.4	12.3	195.8	1909
8.5	1.9	18.3	12.6	206.3	1910
11.1	2.6	18.5	13.4	218.7	1911
12.3	2.9	18.9	13.6	222.0	1912
14.4	3.5	20.8	15.0	245.8	1913
15.5	4.3	18.8	16.6	266.9	1914
14.6	4.1	18.7	15.9	256.2	1915
15.8	3.9	22.2	15.3	251.2	1916
16.8	4.3	24.8	17.0	278.5	1917
15.3	3.7	23.6	14.9	246.7	1918
14.1	3.0	18.9	12.5	208.2	1919
13.7	2.3	16.2	10.2	172.1	1920
14.7	3.3	14.3	13.9	222.6	1921
14.4	3.5	14.2	14.8	232.8	1922
16.2	3.6	17.6	15.6	244.1	1923
17.1	4.3	16.9	17.8	274.5	1924
17.7	4.3	18.8	18.2	278.3	1925
20.6	4.5	23.8	19.6	301.6	1926
22.7	4.9	24.0	21.1	321.7	1927
22.3	5.1	21.1	22.2	330.1	1928
24.9	5.9	20.1	25.4	374.1	1929
22.2	5.3	16.5	23.9	338.9	1930
14.7	4.7	12.9	21.8	292.6	1931
14.0	4.9	12.3	22.6	298.4	1932
14.9	5.6	13.3	25.1	334.0	1933
15.2	5.2	17.0	24.3	321.6	1934
17.8	6.1	15.6	27.9	368.6	1935
20.7	7.4	13.7	32.7	431.9	1936
23.6	8.1	13.1	35.1	468.8	1937
24.5	8.9	12.8	38.3	506.8	1938
24.8	9.1	11.4	39.2	517.5	1939

Notes: * *Includes coaching, ferry, and motoring services provided by railways.*
** *Includes health, education, utilities, furniture, furnishings and household equipment and operation, cultural and personal services, and other goods and services not included elsewhere.*

Table A1.6 Value and annual growth rate of GFCE at current and constant 1914 prices in Straits$ millions

Year	Current prices				Other outlays less non-commodity sales and commodities produced	GFCE
	Output of producers of government services					
	Compensation of employees	Intermediate consumption	Consumption of fixed capital (depreciation)	Total		
1	2	3	4	5=2+3+4	6	7=5-6
1900	4.7	1.7	0.3	6.6	0.1	6.5
1901	6.2	2.2	0.3	8.7	0.1	8.6
1902	5.6	2.0	0.3	7.9	0.1	7.8
1903	6.3	2.3	0.4	8.9	0.1	8.8
1904	6.7	2.6	0.4	9.7	0.1	9.6
1905	7.1	2.9	0.4	10.5	0.1	10.3
1906	6.6	2.7	0.4	9.7	0.1	9.6
1907	7.1	2.9	0.4	10.4	0.2	10.2
1908	7.7	3.3	0.5	11.5	0.2	11.3
1909	7.8	3.4	0.5	11.7	0.2	11.5
1910	8.1	3.7	0.5	12.3	0.2	12.1
1911	8.7	4.0	0.5	13.2	0.2	13.0
1912	9.6	4.4	0.6	14.6	0.3	14.4
1913	10.6	5.0	0.6	16.2	0.3	15.9
1914	11.3	5.1	0.7	17.1	0.3	16.8
1915	11.5	4.7	0.7	16.9	0.3	16.6
1916	11.7	5.1	0.7	17.4	0.3	17.1
1917	12.1	5.1	0.7	18.0	0.4	17.6
1918	13.8	6.5	0.8	21.1	0.5	20.6
1919	17.4	7.7	1.0	26.2	0.5	25.7
1920	25.8	8.9	1.4	36.2	0.6	35.5
1921	28.8	11.0	1.7	41.5	0.7	40.8
1922	24.8	10.5	1.5	36.7	0.7	36.1
1923	25.1	10.6	1.5	37.2	0.8	36.5
1924	26.2	11.9	1.6	39.6	0.8	38.8
1925	27.8	12.7	1.7	42.2	1.0	41.2
1926	29.7	13.4	1.8	44.9	1.3	43.6
1927	34.2	16.4	2.1	52.7	1.4	51.3
1928	36.0	16.7	2.2	54.8	1.6	53.2
1929	39.0	17.9	2.4	59.2	1.5	57.8
1930	39.8	16.9	2.4	59.1	1.6	57.5
1931	39.8	17.3	2.4	59.5	1.4	58.1
1932	35.1	13.5	2.0	50.5	1.3	49.3
1933	33.4	11.1	1.9	46.4	1.2	45.2
1934	32.6	10.6	1.8	45.0	1.3	43.7
1935	33.2	12.0	1.9	47.1	1.4	45.6
1936	34.6	13.2	2.0	49.8	1.5	48.3
1937	37.1	14.4	2.1	53.6	1.7	51.9
1938	40.1	15.6	2.3	57.9	1.7	56.2
1939	41.4	17.6	2.5	61.5	1.7	59.8

Table A1.6 (cont'd) **Value and annual growth rate of GFCE at current and constant 1914 prices in Straits$ millions**

Deflator	Constant prices	Annual growth rate (%)		
		GFCE		
Consumer price index	GFCE	Current prices	Constant prices 1914=100	Year
1914=100	Value	(%)	(%)	
8	9=7/8*100	10	11	
91.8	7.1	na	na	1900
90.0	9.6	32.2	34.8	1901
95.6	8.1	−10.1	−15.4	1902
96.7	9.1	13.8	12.5	1903
96.5	10.0	9.0	9.3	1904
93.6	11.0	7.4	10.7	1905
90.5	10.6	−7.5	−4.3	1906
95.2	10.7	6.8	1.5	1907
96.0	11.7	10.3	9.4	1908
91.5	12.6	2.1	7.2	1909
91.4	13.2	4.9	5.0	1910
97.2	13.4	7.6	1.2	1911
104.2	13.8	10.5	3.0	1912
105.0	15.1	10.7	10.0	1913
100.0	16.8	5.9	11.1	1914
107.4	15.4	−1.5	−8.2	1915
116.0	14.7	3.0	−4.7	1916
120.1	14.7	3.1	−0.4	1917
143.7	14.3	16.7	−2.4	1918
184.6	13.9	25.0	−2.7	1919
240.0	14.8	38.2	6.3	1920
175.9	23.2	15.0	56.9	1921
154.3	23.4	−11.7	0.7	1922
151.2	24.1	1.1	3.2	1923
151.0	25.7	6.4	6.6	1924
155.4	26.5	6.1	3.1	1925
162.1	26.9	5.9	1.6	1926
158.7	32.3	17.5	20.0	1927
156.8	34.0	3.9	5.2	1928
153.9	37.5	8.5	10.5	1929
145.5	39.5	−0.4	5.4	1930
117.7	49.4	1.0	24.9	1931
101.0	48.8	−15.2	−1.2	1932
93.0	48.6	−8.3	−0.4	1933
95.8	45.6	−3.3	−6.1	1934
102.3	44.6	4.4	−2.2	1935
100.1	48.2	5.8	8.1	1936
108.3	48.0	7.6	−0.6	1937
103.5	54.4	8.3	13.3	1938
104.6	57.2	6.4	5.3	1939

Table A1.7 GFCF by type at current prices in Straits$ millions

Year	Construction	Machinery and equipment	Cultivated assets*	GFCF**
1	2	3	4	5=2+3+4
1900	5.3	2.5	0.4	8.2
1901	8.8	2.9	0.6	12.3
1902	7.9	2.2	0.8	10.9
1903	9.2	2.8	1.0	12.9
1904	10.6	1.6	1.4	13.6
1905	12.7	1.4	1.7	15.9
1906	10.9	4.1	3.6	18.6
1907	15.1	8.0	5.5	28.6
1908	22.0	7.9	8.2	38.0
1909	12.3	4.2	9.4	26.0
1910	20.4	5.8	17.2	43.4
1911	16.8	8.6	22.6	48.0
1912	25.0	10.1	26.6	61.7
1913	52.2	18.0	29.0	99.2
1914	38.5	17.8	23.2	79.5
1915	18.8	6.8	26.0	51.7
1916	15.1	8.0	25.6	48.7
1917	28.1	7.3	36.5	71.9
1918	20.0	5.7	36.7	62.4
1919	26.4	12.7	33.6	72.8
1920	66.2	30.8	33.0	130.0
1921	56.2	29.6	31.0	116.8
1922	23.4	14.2	30.5	68.2
1923	21.4	12.9	22.7	57.0
1924	19.6	11.1	25.4	56.1
1925	32.0	21.7	24.5	78.1
1926	40.6	31.8	29.7	102.1
1927	60.1	31.8	44.8	136.6
1928	71.9	31.0	41.0	143.9
1929	64.6	28.2	42.1	134.9
1930	40.0	19.1	40.8	99.9
1931	31.1	11.1	22.7	65.0
1932	19.1	6.1	19.8	45.0
1933	12.8	4.9	14.9	32.6
1934	11.5	8.4	13.5	33.4
1935	15.0	11.0	12.8	38.8
1936	17.5	12.8	14.6	44.9
1937	26.8	21.0	16.3	64.1
1938	31.7	23.5	15.3	70.5
1939	33.6	20.6	28.7	82.9

Notes: * Relates to plantation, orchard, and vineyard development.
** Excludes land improvement, breeding stock, draught animals, dairy cattle, and the like, which is deemed to be negligible or is conceivably zero.

Table A1.8 **GFCF by type at constant 1914 prices in Straits$ millions**

Year	Construction	Machinery and equipment	Cultivated assets*	GFCF**
1	2	3	4	5=2+3+4
1900	3.5	2.5	0.4	6.5
1901	6.3	3.0	0.8	10.1
1902	5.5	2.4	1.0	8.8
1903	6.8	3.0	1.2	11.0
1904	8.1	1.8	1.7	11.6
1905	10.0	1.5	2.1	13.7
1906	11.0	4.5	4.3	19.9
1907	14.3	8.5	6.3	29.1
1908	20.6	8.1	8.6	37.3
1909	12.9	4.5	9.9	27.3
1910	22.7	6.1	18.0	46.8
1911	17.5	8.9	23.7	50.0
1912	25.3	10.0	27.9	63.2
1913	46.5	17.2	29.3	92.9
1914	38.5	17.8	23.2	79.5
1915	16.9	5.4	26.0	48.2
1916	10.2	5.3	25.6	41.1
1917	14.5	3.7	31.2	49.5
1918	7.5	2.6	30.9	41.0
1919	10.6	5.1	27.3	43.0
1920	19.7	12.1	26.8	58.6
1921	19.4	16.6	24.6	60.5
1922	14.9	10.5	25.7	51.0
1923	16.5	10.0	19.1	45.7
1924	14.8	8.5	17.7	40.9
1925	25.0	16.6	17.0	58.6
1926	32.3	24.9	19.0	76.2
1927	47.9	24.4	28.7	100.9
1928	56.4	23.5	26.3	106.2
1929	51.0	20.8	23.2	95.1
1930	34.7	15.4	27.8	77.9
1931	30.8	9.6	21.1	61.5
1932	19.1	5.3	20.8	45.2
1933	14.6	4.4	14.5	33.5
1934	15.9	7.1	13.8	36.8
1935	21.3	9.2	10.6	41.1
1936	25.0	10.0	10.6	45.6
1937	38.7	14.3	10.5	63.5
1938	39.5	15.9	9.9	65.3
1939	41.0	13.3	18.5	72.9

Notes: * *Relates to plantation, orchard, and vineyard development.*
        ** *Excludes land improvement, breeding stock, draught animals, dairy cattle, and the like, which is deemed to be negligible or is conceivably zero.*

Table A1.9 Exports and imports of goods and services at current prices in Straits$ millions*

Year	Malaya's exports			Malaya's imports		
	Goods	Services**	Total	Goods	Services**	Total
1	2	3	4=2+3	5	6	7=5+6
1900	99.6	3.1	102.7	69.4	4.4	73.8
1901	102.4	3.2	105.6	66.0	4.2	70.2
1902	121.3	3.8	125.1	74.7	4.8	79.5
1903	119.6	3.7	123.3	84.3	5.4	89.7
1904	104.9	3.2	108.2	79.1	5.0	84.1
1905	119.5	3.7	123.2	84.8	5.4	90.2
1906	129.9	4.0	133.9	89.7	5.7	95.5
1907	134.0	4.1	138.2	97.4	6.2	103.6
1908	116.4	3.6	120.0	91.5	5.8	97.3
1909	127.1	3.9	131.0	87.5	5.6	93.1
1910	162.9	5.0	167.9	101.3	6.5	107.7
1911	184.5	5.7	190.2	127.0	8.1	135.1
1912	226.2	7.0	233.2	154.9	9.9	164.8
1913	218.9	6.8	225.7	163.6	10.4	174.0
1914	188.9	5.8	194.7	139.0	8.9	147.8
1915	244.9	7.6	252.5	132.5	8.5	141.0
1916	322.5	10.0	332.5	161.4	10.3	171.7
1917	395.7	10.7	406.4	179.6	11.5	191.1
1918	358.3	11.1	369.4	196.9	12.6	209.4
1919	452.5	14.0	466.5	254.2	16.2	270.4
1920	470.3	14.5	484.8	364.6	23.3	387.9
1921	217.5	6.7	224.3	198.1	12.6	210.7
1922	247.3	7.6	255.0	173.5	11.1	184.6
1923	366.7	11.3	378.1	205.6	13.1	218.7
1924	385.0	11.9	396.9	231.9	14.8	246.7
1925	725.9	16.3	742.2	311.4	19.9	331.3
1926	766.1	23.7	789.8	382.3	24.4	406.7
1927	588.7	18.2	606.9	385.2	24.6	409.7
1928	468.7	14.5	483.2	384.3	24.5	408.9
1929	586.7	18.1	604.8	403.8	25.8	429.6
1930	371.5	11.5	382.9	330.8	21.1	351.9
1931	222.2	6.9	229.0	212.4	13.6	226.0
1932	163.7	5.1	168.8	156.9	10.0	166.9
1933	208.1	6.4	214.6	159.2	10.2	169.3
1934	347.4	10.7	358.2	206.1	13.2	219.3
1935	341.7	10.6	352.2	217.5	13.9	231.3
1936	430.2	13.3	443.5	244.4	15.6	260.0
1937	624.0	19.3	643.3	330.7	21.1	351.8
1938	355.8	11.0	366.8	287.1	18.3	305.4
1939	474.7	14.7	489.4	316.2	20.2	336.4

Notes: * The trade balance may be computed as exports minus imports.
** Exports and imports of services is assumed to be, in general, 3% and 6% of total exports and imports of goods and services respectively, based on statistical evidence.

Table A1.10 Exports and imports of goods and services at constant 1914 prices in Straits\$ millions*

Year	Malaya's exports			Malaya's imports		
	Goods	Services	Total	Goods	Services	Total
1	2	3	4=2+3	5	6	7=5+6
1900	81.8	3.5	85.3	76.2	5.0	81.2
1901	95.7	3.5	99.2	73.7	4.7	78.3
1902	113.2	4.1	117.3	74.1	5.2	79.4
1903	106.9	4.0	110.9	93.1	5.9	98.9
1904	93.2	3.5	96.7	90.1	5.4	95.4
1905	97.5	3.9	101.4	92.9	5.8	98.7
1906	83.1	4.2	87.3	107.2	6.0	113.2
1907	90.6	4.3	94.9	112.1	6.4	118.5
1908	100.5	3.8	104.3	105.8	6.1	111.9
1909	85.7	4.1	89.8	104.1	5.8	109.9
1910	88.1	5.2	93.3	94.4	6.6	101.0
1911	113.6	5.8	119.4	108.3	8.3	116.6
1912	137.6	7.0	144.6	145.4	9.9	155.3
1913	162.5	6.8	169.3	157.7	10.5	168.1
1914	188.9	5.8	194.7	139.0	8.9	147.8
1915	259.5	7.2	266.7	133.5	8.0	141.5
1916	246.3	9.0	255.3	143.7	9.3	153.0
1917	293.9	7.9	301.7	118.8	8.4	127.2
1918	367.6	7.2	374.9	127.2	8.2	135.4
1919	421.7	7.8	429.5	121.6	9.0	130.6
1920	422.4	7.0	429.4	122.6	11.2	133.8
1921	444.0	3.4	447.4	82.7	6.4	89.1
1922	518.7	4.4	523.0	82.5	6.3	88.9
1923	467.0	6.9	473.9	139.9	8.0	147.8
1924	462.1	7.3	469.4	151.1	9.0	160.2
1925	409.7	10.0	419.7	203.7	12.2	215.8
1926	574.5	14.6	589.1	232.7	15.1	247.8
1927	521.0	11.4	532.4	235.7	15.5	251.2
1928	722.4	9.2	731.6	246.6	15.5	262.1
1929	991.1	11.7	1,002.7	266.3	16.6	282.8
1930	1,012.8	7.6	1,020.4	228.6	13.9	242.5
1931	972.2	4.6	976.8	175.4	9.2	184.5
1932	805.4	3.5	808.9	135.4	6.9	142.3
1933	798.9	4.5	803.4	154.6	7.1	161.7
1934	897.7	7.6	905.3	206.2	9.3	215.5
1935	854.1	7.5	861.6	215.3	9.9	225.1
1936	943.4	9.5	952.9	242.8	11.1	253.9
1937	1,143.0	13.5	1,156.5	318.7	14.8	333.5
1938	864.1	7.6	871.7	319.4	12.7	332.0
1939	917.8	9.9	927.7	330.9	13.6	344.5

Note: * The trade balance may be computed as exports minus imports.

Table A1.11 Price indices used in the deflation of the various components of GDP from current to constant 1914 prices

	GFCE	PFCE							
		Consumer price indices by major consumption categories							
	Consumer price index (overall)	Food	Beverages and tobacco	Clothing	Rent	Domestic servants	Transport	Clubs	Consumer price index (overall)
Year									
1	2	3	4	5	6	7	8	9	10
1900	92	96	73	80	75	75	108	99	92
1901	90	91	69	98	77	73	107	97	90
1902	96	96	78	107	78	82	107	98	96
1903	97	98	82	104	80	82	107	104	97
1904	97	96	78	117	81	79	107	95	97
1905	94	94	66	109	83	79	107	93	94
1906	91	90	69	103	85	82	107	87	91
1907	95	95	66	108	86	91	105	86	95
1908	96	97	62	108	88	91	105	87	96
1909	92	92	61	97	86	91	104	85	92
1910	91	91	70	99	86	91	103	89	91
1911	97	98	82	101	85	91	103	96	97
1912	104	108	84	103	86	91	103	100	104
1913	105	108	99	100	93	91	100	105	105
1914	100	100	100	100	100	100	100	100	100
1915	107	104	97	138	102	104	102	91	107
1916	116	110	147	161	104	104	103	104	116
1917	120	118	129	144	105	113	109	114	120
1918	144	140	175	190	117	117	113	134	144
1919	185	189	201	230	127	117	123	147	185
1920	240	251	244	292	156	156	127	164	240
1921	176	168	239	237	162	156	123	177	176
1922	154	145	237	183	184	156	112	177	154
1923	151	145	201	164	213	156	95	169	151
1924	151	146	188	157	223	156	99	164	151
1925	155	151	186	158	233	156	105	164	155
1926	162	160	190	158	245	156	104	162	162
1927	159	155	183	155	267	156	94	160	159
1928	157	151	183	152	292	156	93	160	157
1929	154	149	180	141	294	156	90	155	154
1930	146	140	171	140	271	153	86	156	146
1931	118	104	174	135	233	138	96	161	118
1932	101	87	168	115	190	125	89	160	101
1933	93	80	151	110	166	116	85	158	93
1934	96	84	151	104	166	124	85	160	96
1935	102	94	140	104	166	127	82	158	102
1936	100	91	140	103	166	126	80	157	100
1937	108	102	140	109	169	130	81	158	108
1938	104	94	140	110	178	128	82	159	104
1939	105	93	151	120	194	128	82	153	105

Table A1.11 (cont'd) **Price indices used in the deflation of the various components of GDP from current to constant 1914 prices**

GFCF			Exports of goods and services		Imports of goods and services		
Cultivated assets	Construction	Machinery and equipment	Goods	Services	Goods	Services	
Wage indices of agricultural sector workers	Import unit value index of cement Federated Malay States	Price index of capital goods UK	Export unit value index	Price indices of 'transport and communication' and 'other services' UK	Import unit value index Federated Malay States	Price indices of 'transport and communication' and 'other services' UK	Year
11	**12**	**13**	**14**	**15**	**16**	**17**	
80	149	102	122	89	91	89	1900
80	140	97	107	90	90	90	1901
84	144	93	107	91	101	91	1902
84	136	91	112	92	91	92	1903
82	131	91	113	94	88	94	1904
82	127	91	123	94	91	94	1905
84	98	91	156	95	84	95	1906
88	105	94	148	97	87	97	1907
96	107	97	116	96	87	96	1908
96	95	94	148	96	84	96	1909
96	90	94	185	98	107	98	1910
96	96	97	162	98	117	98	1911
96	99	101	164	100	107	100	1912
99	112	105	135	100	104	100	1913
100	100	100	100	100	100	100	1914
100	112	128	94	105	99	105	1915
100	147	152	131	111	112	111	1916
117	193	196	135	136	151	136	1917
119	267	215	98	154	155	154	1918
123	249	252	107	180	209	180	1919
123	336	253	111	208	298	208	1920
126	290	179	49	197	240	197	1921
119	158	135	48	175	210	175	1922
119	130	128	79	165	147	165	1923
144	133	131	83	164	154	164	1924
144	128	130	177	163	153	163	1925
156	126	128	133	162	164	162	1926
156	126	130	113	159	163	159	1927
156	127	132	65	158	156	158	1928
181	127	136	59	156	152	156	1929
147	116	124	37	152	145	152	1930
108	101	115	23	148	121	148	1931
95	100	115	20	145	116	145	1932
103	88	111	26	143	103	143	1933
98	72	117	39	142	100	142	1934
120	70	120	40	141	101	141	1935
138	70	128	46	140	101	140	1936
155	69	147	55	143	104	143	1937
155	80	148	41	145	90	145	1938
155	82	155	52	149	96	149	1939

References

Abraham, W. I. 1969. *National Income and Economic Accounting.* New York: Prentice-Hall.

Abraham, W. I. and M. S. Gill. 1969a. 'New Measures of Economic Growth and Structural Change of the Malaysian Economy in the Post-1960 Period.' *Malayan Economic Review* (April), pp. 65–79.

———— 1969b. 'The Growth and Composition of Malaysia's Capital Stock.' *Malayan Economic Review* (October), pp. 44–54.

Akers, C. E. 1914. *The Rubber Industry in Brazil and the Orient.* London: Methuen & Company.

Albers, R. M. 2002. *Machinery Investment and Economic Growth: The Dynamics of Dutch Development 1800–1913.* Amsterdam: Aksant Academic Publishers.

Allen, L. A. 1938. *Proclamations, Order, Notices, Rules, Regulations, Declarations, Appointments, Forms and By-laws in Force on 31st day of December 1935 made under the Laws of the Federated Malay States and of each of them prepared under the Authority of the Revised Edition of the Laws Enactment, 1932, Vol. 5 containing the Subsidiary Legislation made under Enactments, Ch. 138–161.* (Diet Scales of Government Hospitals 1936–Ch. 154). Kuala Lumpur: Government Printers.

Allen, R. C. 2009. *The British Industrial Revolution in Global Perspective.* Cambridge: Cambridge University Press.

Andaya, B. W. and Andaya L. Y. 2001. *A History of Malaysia*, 2nd edn. University of Hawaii Press.

Asian Development Bank. 1999. 'Interpreting the Asian Financial Crisis', *Economic Development Resource Centre Briefing Notes Number 10.* Manila: Asian Development Bank.

Athukorala, P. and Menon, M. 1996. 'Foreign Investment and Industrialization in Malaysia: Exports, Employment and Spillovers.' *Asian Economic Journal* 10/11, pp. 29–44.

Azrai Abdullah, Izdihar Baharin and Rizal Yaakop. 2012. 'The Transformation of Perak's Political and Economic Structure in the British Colonial Period in Malaya, 1874–1957.' *Malaysian Journal of History, Politics, and Strategy,* Vol. 39/2 (December), pp. 63–72.

Baker, J. 2008. *Crossroads: A Popular History of Malaysia and Singapore.* Singapore: Marshall Cavendish Editions.

Balassa, B. 1964. *Trade Prospects for Developing Countries.* Illinois: Homewood.

Bank Negara Malaysia. 2016. *Bank Negara Annual Report 2015.* Kuala Lumpur. [http://www.bnm.gov.my/files/publication/ar/en/2015/ar2015_book.pdf], accessed 17 September 2016.

Barber, A. 2008. *Malaya: The Making of a Nation 1510–1957.* Kuala Lumpur: AB&A.

Barlow, C. 1978. *The Natural Rubber Industry: Its Development, Technology, and Economy in Malaysia.* Kuala Lumpur: Oxford University Press.

Barlow, C., Jayasriya, S. and Tan, C. S. 1994. *The World Rubber Industry.* London: Routledge.

Barlow, H. 1995. *Swettenham.* Kuala Lumpur: Southdene.

Bauer, P. T. 1961. *Indian Economic Policy and Development.* Great Britain: George Allen and Unwin Ltd.

Benham, F. C. 1951. *The National Income of Malaya, 1947–1949.* Singapore: Government Printers.

Bhanoji Rao, V. V. 1976. *National Accounts of West Malaysia, 1947–1971.* Singapore: Heinemann Educational Books.

_____ 1980. *Malaysia, Development Pattern and Policy, 1947–1971.* Singapore: Singapore University Press.

Birdsall, N. M., Campos, J. E., Kim, C. K., Corden, W. M. and MacDonald, L. (eds.). 1993. *The East Asian Miracle: Economic Growth and Public Policy – Main Report.* Washington: The World Bank.

Bolt, J. and Van Zanden, J. L. 2014. 'The Maddison Project: Collaborative Research on Historical National Accounts', *The Economic History Review,* 67, 3: pp. 627–651.

Boomgaard, P. and Brown, I. (eds.). 2000. *Weathering the Storm, The Economies of Southeast Asia in the 1930s Depression.* Singapore: Institute of Southeast Asian Studies.

Booth, A. 2016. *Economic Change in Modern Indonesia: Colonial and Post-colonial Comparisons.* Cambridge: Cambridge University Press.

Bosworth, B. P. and Collins, S. M. 2003. *The Empirics of Growth: An Update.* Brookings Institution. [http://www.brookings.edu/~/media/research/files/papers/2003/9/22 globaleconomics–bosworth/20030307.pdf], accessed 5 June 2016.

Bosworth, B. P., Collins, S. M. and Chen, Y. C. 1995. 'Accounting for Differences in Economic Growth.' Brookings Discussions Papers in *International Economics,* Vol. No. 115 (October), Washington: The Brookings Institution.

Brunner, K. 1981. *The Great Depression Revisited.* Boston: Martinus Nijhoff Publishing.

Bullard, J. 2012. 'Inflation Targeting in the USA', *Federal Reserve Bank of St Louis,* (February) 2012. [https://www.stlouisfed.org/~/media/Files/PDFs/Bullard/remarks/Bullard_Inflation_Targeting_in_the_USA_06Feb2012_final.pdf], accessed August 2016.

Burns, P. L. 1982. 'Capitalism and the Malay States'. In Hamza Alavi *et al.* (eds.). *Capitalism and Colonial Production,* London: Croom Helm.

Caldwell, J. C. 1963. 'Urban Growth in Malaya: Trends and Implications.' *Population Review* 7, pp. 39–50.

Carroll, C. D. 1997. 'Buffer Stock Saving and the Life Cycle/Permanent Income Hypothesis,' *Quarterly Journal of Economics,* CXII (1), pp. 1–56.

Carroll, C. D. and Summers, L. H. 1991. 'Consumption Growth Parallels Income Growth: Some New Evidence', In Bernheim B. D. and Shoven J. B., (eds.). *National Saving and Economic Performance.* Chicago: The University of Chicago Press.

Carter, S. B., *et al.* 2006. *Historical Statistics of the United States: Millennial Edition,* Vol. 3 (*Economic Structure and Performance*), Vol. 4 (*Economic Sectors*), and Vol. 5 (*Governance and International Relations*). New York: Cambridge University Press.

Cavalcanti, T. V. V., Mohaddes, K. and Raissi, M. 2012. 'Commodity Price Volatility and the Sources of Growth.' *IMF working paper 12/12.* Washington DC.

Cavendish, A. 1911. *Report on the Census of Kedah and Perlis, 1911.* Penang: The Criterion Press Ltd.

Chai, H. 1977. *Education and Nation–Building in Plural Societies: The West Malaysian Experience.* Canberra: Australian National University.

Cheah, B. K. 2001. *Early Modern History 1800–1940.* The Encyclopedia of Malaysia, Vol. 7. Singapore: Archipelago Press.

Cole, D. C., Kim, M. J., Kwang S. K, Mason, E. S. and Perkins, D. H. 1989. *Studies in the Modernisation of the Republic of Korea: 1945–1975. The Economic and Social Modernisation of the Republic of Korea.* Cambridge: Harvard University Press.

Coyle, D. 2014. *GDP: A Brief but Affectionate History.* Princeton University Press.

Crafts, N. F. R. 1985. 'Income Elasticities of Demand and Release of Labour by Agriculture During the British Industrial Revolution: A Further Appraisal'. In *The Economics of the Industrial Revolution*, Mokyr, J. (ed.). United States: Rowman and Littlefield Publishers Inc., pp. 151–163.

Curtis, M. 2003. *Web of Deceit—Britain's Real Role in the World.* London: Vintage Books.

Dabušinskas, A., Kulikov D. and Randveer, M. 2012. 'The Impact of Volatility on Economic Growth'. *Working Papers of Eesti Pank*, No. 7/2012. [http://www.eestipank.ee/en/publication/working–papers/2012/72012-aurelijus-dabusinskas-dmitry-kulikov-martti-randveer-impact-volatility-economic-growth], accessed 17 June 2016.

Darwin, J. 2013. *Unfinished Empire, the Global Expansion of Britain.* London: Penguin Books.

Dawe, D. C. 1993. '*Essays on Price Stabilization and the Macroeconomy in Low Income Countries.*' Ph.D. dissertation. Cambridge, Mass.: Harvard University.

———— 1996. 'A New Look at the Effects of Export Instability on Investment and Growth', *World Development 24* (12), 1905–1914.

Deaton, A. S. 1991. 'Saving and Liquidity Constraints.' *Econometrica* (59), pp. 1221–1248.

———— 2013. *The Great Escape: Health, Wealth, and the Origins of Inequality.* Princeton and Oxford: Princeton University Press.

Del Tufo, M. V. 1949. *A Report on the 1947 Census of Population, Malaya (Comprising the Federation of Malaya and the Colony of Singapore).* London: Crown Agents for the Colonies.

Department of Statistics-Malaysia. 1965. *National Accounts of the States of Malaya, 1955–1963.* Kuala Lumpur: Government Printers.

———— 1966. *National Accounts of West Malaysia, 1960–1965.* Kuala Lumpur: Government Printers.

———— 1967 (various years). *Survey of Construction Industries, Peninsular Malaysia, 1966.* Kuala Lumpur: Government Printers.

———— 1972. *National Accounts of West Malaysia, 1960–1968.* Kuala Lumpur: Government Printers.

———— 1975. *National Accounts of Peninsular Malaysia, 1960–1971,* Kuala Lumpur: Government Printers.

———— 1987. *National Income Estimates of Malaysia, 1987.* Unpublished.

Department of Statistics-Singapore. 1950. 'Cost of Living Pilot Survey, 12th August to 11th September, 1948 Singapore.' *Average Prices, Declared Trade Values, Exchange and Currency, Volume and Average Values of Imports and Exports, Market Prices, and Cost of Living for the years 1947 and 1948.* Singapore: Government Printing Office, Appendix B, pp. 78–136.

_____ 1952. *Average Prices, Declared Trade Values, Exchange and Currency, Volume and Average Values of Imports and Exports, Market Prices, and Cost of Living for the year 1951*, Malaya. Singapore: Government Printers.

Derksen, J. B. D. and Tinbergen, J. 1945. 'Calculations of the Economic Significance of the Netherlands Indies to the Netherlands'. *Monthly Bulletin of the Central Bureau of Statistics* (40), pp. 210–216.

Drabble, J. H. 1973. *Rubber in Malaya, 1876–1922: The Genesis of the Industry.* Kuala Lumpur: Oxford University Press.

_____ 2000. *An Economic History of Malaysia, c. 1800–1990: The Transition to Modern Economic Growth.* London: Macmillan Press.

Economic Planning Unit-Malaysia. 1966. *First Malaysia Plan, 1966–1970*, Kuala Lumpur. Government Printers.

_____ 1974. *Mid-term Review of the Second Malaysia Plan. 1971–1975.* Kuala Lumpur: Government Printers.

_____ 1989. *Mid-term Review of the Fifth Malaysia Plan 1986–1990.* Kuala Lumpur: Government Printers.

_____ 2015. *Eleventh Malaysia Plan 2016–2020 Anchoring Growth on People.* Kuala Lumpur: Government Printers.

_____ 2016. *Percentage Distribution of Households by Income Class, Malaysia, 1970–2014.* [http://www.epu.gov.my/documents/10124/86c5eb08–104c–47d3–b238–b2c3e32761b7], accessed 20 August 2016.

Eichengreen, B., Perkins, D. H. and Shin, K. 2012. *From Miracle to Maturity: The Growth of the Korean Economy.* Cambridge: Harvard University Press.

Engel, E. 1857. *Die Produktions– und Consumtionsverhältnisse des Königreichs Sachsen*, reprinted with Engel (1895), Anlage I, pp. 1–54.

Faulkner, H. U. 1959. *American Economic History.* New York: Harper & Brothers Publishers.

Feinstein, C. H. 1972. *National Income, Expenditure, and Output of the United Kingdom, 1855–1965.* Cambridge: Cambridge University Press.

Felipe, J. 1998. *Singapore's Aggregate Production Functions and Its (Lack of) Policy Implications.* Economics and Development Resource Center. Manila: Asian Development Bank.

Fell, H. 1960. *1957 Population Census of the Federation of Malaya, Report No. 14.* Kuala Lumpur: Department of Statistics-Federation of Malaya.

Figart, D. M. 1925. *The Plantation Rubber Industry in the Middle East.* Washington, DC: US Government Printing Office.

Fogel, R. F. 2001. '*Simon S. Kuznets 1901–1985: A Biographical Memoir—National Academy of Science, Biographical Memoirs, Vol. 79.* Washington, DC: The National Academy Press.

Friedman, M. and Schwartz, A. 1963. *A Monetary History of the United States 1867–1960.* Princeton: Princeton University Press.

Ghesquiere, H. 2007. *Singapore's Success: Engineering Economic Growth.* Singapore: Thomson Learning.

Grist, D. H. 1950. *An Outline of Malayan Agriculture.* Letchworth, Herts: Garden City Press.

Gullick, J. M. 1998. *A History of Selangor, 1766–1939.* Selangor: The Malaysian Branch of the Royal Asiatic Society.

_____ 2003. *A History of Negri Sembilan.* Selangor: The Malaysian Branch of the Royal Asiatic Society.

Hagan, J. and Wells, A. D. 2005. 'The British and Rubber in Malaya, c1890–1940', in G. Patmore, J. Shields, and N. Balnave (eds.). *The Past is Before Us: Proceedings of the Ninth National Labour History Conference*, ASSLH, Business and Labour History Group. Sydney: University of Sydney.

Hare, G. T. 1902. *Census of The Population, The Federated Malay States, 1901*. Kuala Lumpur: Government Printers.

Harper, T. N. 1999. *The End of Empire and the Making of Malaya*. Cambridge: Cambridge University Press.

Harvie, C. H. 1960. *National Accounts of the Federation of Malaya 1955–1960*. Kuala Lumpur: Department of Statistics, Federation of Malaya.

Hassan Osman Rani. 2007. *The Economy*. The Encyclopedia of Malaysia, Vol. 13. Singapore: Archipelago Press.

Heath, R. G. 1951. *Malayan Agricultural Statistics 1949*. Kuala Lumpur: Department of Agriculture, Federation of Malaya.

Heussler, R. 1981. *British Rule in Malaya, The Malayan Civil Service and Its Predecessors, 1867–1942*. Oxford: Clio Press.

Hirschman, C. 1988. 'Ownership and Control of the Malaysian Economy Revisited: A Review of Research in the 25 Years Since the Publication of J. J. Puthucheary's Classic', In D. Puthucheary and Jomo, K. S. (eds.). *No Cowardly Past: James J. Puthucheary's Writings, Poems, and Commentaries*.

Hjerppe, R. 1989. *The Finnish Economy 1860–1985, Growth and Structural Change*. Helsinki: Government Printing Centre.

Ho, T. M. 2009. *Ipoh When Tin Was King*. Ipoh: Perak Academy.

Horlings, E. 1995. *The Economic Development of the Dutch Service Sector 1800–1850, Trade and Transport in a Premodern Economy*. Amsterdam: The Netherlands Economic History Archives.

Hunter, W. C., Kaufman, G. G. and Krueger, T. H. (eds.). 1999. *The Asian Financial Crisis: Origins, Implications and Solutions*. New York: Springer Science+Business Media, LLC.

Imbs, J. 2007. 'Growth and Volatility.' *Journal of Monetary Economics,* Vol. 54, No.7.

Innes, J. R. 1901. *Report on the Census of the Straits Settlements, 1901*. Singapore: Government Printing Office.

International Bank for Reconstruction and Development. 1955. *The Economic Development of Malaya*. Report of a mission organised by the International Bank for Reconstruction and Development at the request of the Government of the Federation of Malaya, the Crown Colony of Singapore and the United Kingdom. Baltimore: Johns Hopkins Press.

International Rubber Study Group. (various years). *Rubber Statistical Bulletin*. [http://www.rubberstudy.com/pub-stats-bulletin.aspx], accessed 1 March 2016.

International Tin Council. 1968. *Statistical Year Book*.

——— (various years). *Annual Report*.

——— (various years). *Tin Statistics*.

International Tin Statistics. 1991. Bulletin No. 1, July 1991 and No. 16–17, January–October 1996.

Jackson, J. C. 1968. *Sarawak: A Geographical Survey of a Developing State*. London: University of London Press.

Jawaharlal, D. N. 2011. 'The Financial Crisis, the Great Recession and the Developing World', *Global Policy*, January 2011.

Jomo, K. S. 1986. *A Question of Class: Capital, the State, and Uneven Development in Malaya*. Singapore: Oxford University Press.

Jomo, K. S. (ed.). 1990a. *Undermining Tin, the Decline of Malaysian Pre-eminence.* Sydney: Transnational Corporations Research Project.

———— 1990b. *Growth and Structural Change in the Malaysian Economy.* Hong Kong: The Macmillan Press Ltd.

Jomo, K. S. and Tan, J. 2011. 'Lessons from Privatisation' in *Malaysia: Policies and Issues in Economic Development.* Kuala Lumpur: Institute of Strategic and International Studies, 329, pp. 362.

Karabell, Z. 2014. *The Leading Indicators: A Short History of the Numbers That Rule Our World.* Simon & Schuster Paperbacks.

Kaur, A. 1985. *Bridge and Barrier: Transport and Communications in Colonial Malaya, 1870–1957.* Singapore: Oxford University Press.

Kennedy, J. 2007. *History of Malaya.* Kuala Lumpur: Reprinted Synergy Media.

Khoo, K. K. 1977. 'The Great Depression: The Malaysian Context', In Khoo, K. K. (ed.). *The History of South, South East and East Asia: Essays and Documents.* Kuala Lumpur: Oxford University Press, pp. 78–94.

Khoo, K. K. 2003. *Taiping, The Vibrant Years.* Kuala Lumpur: OFA Desyne.

Kim, J. I., and L. Lau. 1994. 'The Sources of Economic Growth of the East Asian Newly Industrialized Countries.' *Journal of the Japanese and International Economies,* Vol. 8, pp. 235–271.

Kinney, W. P. 1975. *Aspects of Malayan Economic Development, 1900–1940.* Ph.D thesis. London: The University of London.

Kratoska, P. H. 1998. *The Japanese Occupation of Malaya, 1941–1945.* London: Hurst & Company.

Krugman, P. 1994. 'The Myth of Asia's Miracle.' *Foreign Affairs* (November/December), pp. 62–78.

———— 2008. The *Return of Depression Economics and the Crisis of 2008.* New York: W.W. Norton.

———— 2012. *Filters and Full Employment (Not Wonkish, Really).* [http:// krugman.blogs.nytimes.com/2012/07/11/filters-and-full-employment-not- wonkish-really/], accessed June 2016.

Kwang, S. K. and Roemer M. 1981. *Growth and Structural Transformation, Studies in the Modernisation of the Republic of Korea: 1945–1975.* Cambridge: Harvard University Press.

Lau, Albert. 1991. *The Malayan Union Controversy 1942–1948.* Singapore: Oxford University Press.

Llaudes, R., Salman, F. and Chivakul, M. 2010. 'The Impact of the Great Recession on Emerging Markets', *IMF Working Paper* WP/10/237, October 2010.

Lee, H. G. 2007. 'Ethnic Politics, National Development and Language Policy in Malaysia', In Lee, H. G. and Leo, S. (eds.). *Language, Nation, and Development in Southeast Asia.* Singapore: Institute of Southeast Asian Studies.

Lee, K. H. and Tan, C. B. (eds.). 2000. *The Chinese in Malaysia.* Kuala Lumpur: Oxford University Press

Lee, S. A. 1968. *Economic Growth and The Public Sector in Malaya and Singapore, 1948–1960.* Singapore: Oxford University Press.

Lee, S. Y. 1990. *The Monetary and Banking Development of Singapore and Malaysia.* Singapore: Singapore University Press, National University of Singapore.

Leete, R. 1996. *Malaysia's Demographic Transition: Rapid Development, Culture and Politics.* Kuala Lumpur: Oxford University Press.

_____ 2007. *Malaysia from Kampung to Twin Towers: 50 Years of Economic and Social Development.* Selangor Darul Ehsan: Oxford Fajar.

Li, D. J. 1982. *British Malaya, An Economic Analysis.* Kuala Lumpur: Institute of Social Analysis (INSAN).

Lim, C. Y. 1967. *Economic Development of Modern Malaya.* Kuala Lumpur: Oxford University Press.

Lim, D. 1973. *Economic Growth and Development in West Malaysia 1974–1970.* Kuala Lumpur: Oxford University Press.

_____ 2011. 'Economic Development: A Historical Survey,' in *Malaysia: Policies and Issues in Economic Development.* Kuala Lumpur: Institute of Strategic and International Studies.

Lim, T. G. 1977. *Peasants and Their Agricultural Economy in Colonial Malaya 1874–1941.* Kuala Lumpur: Oxford University Press.

Loh, K. W. 1988. *Beyond the Tin Mines: Coolies, Squatters and New Villages in the Kinta Valley.* Singapore: Oxford University Press.

MacBean, A. I. 1966. *Export Instability and Economic Development.* Cambridge: Harvard University Press.

Maddison, A. 2003. *The World Economy: Historical Statistics.* Paris: Organisation for Economic Co-operation and Development.

Mahadevan, R. 2007. *Sustainable Growth and Economic Development, A Case Study of Malaysia.* Cheltenham: Edward Elgar Publishing.

Manderson, L. 1996. *Sickness and the State: Health and Illness in Colonial Malaya, 1870–1940.* Melbourne: Oxford University Press.

Mankiw, N.G., Romer, D. and Weil D. N. 1992. A Contribution to the Empirics of Economic Growth. *The Quarterly Journal of Economics,* (May). [http://eml.berkeley.edu/~dromer/papers/MRW_QJE1992.pdf], accessed 1 June 2016.

Marks, T. 1997. *The British Acquisition of Siamese Malaya, 1896–1909.* Bangkok: White Lotus Press.

Marriott, H. 1911a. *Census Report of the Straits Settlements, 1911.* Singapore: Government Printing Office.

_____ 1911b. *Report on the Census of the State of Johore, 1911.* Johore Bahru: Government Printing Office.

Mayer, J. 2002. 'The Fallacy of Composition: A Review of the Literature', *World Economy,* 26, pp. 2.

McFadyean, A. 1944. *The History of Rubber Regulation, 1934–1943.* London: George Allen & Unwin Ltd.

Miller, J. I. 1931. *Family Budget 1930,* In W. C. Huggard, *Report of the Commission on the Temporary Allowances 1931.* Singapore: Government Printing Office.

Mills, L. A. 1958. *Malaya: A Political and Economic Appraisal.* Minneapolis: University of Minnesota Press.

Milner, A. C. 1994. *The Invention of Politics in Colonial Malaya: Contesting Nationalism and the Expansion of the Public Sphere.* Cambridge: Cambridge University Press.

Mizoguchi, T. and Umemura, M. (eds.). 1988. *Basic Economic Statistics of Former Japanese Colonies, 1895–1938. Estimates and Findings.* Tokyo: Toyo Keizai Shinposha.

Mohamed Ariff. 1972. *Export Trade and the West Malaysian Economy – An Enquiry into the Economic Implication of Export Instability.* Kuala Lumpur: University of Malaya.

_____ 1991. *The Malaysian Economy: Pacific Connections*. Singapore: Oxford University Press.

Mokyr, J. 1985. 'The Industrial Revolution and the New Economic History', In Joel Mokyr (ed.). *The Economics of the Industrial Revolution*. United States of America: Rowman & Littlefield Publishers, pp. 1–51.

Nadarajah, N. 2000. *Johore and the Origins of British Control, 1895–1914*. Ipoh: Arenabuku.

Naing, T. H. 2009. *Economic Policy, Growth and Inequality in Malaysia, 1900–2005*. Ph.D. thesis. Kuala Lumpur: University of Malaya.

Nathan, J. E. 1922. *The Census of British Malaya (The Straits Settlements, Federated Malay States, and Protected States of Johore, Kedah, Perlis, Kelantan, Trengganu, and Brunei), 1921*. London: Waterloo and Sons Ltd.

National Library Board of Singapore. 2014. *Monopolies Department Begins Operations, 1 January 1910*. [http://eresources.nlb.gov.sg/history/events/07c3c57d-55ed-48db-b4ff-e90bf0391504], accessed 14 April 2016.

O'Brien, P. K. and University of London. 1999. *Philip's Atlas of World History*. London: George Philip.

Ooi, J. 1961. 'Rubber Industry of the Federation of Malaya.' *The Journal of Tropical Geography* 15, pp. 47.

Perkins, D. H. 2013. *East Asian Development, Foundations and Strategies*. Cambridge Mass.: Harvard University Press.

Perkins, D. H., Radelet, S., Lindauer, D. L. and Block, S. A. 2013. *Economics of Development*, 7th edn. New York: W. W. Norton & Company.

Pesaran, M. H. and Harcourt, G. C. 2000. 'Life and Work of John Richard Nicholas Stone 1913–1991,' *The Economic Journal* 110, pp. 461.

Pesaran, M. H. and Pesaran, B. 1997. *Working with Microfit 4.0: Interactive Econometric Analysis* (Windows Version). Oxford: Oxford University Press.

Phillips, P. C. B. and Jin, S. 2015. 'Business Cycles, Trend Elimination and the HP Filter'. *Cowles Foundation Discussion Paper*, No. 2005, June 2015.

Piketty, T. 2014. *Capital in the Twenty-first Century*. Cambridge, Mass.: The Belknap Press of Harvard University Press.

Pountney, A. M. 1911. *The Census of the Federated Malay States: Review of the Census Operations and Results Including Tables Exhibiting the Population by Sex, Age, Race, Birthplace, Religion and Occupation*. London: Darling & Son, Ltd.

_____ 1911b. *The Census of the Federated Malay States, 1911*. London: His Majesty's Stationery Office.

Purcell, V. 1967. *Malaysia*. New York: Walker and Company.

Puthucheary, J. J. 1960. *Ownership and Control in the Malayan Economy: A Study of the Structure of Ownership and Control and its Effects on the Development of Secondary Industries and Economic Growth in Malaya and Singapore*. Singapore: Eastern Universities Press.

Rais Yatim. 2007. 'The Road to Merdeka'. In Harding, A. and Lee, H. P. (eds.). *Constitutional Landmarks in Malaysia, the First 50 Years 1957–2007*. Singapore: LexisNexis, pp. 1–24.

Raja Nazrin. 2000. *Essays on Economic Growth in Malaysia in the Twentieth Century*. Ph.D. dissertation. Cambridge, Mass.: Harvard University.

_____ 2001. 'Preliminary GDP Statistics of Malaya, 1895–1939: Progress and Perspectives', paper presented at the *International Workshop on 'Modern*

Economic Growth and Distribution in Asia, Latin America and the European Periphery: A Historical National Accounts Approach', 16–18 March 2001, Tokyo.

———. 2002. 'Historical GDP Statistics of Malaya, 1900–1939: Progress and Perspectives.' Presented at the *XIII International Economic History Congress*, Buenos Aires.

———. 2006. 'Methodology for Deriving the Domestic Private Final Consumption Expenditure Series of Malaya, 1900–1939.' Presented at the *XIV International Economic History Congress*, Helsinki.

Ramasamy, P. 1994. *Plantation Labour, Unions, Capital, and the State in Peninsular Malaysia*. Kuala Lumpur: Oxford University Press.

Ramey, G. and Ramey, V. A. 1995. 'Cross-Country Evidence on the Link Between Volatility and Growth'. *The American Economic Review*, Vol. 85, No. 5 (December), American Economic Association, pp. 1138–1151.

Rasiah, R. 1995. *Foreign Capital and Industrialisation in Malaysia*. Basingstoke: Macmillan.

Ravn, M. O. and Uhlig, H. 2002. 'On Adjusting the Hodrick-Prescott Filter for the Frequency of Observations.' *The Review of Economics and Statistics*.

Rodrik, D. 2008. *What use is sources-of-growth accounting?* [http://rodrik.typepad.com/dani_rodriks_weblog/2008/02/what-use-is-sou.html], accessed 15 June 2016.

———. 2014. 'The Past, Present, and Future of Economic Growth', in F. Allen and others, *Towards a Better Global Economy: Policy Implications for Citizens Worldwide in the 21st Century*. Oxford and New York: Oxford University Press.

Sachs, J. D. and Warner, A. M. 1995. 'Natural Resource Abundance and Economic Growth.' *National Bureau of Economic Research Working Paper 5398*.

Saw, S. H. 1988. *The Population of Peninsular Malaysia*. Singapore: Singapore University Press.

Schumpeter, J. A. 1934. *The Theory of Economic Development: An Inquiry into Profits, Capital, Credit, Interest and the Business Cycle*. Harvard Economic Studies 46. Translated by Redvers Opie.

Shaharil Talib. 1984. *After its Own Image, the Trengganu Experience 1881–1941*. Singapore: Oxford University Press.

———. 1995. *History of Kelantan 1890–1940*. Selangor: The Malaysian Branch of the Royal Asiatic Society.

Sidhu, M. S. and Jones, G. W. 1981. *Population Dynamics in a Plural Society: Peninsular Malaysia*. Kuala Lumpur: University of Malaya Co-operative Bookshop.

Smith, T. E. 1952. *Population Growth in Malaya*. London: Royal Institute of International Affairs.

Smits, J., Horlings, E. and Van Zanden, J. L. 2000. *Dutch GNP and Its Components, 1800–1913*. Netherlands: Groningen University Press.

Solow, R. M. 1957. 'Technical Change and the Aggregate Production Function', *The Review of Economics and Statistics*, Vol. 39, No. 3 (August 1957), pp. 312–320. The MIT Press Stable.

Stiglitz, J., Sen, A. and Fitoussi, J. P. 2009. *Mismeasuring Our Lives: Why GDP Doesn't Add Up, Report of the Commission on the Measurement of Economic Performance and Social Progress*. Commission on the Measurement of Economic Performance and Social Progress. [http://www.stiglitz-sen-fitoussi.fr/en/index.htm] accessed Jun 2016.

Stone, R. *et al.* 1966. *The Measurement of Consumers' Expenditure and Behaviour in the United Kingdom, 1920–1938, Vol. II*. Cambridge: Cambridge University Press.

Sugimoto, I. 2009. '*Economic Growth of Singapore in the Twentieth Century: Historical GDP Estimates and Empirical Investigations on Economic Instability and Government Fiscal Behavior*'. Ph.D. dissertation. University of Malaya, Kuala Lumpur

_____ 2011. 'Economic Growth of Singapore in the Twentieth Century: Historical GDP Estimates and Empirical Investigations'. *Economic Growth Research Centre Monograph Series*, Vol. 2. Singapore: World Scientific Publishing.

_____ 2015. 'The Reconstruction of Singapore's GDP, 1900–60: Estimates and Trends', *Macroeconomic Review*, Monetary Authority of Singapore. April 2015, pp. 2–8.

Swettenham, F. A. 1975. *British Malaya: An Account of the Origin and Progress of British Influence in Malaya*. New York: AMS Press.

Tan E. C. 2014. 'Malaysia's Economic Growth and Development: Challenges and the Way Forward'. *The Singapore Economic Review*, Vol. 59, No. 3. World Scientific Publishing Company.

Tan, E. C. and Mohamed Ariff. 2001. 'Structural Change in the Malaysian Manufacturing Industry,' In C. Barlow (ed.). *Modern Malaysia in the Global Economy: Political and Social Change into the 21st Century*. Cheltenham: Edward Edgar Publishing, pp. 59–73.

Tate, D. J. M. 1996. *The RGA History of the Plantation Industry in the Malay Peninsula*. Kuala Lumpur: Oxford University Press.

Thio, E. 1969. *British Policy in the Malay Peninsula, 1880–1910: Volume I, the Southern and Central States*. Kuala Lumpur: University of Malaya Press.

Timmer, C. P. 1989. 'Food Price Policy: The Rationale for Government Intervention.' *Food Policy*, vol. 14, no. 1 (February), pp. 17–27.

Timmer, C. P., Block, S. and Dawe, D. 2010. 'Long–run Dynamics of Rice Consumption, 1960–2050', Chapter 1.6, In S. Pandey, D. Byerlee, D. Dawe, A. Dobermann, S. Mohanty, S. Rozelle, and B. Hardy (eds.). *Rice in the Global Economy: Strategic Research and Policy Issues for Food Security*. Los Banos (Philippines): International Rice Research Institute, pp.139–174.

Thoburn, J. T. 1977. *Primary Commodity Exports and Economic Development: Theory, Evidence and a Study of Malaysia*. London: John Wiley & Sons.

_____ 1994. *Tin in the World Economy*. Edinburgh: Edinburgh University Press.

United Nations Country Team, Malaysia Economic Planning Unit-Malaysia. 2005. *Malaysia—Achieving the Millennium Development Goals: Successes and Challenges*. Kuala Lumpur.

United Nations Department of Economic and Social Affairs. 1953. *A System of National Accounts and Supporting Tables, Studies in Methods Series F, No. 2*. New York: United Nations.

_____ 1968. *A System of National Accounts, Studies in Methods Series F, No. 2, Rev. 3*. New York: United Nations.

_____ 1986. *Handbook of National Accounting, Accounting for Production: Sources and Methods, Studies in Methods Series F, No. 39*. New York: United Nations.

United Nations Development Programme-Malaysia. 2007. *Malaysia, Measuring and Monitoring Poverty and Inequality*. Kuala Lumpur: United Nations Development Programme-Malaysia.

_____ 2014. *Malaysia Human Development Report 2013, Redesigning an Inclusive Future*. Kuala Lumpur: United Nations Development Programme-Malaysia.

United Nations, European Commission, International Monetary Fund, Organisation for Economic Co-operation and Development and World Bank. 2009. *System of National Accounts 2008*. New York: United Nations. [http://unstats.un.org/unsd/nationalaccount/docs/SNA2008.pdf], accessed 1 February 2016.

United States Department of Commerce. 1975. *Historical Statistics of the United States, Colonial Times to 1970*. Washington DC: Bureau of Census.

Van der Eng, P. 2001. 'Long-term Trends in Gross Domestic Expenditure in Indonesia'. International Workshop on *Modern Economic Growth and Distribution in Asia, Latin America and the European Periphery: A Historical National Accounts Approach*. Tokyo, March 2001.

Van Zanden, J. L. 2004. 'Global Economic History: A Personal View on the Agenda for Future Research', In Sakari Heikkinen and Jan Luiten van Zanden (eds.). *Explorations in Economic Growth*. Amsterdam: Aksant Academic Publishers, pp. 265–384.

Vlieland, C. A. 1932. *A Report on the 1931 Census and on Certain Problems of Vital Statistics, British Malaya (The Colony of the Straits Settlements and the Malay States Under British Protection, namely the Federated Malay States of Perak, Selangor, Negri Sembilan, and Pahang and the States of Johore, Kedah, Kelantan, Trengganu, Perlis, and Brunei)*. London: Crown Agents for the Colonies.

Walters, D. 1960. *Report to U. N. on National Accounts of the Federation of Malaya 1955–1959*. Kuala Lumpur: Department of Statistics-Malaysia (unpublished).

Wdcf. 2010. *Malaysia Tree Diagram*. [https://commons.wikimedia.org/wiki/File:Malaysia_Tree_Diagram.png], accessed 1 February 2016.

Wharton Jr., C. R. 1963, 'Rubber Supply Conditions: Some Policy Implications', In T. H. Silcock and E. K. Fisk (eds.). *The Political Economy of Independent Malaya*. Long, Angus and Robertson.

Willis, J. F. and Primack, M. L. 1989. *An Economic History of the United States*, 2nd edn. New Jersey: Prentice-Hall.

Winstedt, R. O. 1992. *A History of Johore, 1365–1941*. Selangor: The Malaysian Branch of the Royal Asiatic Society.

Wong, D. 2004. *HSBC: Its Malaysian Story*. Singapore: Editions Didier Millet.

Wong, L. K. 1965. *The Malayan Tin Industry to 1914*. Tucson: University of Arizona Press.

World Bank. 1993. *The East Asian Miracle: Economic Growth and Public Policy*. Oxford: Oxford University Press.

———— n. d. World Development Indicators. [http://databank.worldbank.org/data/reports.aspx?source=2&country=MYS&series=&period=], accessed 30 March 2016.

Wu, X. A. *Chinese Business in the Making of a Malay State, 1882–1941*. London: RoutledgeCurzon. Yip, Y. H. 1969. *Development of the Tin Mining Industry of Malaya*. Kuala Lumpur: University of Malaya Press.

Young, A. 1992. 'A Tale of Two Cities: Factor Accumulation and Technical Change in Hong Kong and Singapore.' *National Bureau of Economic Research, Macroeconomics Annual, Volume 7*. Cambridge: MIT Press.

———— 1995. 'The Tyranny of Numbers: Confronting the Statistical Realities of the East Asian Growth Experience.' *Quarterly Journal of Economics* (August), pp. 641–680.

Zainal Aznam Yusof. 2011. 'The Developmental State: Malaysia,' In Paul Collier and Anthony J. Venables (eds.). *Plundered Nations? Successes and Failures in Natural Resource Extractions*. London: Palgrave Macmillan.

Zainal Aznam Yusof and Bhattasali, D. 2008. 'Economic Growth and Development in Malaysia: Policy Making and Leadership'. *Working Paper 2, Commission on Growth and Development*. Washington DC: International Bank for Reconstruction and Development.

Historical Administrative and Annual Reports

British Malaya

_____ 1921–1925, 1928, 1931, 1934 and 1937. *Return of Foreign Imports and Exports, British Malaya*.

_____ 1928–1939. *The Foreign Trade of Malaya*, 1928–1939. Singapore: Government Printing Office.

Federated Malay States

_____ 1900–1930. *Annual Report, Federated Malay States*. Kuala Lumpur: Government Printers.

_____ 1900–1909. *Federated Malay States Government Gazette*, Selangor: Government Printers.

_____ 1902–1903. *Annual Report of the Inspector of Coconut Trees, Federated Malay States*. Government Printers.

_____ 1902, 1906–1907. *Annual Report, Lands, Mines and Surveys, Federated Malay States*. Government Printers.

_____ 1902–1939 (various years). *Annual Report, Federated Malay States Railways*. Government Printers.

_____ 1903–1909, 1911–1914, and 1916–1933. *Annual Report on the Trade and Customs Department, Federated Malay States*. Government Printers.

_____ 1904–1906. *Annual Report of the Inspector of Coconut Plantations, Federated Malay States*. Government Printers.

_____ 1905, 1911–1913, 1918–1928 and 1930–1937. *An Annual Report on Education in the Federated Malay States*. Government Printers.

_____ 1905–1908 and 1911–1919. *Report of the Director of Agriculture, Federated Malay States*. Government Printers.

_____ 1908–1909. *Public Works Department Annual Report, Federated Malay States*. Government Printers.

_____ 1910–1939. *Federated Malay States Government Gazette*. Government Printers

_____ 1911–1923. *Annual Medical Report, Federated Malay States*. Government Printers.

_____ 1912. 'Rubber in Malaya, 1911', *Agricultural Bulletin of the Federated Malay States*, Vol. 1, No. 2, (September), pp. 1–8.

_____ 1912–1915, 1917–1918, 1920. *Agricultural Bulletin of the Federated Malay States*. Government Printers.

_____ 1913. *Federated Malay States Railways Annual Report 1913, Supplement to the Federated Malay States Government Gazette*. Kuala Lumpur: Government Printers.

—— 1914–1915. 'Statistics of crops, acreages for the year 1914', *Agricultural Bulletin of the Federated Malay States*, Vol. 3, pp. 481–494.

—— 1914, 1918, and 1924–1928. *Annual Report, Mines Department, Federated Malay States*. Government Printers.

—— 1918 and 1930–1939. *Financial Statements, Federated Malay States*. Kuala Lumpur: Government Printers.

—— 1920. *Budget for 1920–1921*, Vol. 8, No. 3, (October), pp. 44–85.

—— 1922–1927. *Auditor-General's Report on the Public Accounts for the Federated Malay States*. Government Printers.

—— 1922–1939. *Annual Report of the Electrical Board/Department, Federated Malay States*. Kuala Lumpur: Government Printers.

—— 1923. *Report of a Committee Appointed to Consider the Alleged Shortage of Houses*. Kuala Lumpur: Government Printers.

—— 1924–1938. *Annual Report on the Medical Department, Federated Malay States*, Kuala Lumpur: Government Printers.

—— 1925. *Report on the Public Accounts, Federated Malay States for the year ended 31st December*, Kuala Lumpur: Government Printers.

—— 1925. *Report on the Administration of the Mines Department and on the Mining Industries*. Kuala Lumpur: Government Printers.

—— 1927. *Public Works Department Annual Report, Supplement to the Federated Malay States Government Gazette, July 6, 1928, pp. 1, 9*. Kuala Lumpur: Government Printers.

—— 1928. *Public Works Department Annual Report, 1927, Supplement to the Federated Malay States Government Gazette*. Kuala Lumpur: Government Printers.

—— 1928–1929. *Report of the Auditor-General, Federated Malay States on the Revenue and Expenditure and on the Audit of the Accounts*. Government Printers.

—— 1931–1938. *Annual Report on the Social and Economic Progress of the People of the Federated Malay States*. Kuala Lumpur: Government Printers.

—— 1931–1940. *Malayan Agricultural Statistics*. Kuala Lumpur: Caxton Press Ltd.

—— 1932a. *Report of the Federated Malay States Retrenchment Commission appointed by His Excellency the High Commissioner on the 9th March, 1932*. Kuala Lumpur: Government Printers.

—— 1932b. *Report of Proceedings of The Third Inter-Departmental Agricultural Conference, Appendix 19*. Kuala Lumpur: Government Printers.

—— 1934–1939. *Annual Report on the Customs and Excise Department, Federated Malay States*. Government Printers.

—— 1935–1938. *Annual Report on the Departments of Agriculture Malaya*. Kuala Lumpur: Government Printers.

—— 1936. *Supplement to the Federated Malay States Government Gazette*. Government Printers.

—— 1939. *Supplement to the Federated Malay States Government Gazette*. Government Printers.

—— 1946–1947. *Annual Report of the Electricity Department, Malayan Union*. Kuala Lumpur: Government Printers.

—— (various years). *Federated Malay States, Quarterly Returns of Imports into the Federated Malay States*. Government Printers.

Federation of Malaya

_____ 1948. *Annual Report of the Electricity Department, Federation of Malaya.* Kuala Lumpur: Government Printers.

_____ 1949. *Annual Report, Labour Department, Federation of Malaya.* Government Printers.

_____ 1951. *Mines Department, Bulletin of Statistics Relating to the Mining Industry of Malaya, 1950.* Kuala Lumpur: Government Press.

_____ 1959. *Household Budget Survey of the Federation of Malaya, 1957–1958.* Kuala Lumpur: Government Printers.

_____ 1961. *The Second Five-year Plan, Federation of Malaya,* 1957–1958. Kuala Lumpur: Government printer.

Johore

_____ 1910–1939. *Annual Report, State of Johore.* Johore Bahru: Government Printers.

_____ 1922–1926 and 1929–1930. *Territorial Medical Report, State of Johore.* Johore Bahru: Government Printers.

_____ 1925, 1929–1930. *Annual Report, Agricultural Department, State of Johore.*

_____ 1927–1928. *Annual Medical Report, State of Johore.* Johore Bahru: Government Printers.

_____ 1930 and 1937. *Colonial Annual Report, Survey of Agriculture, State of Johore.* Government Printers.

_____ 1931–1934 and 1936. *Annual Medical Report, State of Johore.* Johore Bahru: Government Printers.

_____ 1933. *Annual Report, Labourer's Specimen Monthly Budget.* Government Printers.

_____ 1935. *Annual Medical Report, State of Johore.* Singapore: Malaya Publishing House Ltd.

_____ 1937 and 1938. *Annual Medical Report, State of Johore.* Singapore: Singapore Printers Ltd.

_____ 1939. *Annual Medical Report, State of Johore.* Singapore: D. Geststhner Eastern Ltd.

Kedah and Perlis

_____ 1906–1907. *Report on the Administration of the State of Kedah.* Government Printers.

_____ 1909–1916. *The Annual Report of the Adviser to the Kedah Government with The Annual Report of the Adviser to the Perlis Government.* Government Printers.

_____ 1917–1931. *The Annual Report of the British Adviser to the Kedah Government with The Annual Report of the British Adviser to the Perlis Government.* Government Printers.

_____ 1930–1935 (various years). *Report of the Medical Health Departments, States of Kedah and Perlis.* Alor Star: Kedah Government Printers.

_____ 1932–1934. *Annual Report on the Social and Economic Progress of the People of the State of Kedah and of the People of the State of Perlis.* 1932–1939. Government Printers.

_____ 1935–1939. *Annual Report on the Social and Economic Progress of the People of the State of Kedah.* Government Printers.

———— 1935–1939. *Annual Report on the Social and Economic Progress of the People of the State of Perlis.* Government Printers.

———— 1936–1939. *Annual Report of the Medical Department, States of Kedah and Perlis.* Alor Star: Kedah Government Printers.

Kelantan

———— 1903–1907. *Report on the State of Kelantan. Government Printers.*

———— 1909–1911 and 1913–1931. *Kelantan Administration Report, State of Kelantan.* Government Printers.

———— 1919. *Annual Medical and Sanitary Report, State of Kelantan.* Government Printers.

———— 1928–1930. *Annual Medical Report, State of Kelantan.* Penang: The Criterion Press Company Ltd.

———— 1931–1933. *Annual Medical Report, State of Kelantan.* Kelantan: Al-Asasiyah Press Company.

———— 1932–1938. *Annual Report on the Social and Economic Progress of the People of Kelantan.* Government Printers.

———— 1934–1936. *Annual Medical Report, State of Kelantan.* Kelantan: The Cheong Fatt Press.

———— 1937–1939. *Annual Medical Report, State of Kelantan.* Government Printers.

———— 1941. *State of Kelantan Estimates.* Government Printers.

Malacca

———— 1918, 1920, and 1922. *Administration Report, State of Malacca, Resident Councillor's Office.* Malacca: Government Printers.

Negri Sembilan

———— 1900 and 1901. *Annual Report, State of Negri Sembilan.* Government Printers.

———— 1900–1909. *Federated Malay States Government Gazette, State of Negri Sembilan.* Government Printers.

———— 1903–1905 and 1907–1934. *Administration Report, State of Negri Sembilan.* Government Printers.

———— 1935 and 1937–1939. *Annual Report on the Social and Economic Progress of the People of Negri Sembilan.* Government Printers.

Pahang

———— 1900 and 1901. *Annual Report of the State of Pahang.* Kuala Lumpur: Selangor Government Printers.

———— 1902–1905, 1907 to 1913, and 1915–1931. *Pahang Administration Report, State of Pahang.* Kuala Lumpur: Government Printers.

———— 1932–1935 and 1937–1939. *Annual Report on the Social and Economic Progress of the People of Pahang, State of Pahang.* Kuala Lumpur: Government Printers.

Penang

———— 1918–1922. *Administration Report, State of Penang.* Resident Councillor's Office, Penang. Government Printers.

———— 1929 and 1938. *Administration Report of the Municipality of George Town, State of Penang.* Municipality Office George Town, Penang: The Criterion Press Co. Ltd.

Perak

_____ 1900–1901 and 1903–1932. *Annual Report, State of Perak*. Government Printers.

_____ 1900–1909. *Federated Malay States Government Gazette, State of Perak*. Government Printers.

_____ 1901. *Railways, Perak and Province Wellesley*. Taiping: Government Printers.

_____ 1933. *Administration Report, State of Perak, 1932*. Kuala Lumpur: Government Printers.

_____ 1933–1939. *Annual Report on the Social and Economic Progress of the People of Perak*. Government Printers.

Selangor

_____ 1900–1931. *Administration Report, Selangor*. Government Printers.

_____ 1932–1939. *Annual Report on the Social and Economic Progress of the People of Selangor*. Government Printers.

Singapore

_____ 1900–1935 and 1939. *Administration Report of the Singapore Municipality*. Singapore: Government Printers.

_____ 1949. *Annual Report, Labour Department, Colony of Singapore*. Government Printers.

Straits Settlements

_____ 1900–1901, 1903–1906, 1908–1914, 1916, 1917 and 1919–1927 (various years). *Report on Trade of the Straits Settlements, Registrar of Imports and Exports, Straits Settlements*. Singapore: Government Printers.

_____ 1900–1938. *Blue Book*. Singapore: Government Printing Office.

_____ 1901–1903, 1905–1907, 1909–1913, 1915–1916, 1918–1924, 1926–1927, and 1930–1938. *Annual Report on Education in the Straits Settlements*. Education Office Straits Settlements. Singapore: Government Printers.

_____ 1901–1902, 1905–1907 and 1909–1911. *Annual Report on Indian Immigration, Straits Settlements*. Indian Immigration Office, Penang.

_____ 1902–1903, 1905–1907, 1910–1931 and 1933–1938. *Registrar of General of Births and Deaths, Straits Settlements*. Singapore: Government Printers.

_____ 1910–1915, 1918, 1927, 1933 and 1934 (various years). *Report on the Government Monopoly Department, Straits Settlements*. Government Printers.

_____ 1910. *Ordinance No. XVI of 1909*. Straits Settlements, Governor. Singapore: Government Printing Office.

_____ 1911. *Ordinance No. V of 1910*. Singapore: Government Printing Office.

_____ 1913, 1914, 1917 and 1919. *Medical Report*. Government Printers.

_____ 1915–1930. *Colonial Annual Report on the Colony of Straits Settlements*. Government Printers.

_____ 1920–1921. *Colonial Annual Report, Straits Settlements*. Colonial Secretary Straits Settlements. Singapore: Government Printers.

_____ 1931. *Annual Report on the Colony of Straits Settlements for the year 1930*. Singapore: Government Printers.

_____ 1931–1938. *Colonial Annual Report of the Social and Economic Progress of the People of the Straits Settlement*. Government Printers.

_____ 1933. *Annual Report on the Social and Economic Progress of the People of the Straits Settlements for the year 1932*. Singapore. Government Printers.

———— 1940–1946. *Registration of Births and Deaths, Malayan Union, Straits Settlement*. Government Printers.

———— 1940. *Financial Statement for the year 1939*. Singapore: Government Printing Office.

Straits Settlements and Federated Malay States

———— 1902–1908, 1911–1913, 1915, 1925–1928, and 1930–1934. *Annual Report, Agricultural Department, Straits Settlement and Federated Malay States*. Government Printers.

———— 1908. *Proceedings of the Commission Appointed to Inquire into Matters Relating to the Use of Opium in the Straits Settlements and the Federated Malay States, Straits Settlements and Federated Malay States Opium Commission*. Singapore: Government Printing Office.

———— 1908–1910 and 1913. *Agricultural Bulletin of the Straits Settlements and Federated Malay States*. Government Printers.

———— 1909. *Agricultural Bulletin of the Straits Settlements and Federated Malay States*, Vol. 8, No. 5, Appendix B.

———— 1910. *Agriculture in the Native States in 1909*, Vol. 10, pp. 311–326.

———— 1919. *Report of the Commissions appointed by His Excellency the Governor of the Straits Settlements and the High Commissioner of the Federated Malay States to Enquire into Certain Matters Relating to the Public Service, to Wit, the Salaries, and the Conditions of Service as Affecting Such Salaries of Certain Officers in the Public Service of the Straits Settlements and the Federated Malay States, and the Provision of Free Passages to Such Officers and to Their Wives and Children When Proceeding From and Returning to the Straits Settlements and Federated Malay States on Leave of Absence, 1919*. Singapore: Government Printing Office.

———— 1921–1923 (various years). *Report of the Secretary for Agriculture, Straits Settlements and Federated Malay States*. Government Printers.

———— 1930. *Reports of Agricultural Field Officers, Department of Agriculture, Straits Settlements and Federated Malay States*. Kuala Lumpur: Government Printers.

———— 1930 and 1932–1934. *Annual Report of the Department of Agriculture, Straits Settlement and Federated Malay States*. Government Printers.

———— 1930. *Annual Report on the Agricultural Department, Straits Settlements and Federated Malay States, Technical Report*. Government Printers.

———— 1939. *An Annual Report on Education in the Straits Settlements and the Federated Malay States for the year 1938, Straits Settlements and Federated Malay States*. Singapore: Government Printers.

———— 1940. *Average Prices, Declared Trade Values, Exchange, and Currency for the year 1939, Malaya*. Singapore: Government Printers.

———— 1941. *Rubber Statistics Handbook, Malaya, 1930–1941*. Singapore: Government Printers.

Trengganu

———— 1913–1914 and 1930–1931. *Annual Report, State of Trengganu*. Government Printers.

———— 1915–1918. *The Annual Report of the British Agent, State of Trengganu*. Government Printers.

———— 1919–1929. *The Annual Report of the British Adviser, State of Trengganu*. Government Printers.

_____ 1927–1934 and 1936–1938. *The Annual Medical and Sanitary Report, State of Trengganu*. Government Printers.

_____ 1929, 1931–1932 and 1941. *Trengganu Estimates, State of Trengganu*. Government Printers.

_____ 1932–1938. *Annual Report on the Social and Economic Progress of the People of Trengganu*. Government Printers.

_____ 1935–1940. *Annual Medical Report, State of Trengganu*. Government Printers.

Miscellaneous

Board of Trade London. 1900–1901. *Statistical Tables Relating to the Colonial and Other Possessions of the United Kingdom*. London: Darling & Son, Ltd.

_____ 1902–1907. *Statistical Tables Relating to British Colonies, Possessions, and Protectorates*. London: Darling & Son, Ltd.

_____ 1908–1911. *Statistical Tables Relating to British Self-governing Dominions, Crown Colonies, Possessions, and Protectorates*. London: Darling & Son, Ltd.

_____ 1913. *Statistical Tables Relating to British Self-governing Dominions, Crown Colonies, Possessions, and Protectorates*, 1912. London: Harrison & Sons.

Department of Statistics-States of Malaya. n.d. *National Accounts of the States of Malaya, 1955–1960*. Kuala Lumpur.

_____ n.d. *National Accounts of the States of Malaya, 1955–1962*. Kuala Lumpur.

Department of Statistics-Malaysia. 1975 (various years). *National Accounts Statistics, Malaysia*, Kuala Lumpur: Government Printers.

_____ 1976. *Monthly Statistical Bulletin of West Malaysia*, Kuala Lumpur: Government Printers.

_____ 1991. *Vital Statistics Time Series, Peninsular Malaysia, 1911–1985*. Kuala Lumpur: Government Printers.

_____ 1999. *Economic Statistics-Time Series, 1999*. Kuala Lumpur: Government Printers.

_____ 2001. *National Accounts Statistics, Malaysia, 2000*. Putrajaya: Government Printers.

_____ 2002. *Census of Construction Industries, Malaysia, 2001*. Kuala Lumpur: Government Printers.

_____ 2002. *Monthly Statistical Bulletin, Malaysia*. Kuala Lumpur: Government Printers.

Secretary for Chinese Affairs Straits Settlements. 1901–1913. *Chinese Protectorate*. Singapore.

_____ 1915–1930. *Protector of Chinese*. Singapore.

_____ 1934. *Annual Report of the Secretary for Chinese Affairs, Straits Settlements for the year 1933*. Singapore.

Index